The Story of
INNOVATION

The Story of
INNOVATION

How Yesterday's Discoveries Lead to Tomorrow's Breakthroughs

JAMES TREFIL

Foreword by Destin Sandlin

NATIONAL
GEOGRAPHIC

WASHINGTON, D.C.

CONTENTS

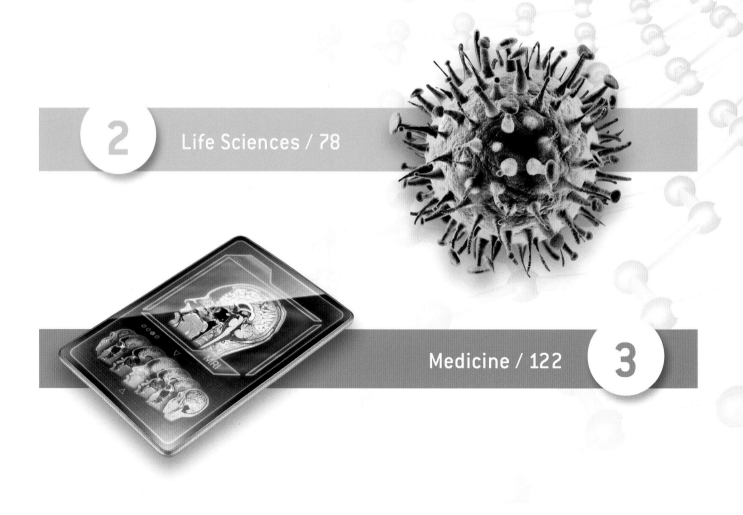

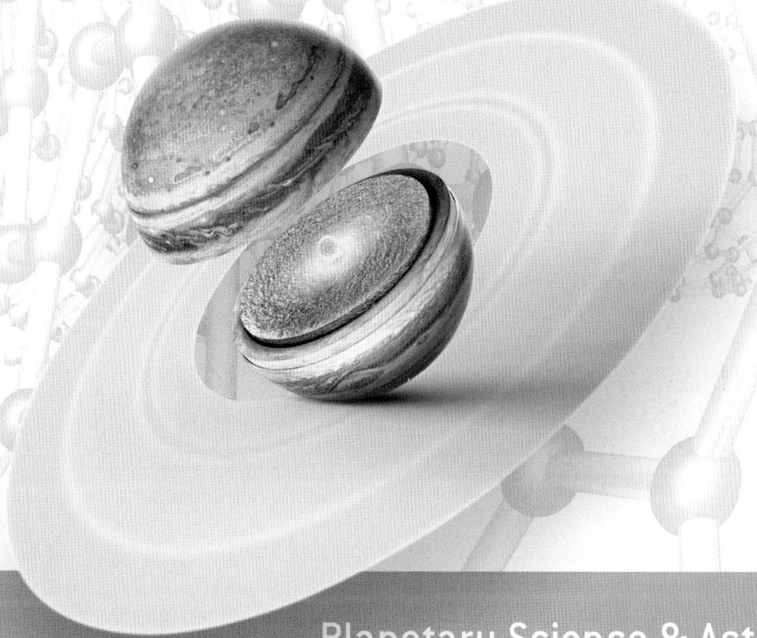

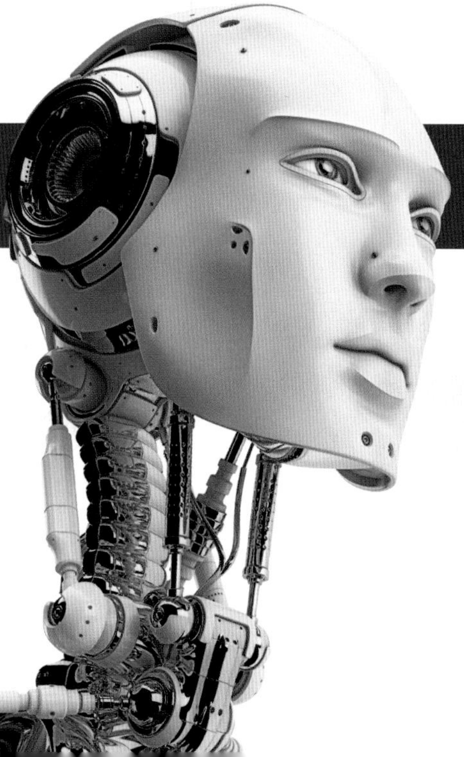

FOREWORD

Destin Sandlin
of *Smarter Every Day*

Innovation is what makes us who we are as humans. Whether it's the kid throwing rocks at a Frisbee stuck in a tree or the engineer designing life-support systems for the International Space Station, we're wired to answer questions and solve problems. Sometimes innovation is born from curiosity; other times it's a form of taking action against "the way things are." It can come from our impulse toward understanding more completely or from wanting to make things work more efficiently. Or it can simply arise from our urge to unravel mysteries for no other reason than to see the beauty of something as it truly is.

Innovation is the human urge to take what the world presents us and change it. This propensity to change things isn't a habit we've picked up recently. Even before there was written language (one of our best innovations, by the way), our ancestors recognized challenges and used the limited tools they had in front of them to craft solutions. They passed on those lessons learned as a gift to successive generations, so each new innovator never truly starts from scratch but stands on the shoulders of those who came before. This fact is perhaps the most alluring aspect of humanity's story. The most trusted and well-worn tools used by this generation were once the unproven solutions to previous generations' problems.

It's easy to imagine that our long shared story is all about the activities of the wealthy and powerful, but a closer look reveals that history has truly been shaped by men and women who never outgrew their simple childlike sense of curiosity and wonder. These sorts of people are driven by a relentless need to know, and by the joy of discovery. Through millennia, innovators—some celebrated but most obscure—have patiently chipped away at question after question and problem after problem to craft the framework of the world we know today. The beauty of that framework is that it wasn't engineered by a handful of elites; rather, it's something we've built together. That is . . . *We, the innovators.*

I say "We" because I believe that the same sense of human curiosity and desire to understand that drove the great innovators of the past is what prompts you or me to crack open a book like this. You're holding this book because you, too, possess the type of spirit that isn't afraid to change things from how they are. Taken in the right frame of mind, the stories you're about to read will stir and inspire; they'll give you a chance to get to know the minds and methods of the giants on whose shoulders we stand. This is a look into the motivations of people who changed things from how they *were* to how they *are*—with an occasional glimpse of how they *will be*.

Remember, this isn't just a story about brilliant ideas and clever problem solving, it's also a story full of optimism about what we have in common, about what makes us human, and what it looks like when *you*, the innovator, are at your best.

Above: Every living thing, including humans, is made from cells. This cutaway illustrates the complexity of even a single cell.

ABOUT THIS BOOK

❶ CHAPTER
Each chapter groups related scientific principles and applications.

❷ SECTIONS
Sections within chapters tell the chronological story of how particular fields of inquiry developed.

There are four types of presentations: The biggest of these are the five chapters, each of which deals with a broad swath of knowledge or applications. Each chapter is split into sections, with each section detailing a smaller field and telling the historical tale about how that field developed. Finally, in each section there will be the story of innovation, interspersed with "Fast Facts" pointing out interesting sidelights. Each section ends with a page titled "On the Horizon," which points out some of the developments we can expect in the future.

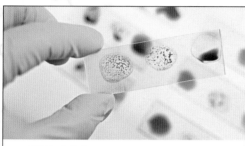

❸ INNOVATIONS
Concise engaging features explain the who, where, what, and how of each scientific and technical breakthrough.

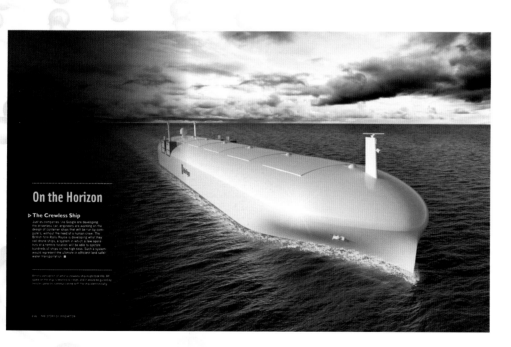

❹ ON THE HORIZON
These features present related developments that are currently in development or achievable in the near future.

Chapter 1
PHYSICAL SCIENCE

Left: Democritus was often called the "laughing philosopher," a characteristic emphasized in this painting.

On one side were philosophers like Parmenides (ca 515 B.C.) and, much later, Plato (ca 428–348 B.C.). Their basic idea was that reality had to be pure and unchanging. Parmenides made the argument by saying that it was impossible that "things that are not are." In other words, it was not possible for true reality to change, since that would involve the appearance of something that "was not" from something that "was." On the other side were a group of philosophers who argued that change was the eternal principle of the universe—that nothing was static and eternal. The most famous of these was a man named Heracleitus of Ephesus (ca 540–ca 480 B.C.).

The most famous of the atomists was a man named Democritus of Abdera (ca 460–ca 370 B.C.). His argument went something like this: If you took the world's sharpest knife and began chopping up a piece of material—a side of cheese, for example—you could cut it in half, then in half again, and so on. Eventually, though, you would come to something that couldn't be divided further. This was the "atom" (literally, "that which cannot be divided"), and the universe was made from atoms and the void. There was something eternal—the atoms themselves—and something always changing—the relationship between atoms. The only part of this theory that survives to modern times is the word "atom." □

▷ ca 400 B.C.

What Is and What Is Not?

The Greek Atom

Sometimes the simplest questions are the hardest to answer, and the question about the ultimate constituents of the universe certainly falls into that category. For the Greeks, this question was not a scientific one in the modern sense, but a philosophical inquiry into the nature of reality. The Greek atomic theory arose as a kind of philosophical compromise between two competing modes of thought.

🔍 Heracleitus summarized his arguments about **universal change** with the epigram **"No man steps into the same river twice."**

MATTER

What is the world made of? This question has haunted scientists and philosophers for millennia.

▷ 1808

Little Bits of Nothing

The Modern Atomic Theory

Throughout the Middle Ages people known as alchemists assembled an impressive body of knowledge about what we call chemical reactions today. This work culminated in the studies of the French chemist Antoine-Laurent Lavoisier (1743–1794). By the turn of the 19th century, some important regularities had been discovered. For one thing it was known that, although many materials could be broken down by chemical processes, there were some that could not be. The latter were called elements and seemed to play a fundamental role in nature. Furthermore, it seemed that the ratios of elements by weight in a given material

were always the same—water was always eight parts oxygen to one part hydrogen, for example.

In 1808 the British scientist John Dalton (1766–1844) published a book titled *A New Chemical Philosophy* that made sense of all of this accumulated knowledge and laid the groundwork for the modern atomic theory. His thesis was simple: Matter was indeed made of atoms, and all of the atoms of a given chemical element were identical to each other and different from the atoms of other chemical elements. Different materials were made by combining atoms together in different proportions.

In Dalton's view his atoms, like those of Democritus, were indivisible—think of them as tiny bowling balls. And although this part of his theory was not destined to survive, the theory itself became the foundation of our modern view of the universe. □

Above: The spectrum of light emitted by neon atoms.

▷ 1859

Knowledge at a Distance

Spectroscopy

Scientists had known since the mid-19th century that different materials give off different combinations of colors when heated. The Bohr atom explains this phenomenon. The energy, and hence the color of light given off by an atom, depends on the spacing of allowed orbits, and this

will differ from atom to atom. The branch of science known as spectroscopy was developed to use this concept to identify substances. Spectroscopy is used today to understand the chemical composition of stars and to monitor concentrations of chemicals in industrial processes, among other things. □

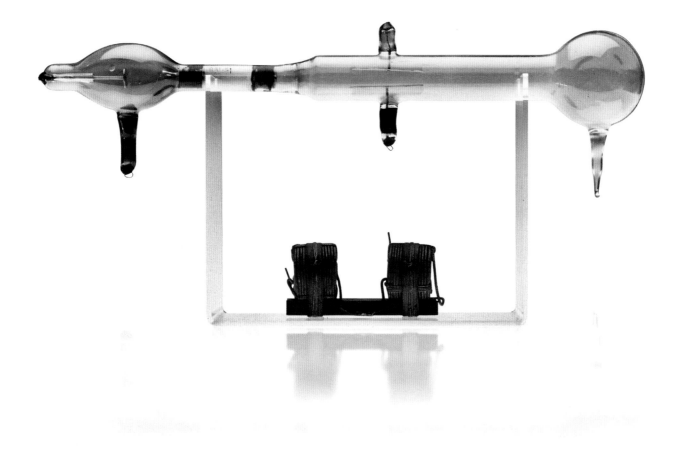

▷ 1897

The Cookie Starts to Crumble

The Discovery of the Electron

Throughout the 19th century the notion of the indivisible atom persisted, although there were suggestions that this might not be the whole story on atoms. The most striking of these phenomena was the appearance of what were called cathode rays. Here's how they worked: A glass tube was prepared with the best vacuum available at the time. At one end of the tube was a wire being heated by an electric current—this was called a cathode. At the other end was a plate kept at high voltage. When current was run through the cathode, streaks of color would appear in the tube as something streamed through and excited the residual atoms. The question was simple: What was streaming through?

The British physicist Sir Joseph John (J.J.) Thomson (1856–1940) set out to answer this question. He set up an apparatus in which whatever was producing the rays passed through a region with both electric and magnetic fields. He made two measurements: one in which he adjusted the fields so that the unknown particle passed through undeflected, and another in which he measured the deflection caused by the electric field alone. From these measurements he was able to show that whatever was streaming through the tube could not be any known particle, but had to be something completely new.

He knew that the new particle had to have a negative electrical charge—information he gleaned from the way it interacted with the electric and magnetic fields. He also knew that it had to be thousands of times lighter than the lightest atom. He named it the electron. For the first time, scientists were confronted with the problem of finding the structure of the atom—in effect, explaining where the electrons came from. □

Above: The original tube used in the discovery of the electron in the late 19th century.

▷ 1897

The Edible Atom

The Raisin Bun Atom

The discovery of the electron forced scientists to ask a simple question: Given that the atom has an internal structure, where do electrons fit in? The first attempt to answer this question worked this way: It was assumed that the positive charge of the atom was spread out in a sphere the size of the atom, and the electrons were embedded in the positive charge like raisins in a bun. The so-called raisin bun atom was a colorful (if short-lived) attempt to understand how the newly divisible atom was put together. ☐

Right: An illustration of the raisin bun atom, which was an early attempt to explain how atoms were put together.

🔍 If the nucleus of an oxygen atom were a **bowling ball** in front of you, the electrons would be **eight grains of sand** in an area the size of a large city.

▷ 1911

The Center Holds

The Discovery of the Nucleus

Ernest Rutherford (1871–1937) has the distinction of being the only scientist to do his most important work *after* he got his Nobel Prize. Born in New Zealand and educated in England, he did pioneering work on radioactivity,

identifying what was called alpha radiation (see page 25) while at McGill University in Montreal. This work led to his being awarded a Nobel Prize in 1908.

Returning to England to take up a position in Manchester, Rutherford began an experiment that was to revolutionize our understanding of the structure of the atom. He put a radioactive source into a lead box with a hole on one side. In this situation, the radioactive particles come out in a beam—think of them as a stream of subatomic bullets. The "bullets" were allowed to hit a thin gold foil and were then detected on the far side. The purpose of the experiment was to determine the size and shape of the diffuse positive charge in the gold atoms.

When Rutherford and his colleagues did the experiment, however, they made an unexpected discovery. Whereas most of the bullets went straight through or were deflected by a small amount—what you would expect from a raisin bun atom—about one in a thousand came bouncing back. It was as if you had shot a pistol into a cloud of steam, and, every once in a while, a bullet came bouncing back at you. Rutherford concluded that most of the mass in the atom had to be concentrated in a small mass—a structure he called the nucleus—and the electrons had to be in orbit. This is the beginning of the modern view of atoms. ☐

Left: A photograph of Ernest Rutherford and some of the scientific apparatus he used.

Things Get Weird
The Bohr Atom

From the start, there were problems with Rutherford's result. If electrons are really circling the nucleus like around the sun, then we know that they have to be emitting light continuously. This means that the electrons would have to lose energy and spiral into the nucleus. Put in the numbers (a favorite homework problem for physics graduate students) and the lifetime of atoms would be measured in seconds. There was an obvious problem.

Niels Bohr (1885–1962) was a young Danish postdoctoral fellow working in England in 1913 when he found a way around this problem. He decided to apply the new science of quantum mechanics (see page 74) to the Rutherford atom. Quantum mechanics says that in the subatomic world everything—mass, energy, and so forth—comes in discrete bundles. Applying these ideas to the electrons in orbit, Bohr found that electrons, unlike planets, cannot occupy just any orbit. There are, in fact, certain well-defined distances from the nucleus where an electron can be found—they are called allowed orbits. So long as electrons stay in these orbits they cannot radiate.

Quantum weirdness comes into the picture when we talk about how electrons can change from one allowed orbit to another. What happens is this: The electron disappears from one orbit, emitting or absorbing light, and reappears in the final orbit *without ever being anywhere in between*. This is called a quantum leap. Don't try to picture the process—there is nothing in our experience like it. ☐

Below: In the Bohr atom, electrons stay in certain well-defined orbits (purple circles) and emit light (yellow wave) when they change from one orbit to another.

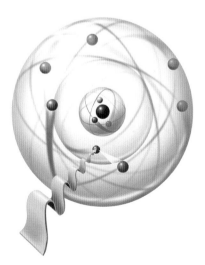

Around and Around
Arrival of the Accelerators

The problem with using cosmic rays to determine the structure of matter is that you can't control them—you have to wait until the one you want shows up. Particle accelerators are the answer to that problem. Starting in 1930 at the University of California at Berkeley, Ernest Orlando Lawrence (1901–1958) spearheaded the development of these machines.

The first Berkeley accelerator was called a cyclotron—a lab nickname name derived from the company name of one of the group's parts suppliers. Imagine a circular set of magnets, one circle over the other, and imagine slicing both in two to produce two sets of D-shaped magnets. A particle introduced into the gap between the *D*'s can be accelerated, but once the particle is in the magnetic field its path will be bent into a circle. Each time the particle comes back to the gap it is accelerated, and its orbit moves farther and farther out until, finally, it is brought out as a beam to run an experiment.

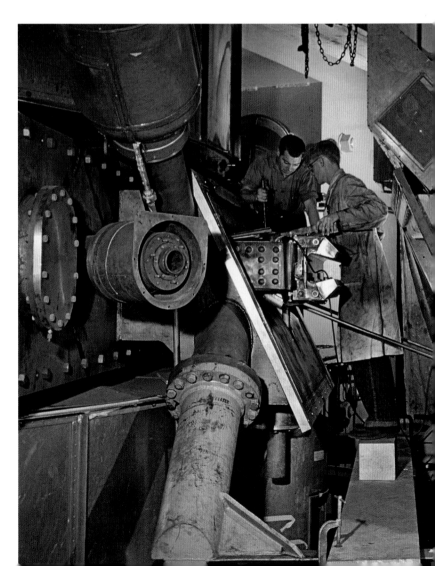

In 1953 an accelerator of a different design went online at Brookhaven National Laboratory on Long Island. In this machine the particles move in a doughnut-shaped chamber, a chamber surrounded by magnets to keep the particles inside the doughnut. Each time the particle passes a specific point it is accelerated and the magnets are strengthened to keep the more energetic particle inside the doughnut. Because the magnets have to be synchronized with the acceleration, such a machine is called a synchrotron. All of the great machines of the late 20th century were of this type.

Finally, you can imagine a synchrotron-type machine made of two rings, with particles traveling in opposite directions in each ring. At the point where the rings intersect, particles collide head on. Such a machine is called a collider. The world's premier machine—the Large Hadron Collider (see page 20) is of this type. ☐

Right: The nucleus of the atom is a mixture of protons (red balls) and neutrons (blue balls).

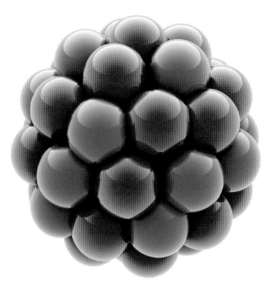

▷ 1932

What's Missing?

The Discovery of the Neutron

Rutherford named the nucleus of the hydrogen atom—the lightest element—the proton ("first one"). But there was a problem. Take carbon as an example. It had six protons in its nucleus, but it weighed 12 times as much as hydrogen. Obviously there was something else in the nucleus. The missing particle was discovered by English physicist James Chadwick (1891–1974) in 1932 in an experiment where subatomic "bullets" produced an uncharged particle when they hit beryllium nuclei. The particle weighed about as much as a proton and was dubbed the neutron ("neutral one"). Neutrons supply the missing piece of the nuclear puzzle. ☐

Left: A technician adjusts the circuits in a cyclotron, the first of which was invented by Ernest O. Lawrence in 1934.

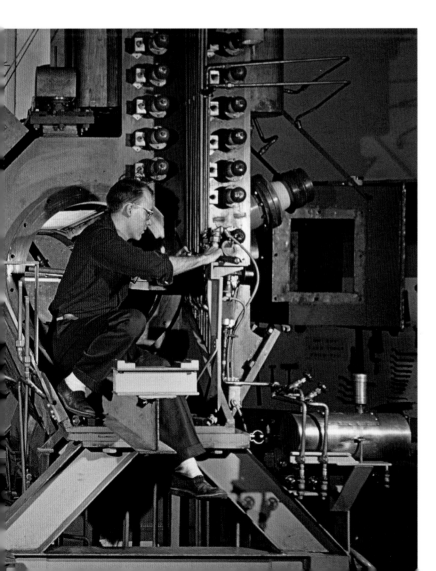

⊕ The English physicist **James Chadwick** received the **Nobel Prize** in 1935 for his **discovery of the neutron.**

Who Ordered This?

New Particles Confuse Things

Earth is constantly being bombarded by particles from space—they're called cosmic rays. Mostly protons, these particles come from the sun, from other stars in our galaxy, and, in a few cases, from other galaxies. Starting in the 1930s, scientists began putting detectors on mountaintops to observe the way these high-energy particles interacted with targets. The basic strategy, which set an example for experimental technique for the rest of the 20th century, was to let a high-energy particle hit a target, and then examine the debris of the collision to learn about the basic structure of matter.

In 1932, Carl Anderson (1905–1991) saw an unusual event in an apparatus placed at the top of Pike's Peak in Colorado. It was the track of a particle as massive as the electron, but with a positive charge. This was the discovery of antimatter, and today we understand that for every particle there is an antiparticle, identical in mass, but opposite in every other way. Since the existence of antimatter had been predicted, the discovery caused no problems for physicists. Anderson received the Nobel Prize in 1936 for the discovery.

Also in 1936, with his then graduate student Seth Neddermeyer (1907–1988), Anderson discovered a much more surprising particle in his cosmic ray apparatus. The new particle was heavier than the electron but lighter than the proton. Called first a mesotron and then a meson, this particle was referred to by the Greek letter *mu* (μ) and is known today as the muon (MEW-on), one of the fundamental particles of nature (see page 68).

By the 1950s, many other kinds of particles had been seen in cosmic ray interactions. The subatomic world was turning out to be a lot more complex than we had expected. □

Where Did All These Particles Come From?

The Particle Zoo

With the advent of the accelerators, it quickly became obvious that the old picture of the nucleus as a bag of protons and neutrons would have to be replaced. Experiments turned up literally hundreds of short-lived "elementary" particles—in fact, by the 1970s, physicists were publishing lists of these particles that resembled a phone book. Three major categories had emerged by 1970: leptons, hadrons, and strange particles.

Leptons ("weakly interacting ones")

These particles, as with electrons and muons, do not take part in the interactions that hold the nucleus together. One more massive particle of this type, the tau, was found. For each of these massive particles there is an uncharged, almost massless particle known as a neutrino, so there are, all told, six leptons.

Hadrons ("strongly interacting ones")

These are particles that exist inside the nucleus. Except for the proton, they are all unstable. They come in two types: baryons ("heavy ones"), whose decay products include at least one proton, and mesons ("intermediate ones") whose decay products do not include a proton. Most of these particles have lifetimes so short that they never leave the nucleus in which they are created.

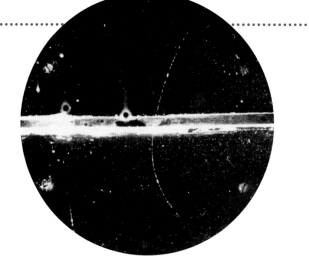

Strange Particles

Some hadrons have "long" lifetimes—lifetimes that allow them to travel macroscopic distances before they decay. Physicists called these strange particles and quantified this term by saying that these particles carried another property—somewhat analogous to electrical charge—that had to change in the decay process. They called this property strangeness. The fact that it took some time for the decay to happen, then, is associated with the time required for the strangeness of the particle to change. □

Above: In the early days of particle physics, cloud chamber pictures like this, showing the tracks of particles, were the main tool scientists had.

▷ 1964

Three Quarks for Muster Mark

The Quark Model

Just as the proliferation of chemical elements was explained by the introduction of elementary particles, with the different elements corresponding to different arrangements of the elementary constituents, the proliferation of elementary particles was explained by the introduction of objects more elementary still, objects called quarks. Introduced independently by physicists Murray Gell-Mann (b 1929) and George Zweig (b 1937), the idea was that there are three quarks, along with their respective antiparticles, and all known hadrons correspond to different arrangements of these three.

The quarks have unusual properties—their electrical charges, for example, are 1/3 and 2/3 the charge on the electron. The two most "ordinary" quarks are called up and down, whereas the third quark, the "strange" quark, carries the strangeness property discussed earlier. The idea is that all hadrons are made from quarks—baryons are a collection of three quarks and mesons a collection of quarks and antiquarks.

Since the original quark model was introduced more particles carrying new properties have been discovered, and the number of quarks has increased to six. The three new quarks are called charm, bottom, and top, respectively. The last of these, the top quark, was discovered in 1995. □

Above: An artist's conception of how three quarks might come together to make a proton. Since the discovery of the first three quarks in 1964, three new ones have been discovered. The top quark—the last to be discovered—was identified in 1995.

▷ 1974

A Mundane Name for a Fantastic Theory

The Standard Model

The prosaically named Standard Model is, at present, our best theoretical understanding of the structure of matter. The best way to picture it is to think of a brick building. There are two important aspects to the building—the bricks, the basic constituents of the structure, and the mortar that holds the bricks together.

In the Standard Model, the "bricks" are quarks and leptons (see page 18). The quarks make up the particles

> 🔍 Bringing **gravity into the picture of forces** described by the Standard Model remains the **greatest outstanding problem** in theoretical physics.

that, in turn, make up the atomic nuclei, whereas the leptons (like the electron) operate outside the nucleus to make atoms. And, although it's not really part of the Standard Model, the atoms combine to make materials.

The phenomena that make up the "mortar" of the universe are the four fundamental forces that operate in nature. Whenever something happens, it is because one of these forces, or some combination of them, is operating:

- Strong force—binds quarks into particles and particles into nuclei
- Electricity and magnetism
- Weak force—governs some radioactive decays
- Gravity

Although these forces seem very different, the Standard Model predicts that at high enough energies some of them will become identical (the technical term is "unify"). The electrical and weak forces unify at energies that can be reached with the most powerful accelerators—an effect that has been seen. The resulting electroweak force unifies with the strong force at much higher energies. We can't verify this directly, but we can confirm other predictions of the model. At the moment, gravity remains odd man out in these unification effects. □

▷ 2010

The Big One

The Large Hadron Collider

The Large Hadron Collider, located at the European Center for Nuclear Research in Geneva, Switzerland, is arguably the most complex technical structure ever built by human beings. Located in a circular tunnel 27 km (17 miles) long buried as far as 500 feet down at the

Above: The Large Hadron Collider, located near Geneva, Switzerland, is the largest and most powerful particle collider in the world.

French–Swiss border, it is designed to produce head-on collisions between counter-rotating beams of protons. The maximum design energy is for collisions to happen at 14 trillion volts. The machine was designed to (1) find the Higgs boson and (2) open the way for physics beyond the Standard Model. ☐

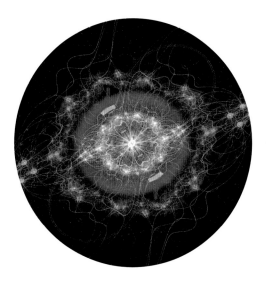

▷ 2012

Seek and Ye Shall Find

The Higgs Boson

In 1964 several theoreticians, most notably Scottish physicist Peter Higgs (b 1929), suggested that certain mathematical problems in the Standard Model could be resolved if one more particle were added to those already discussed here. This hypothetical object became known as the Higgs particle or, in the popular press, the God particle, using a term introduced by physicist Leon Lederman (b 1922) in a book with that title. Finding the Higgs particle became a decades-long quest among particle physicists, a quest that was finally ended in 2012 when the discovery of the Higgs particle at the Large Hadron Collider was announced. Higgs and physicist François Englert (b 1932) shared the Nobel Prize in 2013 for their prediction.

The most interesting thing about the Higgs particle is that it explains, for the first time, why particles have mass. It works this way: The universe is pervaded by a field (called the Higgs field) with which the Higgs par-ticle is associated. Think of the field as being like a thin molasses. Different particles interact with this universal field with different strengths—some interact strongly and are slowed quite a bit by the molasses, whereas others interact less strongly and are slowed down less. We perceive this slowing down as mass—we say that it's harder to get a bowling ball moving than a Ping-Pong ball because the bowling ball is more massive, but we now understand that the bowling ball interacts more strongly with the Higgs field.

Where will this discovery take us? It's hard to say, but the effects on our understanding of a fundamental property of matter could be enormous. ☐

Above: An artist's conception of the Higgs boson.

On the Horizon

▷ String Theory

The progression from materials to atoms to particles to quarks can be thought of as a process analogous to peeling an onion—each layer seems fine until we start looking beneath it to a deeper reality. String theory, in effect, is an attempt to find the layer beneath the quark. The theories involve very complex mathematics, but picture the fundamental unit of the universe to be tiny vibrating strings, with different modes of vibration corresponding to different particles. String theories have the advantage of incorporating gravity, which is no longer odd man out. They have the disadvantage that, in order for the theories to make sense, the strings have to vibrate in 10 or 26 dimensions. Theorists are hoping to see confirmation of string theory predictions at the Large Hadron Collider.

▷ Supersymmetry

Supersymmetry is the name of a property that some theorists think may exist in nature. They predict that there will be another mirrored world made up of what are called supersymmetric particles. These particles combine certain properties of matter that do not appear in the same particle in ordinary matter. The usual custom is to designate the supersymmetric partner of an ordinary particle by putting an *s* in front of the particle's name. Thus in the mirrored world there will be selectrons, squarks, and so on. These particles are expected to be very massive, and none has been seen at this time.

▷ Accelerators on the Drawing Board

You would think that having completed a massive construction project like the Large Hadron Collider, physicists would relax for awhile. In fact, however, some visionary scientists are looking ahead to the next big accelerator project. The International Linear Collider is an example of what such a project might look like.

The machine would accelerate beams of electrons and positrons toward each other (for technical reasons, these particles can't be accelerated in circular machines). These beams would collide at high energies in the middle of the machine. To get meaningful energies, the accelerating track would have to be very long—current design sketches call for the machine to be 31 km (about 20 miles) long. In 2013 an international working group put together a design study that could be presented to governments for support. It remains unknown when, where, and whether such a machine might be built. ■

An artist's conception of what a particle made of strings might look like. The different colored streaks represent the strings that make up the quarks which, in turn, are combined to make particles.

NUCLEAR SCIENCE

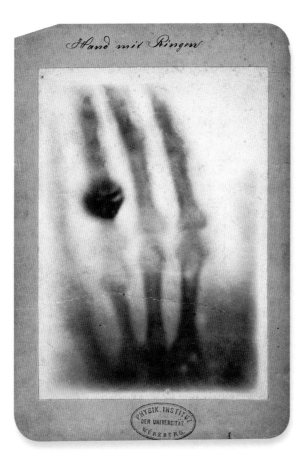

was passing from the tube to the screen. Roentgen called the unknown radiation x-rays to emphasize their mysterious nature. While reaching to adjust a piece of apparatus, he noted a ghostly image of the bones of his hand on the screen. Substituting a photographic plate for the screen, Roentgen took the first x-ray photograph—it was his wife's hand, showing the bones and her wedding ring.

The first radiology department was established at a Glasgow hospital in 1896—one year after x-rays were discovered.

A year later the French physicist Antoine-Henri Becquerel (1852–1908), while trying to investigate the strange new emissions that were showing up, discovered that several different forms of what we would call radiation were coming from atoms. He wrapped a sample of uranium ore in black paper to keep light from triggering reactions, and he discovered that he could still see images of metal objects on a photographic plate. By placing his ore samples in a magnetic field, he found that some of the emitted particles had electrical charge (both positive and negative), whereas some were neutral.

> 🔍 Marie Curie was the **first woman to win a Nobel Prize** and the first person to **win two prizes** — physics (1903) and chemistry (1911).

▷ 1896

It Glows in the Dark
The Discovery of Radioactivity

In 1895 the German physicist Wilhelm Roentgen (1845–1923) was experimenting with the properties of electric current passed through tubes in which a vacuum had been created. He noticed that, even when he had covered the tube, a nearby screen covered with a fluorescent compound glimmered. Obviously, some unknown radiation

Above: The first x-ray photograph taken in 1895. It shows Roentgen's wife's hand with a ring on her finger.

It was the Polish-born physicist Marie Curie (1867–1934), working with her husband Pierre Curie (1859–1906), who coined the term "radioactivity." Working with samples of uranium ore, they were able to establish the existence of two new elements (polonium and radium) and founded the field of science known today as radiochemistry. □

Invisible, deadly, and powerful, nuclear processes power stars and human technology.

▷ 1903

The Philosopher's Stone
Radioactive Decay

Working at McGill University in Montreal, New Zealand–born Ernest Rutherford laid the foundations of modern nuclear theory while investigating the properties of radioactivity. He established the fact that, when a nucleus emits radiation, the number of protons in the nucleus may change, and thus that radioactivity is connected to a process by which atoms can change their chemical identity. He also introduced the concept of half-life to describe the length of time it takes for half of the nuclei in a sample to undergo decay.

🔍 The half-lives of **isotopes** of various elements **vary widely,** from fractions of a second to billions of years.

Rutherford knew that there were three kinds of radioactivity (positively charged, negatively charged, and neutral) and named them alpha, beta, and gamma—the first three letters of the Greek alphabet. His identification of the nature of alpha radiation led to his Nobel Prize in 1908. The modern understanding of radioactive emissions is described in terms of alpha, beta, and gamma emission.

Alpha Emission

Rutherford showed that, when a nucleus emits alpha radiation, it is emitting a particle consisting of two protons and two neutrons—what he identified as the nucleus of a helium atom. This means that, after the emission has occurred, the daughter nucleus will have two less protons and two less neutrons than the original. For example, uranium-238 (92 protons, 146 neutrons) decays by alpha emission to become thorium-234 (90 protons, 144 neutrons).

Beta Emission

In beta emission, one of the neutrons in the nucleus undergoes a process by which it changes into a proton while emitting an electron and a neutrino (see page 18). Since the neutron and the proton have approximately the same mass, beta emission does not change the mass of the daughter nucleus, but it produces a nucleus with one more proton and one less neutron. For example, carbon-14 (6 protons and 8 neutrons) decays by beta emission into nitrogen-14 (7 protons and 7 neutrons). For reference, the electron from the nucleus comes shooting out at high speed and has nothing to do with the electrons already in orbit in the atom.

Gamma Emission

The third kind of emission is just a wave like light or an x-ray. The protons and the neutrons in the nucleus shift around to supply energy for the emission, which can be anything from an x-ray to a high-energy gamma ray. □

Above: In alpha decay, two protons and two neutrons are emitted. Ernest Rutherford was the first to identify the nature of alpha radiation.

▷ 1932

Unstable at the Center

Isotopes

All atoms of the same chemical element have the same number of protons in their nucleus and the same number of electrons in orbit. Soon after he discovered the structure of the atom, Ernest Rutherford realized that, although all atoms of the same chemical element have the same number of protons, they do not have to have the same number of neutrons in their nuclei. Nuclei with the same number of protons but different numbers of neutrons are called isotopes. All chemical elements have many isotopes, most of which are radioactive and hence unstable. The existence of the neutron was confirmed in 1932. ☐

Left: Artist's conception of the deuterium nucleus, an isotope of hydrogen. It contains a proton and a neutron, each made from quarks.

🔍 A standard comment about the possibility of fusion reactions playing a role in the world's energy economy is that **"fusion is the energy source of the future**, and always will be."

▷ 1938

Why Do Stars Shine?

Nuclear Fusion

Just as "fission" refers to a process by which large nuclei are broken up into smaller pieces, "fusion" refers to the process by which small nuclei come together to form larger nuclei, generating energy in the process. In 1938 a young German émigré named Hans Bethe (1906–2005), then at Cornell University, worked out the theoretical framework which showed that the nascent field of nuclear physics could answer an ancient question: Why do stars shine?

Opposite: A star cluster and gas cloud seen through the Hubble Space Telescope. The energy given off by the stars is generated by nuclear fusion. The theoretical framework of fusion, worked out by Hans Bethe, finally explained why stars shine.

Think for a moment of turning your face toward the sun on a warm summer day. The energy you feel had to come from the sun, and it had to come from some process capable of generating that energy for billions of years. No chemical process could do this, but Bethe showed that nuclear fusion could. Basically, the coming together of light nuclei in fusion reactions could supply the energy a star needed to shine.

Today we understand that the exact reactions Bethe worked out are not the main source of stellar energy, but we understand that other fusion reactions are. In the sun, for example, a complex series of fusion reactions turn four hydrogen nuclei (protons) into a helium nucleus (two protons and two neutrons) and a lot of energy. All stars, like the sun, begin their lives by "burning" hydrogen in this way.

Unlike the case with fission, we have not yet found a way to control fusion reactions to supply energy for civilian use. Whether this will remain true in the future is a matter of conjecture. ☐

▷ 1942

Energy Too Cheap to Meter

Nuclear fission

The term "fission" refers to splitting. In principle, every nucleus can be broken up (fissioned) if we supply enough energy, but we normally reserve the term for a particular kind of splitting. It can happen that, when you add up all the masses of the pieces left after a nucleus has been split, the sum is less than the mass of the original nucleus. In this case, Albert Einstein's (1879–1955) famous formula $E = mc^2$ (see page 66) shows that the fission process can supply energy. This is the basic idea behind the nuclear reactor.

One of the isotopes that can yield energy through fission is uranium-235 (92 protons and 143 neutrons).

Above: The cooling towers of a typical nuclear power station. France has the highest reliance on nuclear energy in the world. Nearly 40 percent of the country's energy comes from fission reactors.

Unfortunately, uranium-235 represents only 0.7 percent of naturally occurring uranium, with the rest being primarily the heavier isotope uranium-238. To separate the fissionable material from the rest, the uranium is combined with fluorine to make a gas, which is then introduced to a rapidly spinning centrifuge. The heavier uranium-238 is thrown to the outside, and the lighter uranium-235 collects in the middle. Typically, it takes dozens of centrifuge runs to get to 10 percent uranium-235, which can be used as reactor fuel.

The first nuclear reactor was operated under the stands of the football stadium at the University of Chicago in 1942. Today's reactors are much more sophisticated, but they operate in largely the same way. A neutron strikes the nucleus of a uranium-235 atom, which fissions, producing energy, some debris, and two or three more neutrons. These neutrons pass through a material known as a moderator, usually water, whose function is to slow them down so that they can initiate another fission reaction. This chain reaction produces energy that heats the water, and that energy is eventually used to generate electricity. Today about 20 percent of electricity in the United States is generated by nuclear reactors. ☐

On the Horizon

▷ Nuclear Fusion Reactor

"ITER" used to stand for International Thermonuclear Experimental Reactor, but today it is just taken to be the Latin word for "forward." It is a seven-nation attempt to build the world's first fusion reactor. Designed to produce 500 MW of power while consuming only 50 MW in its operation, ITER is not intended as a commercial power source but as the proof that fusion power can be made to work. It uses powerful magnetic fields to contain a plasma of hydrogen isotopes, which are then heated to the point where fusion begins. The construction of the facility has already started in the Cadarache research center in southern France, and ITER is expected to be operational in 2027—fully 11 years after the original announced completion date.

▷ Superheavy Elements

Naturally occurring elements run up to uranium, which has 92 protons. All elements after uranium are created in laboratories, usually by bombarding a heavy nucleus with an accelerated projectile and hoping that in the resulting maelstrom new elements with more than 92 protons will be made. The result: Today we have seen proton numbers up to 118. These superheavy elements tend to be unstable, often decaying in a matter of microseconds. Theorists predict, however, that when we get to element 126 we will encounter an "island of stability"—elements with half-lives that might be as long as a million years. Such elements could be the basis for an entirely new type of chemistry. ■

A model of the International Experimental Thermonuclear Reactor (ITER). The 35-nation collaborative effort is attempting to prove the feasibility of nuclear fusion as a clean and limitless energy alternative.

CHEMISTRY

▷ ca 350 B.C.

Earth, Fire, Air, and Water

The Greek Elements

As with so many fundamental questions, the first people to ask them were Greeks. As codified by Aristotle (384–322 B.C.), the Greek idea about why materials behave as they do depended on two statements: (1) all materials are made from the fundamental constituents of earth, fire, air, and water; and (2) materials behave as they do because of their innate properties.

For example, if we see a rock fall we attribute it to the effect of the force of gravity. An Aristotelean seeing the same thing would say that what is happening is that the rock is responding to its innate nature, which compels it so seek out the center of the universe.

(And remember, for the Greeks this was the same as the center of Earth.) Similarly, an Aristotelean would say that a flame rose because it was in its nature to seek the outer edge of the universe and would not talk about the density of heated air and the principle of buoyancy.

While the Aristotelean system dominated the universities through the Middle Ages, a group of men called alchemists were accumulating a vast compendium of information about what we would call chemical reactions—information that would eventually lead to the modern science of chemistry. ☐

Above: The four elements that the Greeks believed made up the world: earth, water, air, and fire. The Greek philosopher Aristotle was the first to codify this idea, which remained popular through the Middle Ages.

Modern chemistry built on the efforts of the ancients, analyzing, categorizing, and creating new materials that never existed.

▷ 1789

What Goes in Must Come Out
The Birth of Modern Chemistry

The man who was responsible for compiling the knowledge gained by the alchemists and, through a series of careful experiments, establishing the basic tenets of the modern science of chemistry was the French scientist Antoine-Laurent Lavoisier (1743–1794). Lavoisier was a brilliant man and was elected to the French Academy of Sciences at the age of 25 (for a research paper, believe it or not, on street lighting). His 1789 book, *Elementary Treatise on Chemistry*, became the cornerstone of the new science.

Lavoisier understood that, although most materials can be broken down by chemical means, a few cannot. He introduced the term "element" to describe substances that cannot be broken down. The notion of the existence of chemical elements played a crucial role in the development of the modern atomic theory (see page 13).

Perhaps the most important aspect of Lavoisier's work came from his careful measurement of the weights of materials before and after chemical reactions. For example, in one experiment he sealed some fresh fruit into a jar and measured the weight of the jar as the fruit rotted. Though the fruit was obviously changing during the experiment, the weight of the jar stayed the same. Experiments like this established a very important principle known as the conservation of mass—despite how atoms recombine during a chemical reaction, the actual number of each kind of atom stays the same. If you have two oxygen atoms at the beginning for example, you will have two oxygen atoms at the end.

Above: An engraving of Antoine-Laurent Lavoisier. The 18th-century French scientist was the father of modern chemistry.

Lavoisier was born into an aristocratic family, a fact that obviously helped him pursue his scientific endeavors, but which became a liability during the French Revolution. His participation in an unpopular tax-collecting firm led to his trial and execution by guillotine in 1794. ☐

🔍 When he heard of Lavoisier's execution by guillotine, Italian physicist and mathematician Joseph-Louis Lagrange remarked, **"It took only an instant to cut off his head, but France will not produce another like it for a century."**

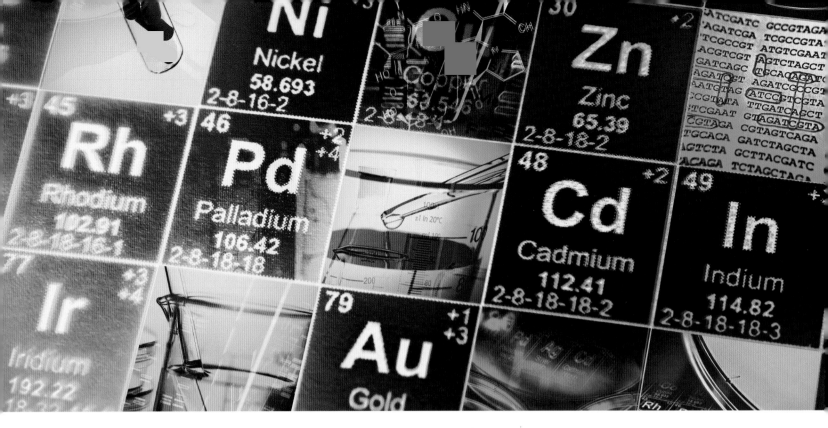

▷ 1869

A Place for Everything and Everything in Its Place

The Periodic Table of the Elements

Throughout the 19th century, more and more chemical elements were discovered, but the chemical landscape was cluttered, with no apparent order or organizing principle among those elements. Dismayed by this situation, a young Russian professor in St. Petersburg, Dmitry Ivanovich Mendeleyev (1834–1907), decided to write a textbook on basic chemistry. He found that there was, in fact, an order to the chemical elements, an order that we now refer to as the periodic table of the elements.

The table works like this: As you read from left to right in any row, the atoms get heavier and the number of protons increases. Thus, in the second row we go from lithium (three

Above: The periodic table of the elements.

protons, four neutrons) to neon (ten protons, ten neutrons). Similarly, if you read down any column you encounter atoms with similar chemical properties. In the first column we find hydrogen, lithium, sodium, and so on. All of these are highly reactive. On the other hand, in the last column (neon, argon, etc.) are what are called noble gases—elements that do not undergo chemical reactions at all. The "periodicity" in the periodic table arises because, when you finish one row, the cycle of chemical properties starts again.

When Mendeleyev first proposed the periodic table, he had no idea why such regularities should have appeared—indeed, today we know that they come from the laws of quantum mechanics (see page 74), which were a half century in the future. There were, however, some missing elements in Mendeleyev's first table, which, in effect, predicted the existence of as yet undiscovered elements. Their ultimate discovery—we call them germanium and scandium today—lent credence to the idea of the table, which was quickly adopted and now hangs in every chemistry classroom in the world. □

⊕ When Dmitry Mendeleyev died, his funeral procession was headed by a group of his **students carrying a copy of the periodic table** in honor of Mendeleyev's having discovered the order of the chemical elements.

Nature Never Made These

Plastics

Plastics are ubiquitous in modern life, so it's hard to imagine a time when they weren't around. They are, however, a product of modern chemistry, not of nature. They are examples of what chemists call polymers—large molecules made up of chains of smaller molecules bound together in various ways. The locking together of these long chains gives plastic materials their shape. Today we hardly think about the prevalence of these materials, but when they were first introduced they were often regarded as cheap (and inferior) substitutes for natural substances like ivory or rubber.

There are two broad classes of plastics—thermosetting and thermoplastic. The former change irreversibly when heated to take on a permanent shape, whereas the latter can be heated and remolded. Both types are in wide use today.

The modern plastics industry is generally regarded as having been started by the American inventor Leo Baekeland (1863–1944) in 1907, when he introduced a material he called Bakelite. A thermosetting plastic, Bakelite was widely used in home plasticware. The standard black telephones that dominated the communication industry in the mid-20th century were often made of Bakelite. Today those early Bakelite utensils fetch high prices in antique stores.

Perhaps the most dramatic success within the plastics story involves nylon, the invention of the American chemist Wallace Carothers (1896–1937). Inspired as a young man by the strength and flexibility of natural fibers, such as those found in spider webs, he founded DuPont Corporation's fundamental research group in 1928—a group that produced many new and profitable materials, such as the artificial rubber neoprene.

In 1935 Carothers introduced the first nylon polymer. It turned out to be an amazingly versatile product. When heated, it could be spun into threads or injected into molds to make everything from women's stockings to parachutes to parts for car bodies.

The following are some common plastics and a few of their uses:

- Polyester—fabrics and textiles
- Polyethylene—supermarket bags, plastic bottles
- Polyvinyl chloride—plumbing pipes, shower curtains
- Polypropylene—yogurt containers, bottle caps
- Polystyrene—packaging "peanuts," plastic tableware
- Polyamides (nylon)—toothbrush bristles, fishing line, fibers
- Polycarbonate—eyeglasses, compact discs, traffic lights
- Polyurethane—car parts, thermal insulation foam, varnish coatings

We could go on, but I think you get the point—plastics are everywhere. ☐

Below: Early portable radios were often made of plastic. The synthetic polymers known as plastics are used everywhere today from toothbrushes and eyeglasses to plumbing pipes and food containers.

▷ 1908

Why Do Atoms Hang Out Together?

The Chemical Bond

The question of how materials can hold together has puzzled scientists for a long time. Some ancient Greeks speculated that atoms had different shapes, and materials made from them were like complex three-dimensional jigsaw puzzles made from those shapes. John Dalton's followers

> 🔍 Although John Dalton **never argued that atoms had hooks on them,** the notion was popularized by his followers.

(see page 13) imaged atoms with little hooks on them for attaching to other atoms. It wasn't, in fact, until the early 20th century that the American chemist Gilbert Lewis (1875–1946) began putting together something that looked like our modern understanding of the chemical bond.

Today we recognize that there are many ways for atoms and molecules to bond together. Each imparts its own special characteristic to the material in which it appears. There are five types of chemical bonds: ionic, covalent, metallic, polar, and van der Waals bonds.

Ionic Bonds

Two atoms can get to a lower energy state if one atom gives up an electron and the other takes it. When this happens, both atoms have an unbalanced electric charge, one positive and one negative. The resulting electrical attraction binds the atoms together. An atom with too many or too few electrons is called an ion; thus the attraction is called an ionic bond. The most familiar ionic bond occurs when a sodium atom gives up an electron to a chlorine atom to form sodium chloride—common table salt. Ionic bonds are often found in minerals.

Covalent Bonds

Atoms can also share pairs of electrons with their nearest neighbors—think of the pair of electrons, one from each atom, shuttling back and forth between the atoms. Quantum mechanics (see page 72) shows that in this situation there will be an attractive force holding the two atoms

Opposite: Copper wire is held together by the metallic bond.
Above: Coal is held together largely by covalent bonds.
Above right: Ordinary table salt is held together by ionic bonds.

together. This is called a covalent bond. Carbon atoms often form covalent bonds, and this type of bond is often found in organic materials.

Metallic Bonds

In some situations, each atom in a substance can give up one or more electrons. These electrons are basically shared by all the atoms in the material. In this case you can think of the material as consisting of a sea of loose electrons in which are embedded the positive ions that are the basic structural components. As the name implies, this type of bond is commonly found in metals.

Polar Bonds

When a molecule forms from different atoms, the overall electrical charge can be neutral, but the charges are unevenly distributed in the molecule so that some parts are more negative and some are more positive. In water, for example, the negative charges tend to be near the oxygen atom, whereas the positive charges are near the hydrogen. Such a molecule is said to be polar. When polar molecules are near each other, they can orient themselves so that the negative part of one is near the positive part of the other. The resulting electrical attraction forms the polar bond.

Van der Waals Bonds

Named for the Dutch physicist Johannes van der Waals (1837–1923), this is a weak force that can exist between neutral atoms. When the atoms approach each other, their electron clouds repel each other, distorting the shape of the atoms. This produces electrical forces between the electrons and the nuclei of the atoms, which can provide a weak bond. In graphite (pencil lead), for example, there are sheets of carbon atoms held together by strong covalent bonds, but the sheets are held together by weak van der Waals forces. When you run the pencil across a piece of paper, the sheets slough off, leaving a visible line of carbon. □

On the Horizon

▷ New Materials

You can think of the processes that lead to commercial development of new materials as being due to either a "push" or a "pull." In a push situation, scientists develop a new material and then look around for a possible application. The people who discovered buckyballs (see page 45), for example, were trying to explain the molecular structure of carbon in red giant stars. They were not trying to find a better way to deliver drugs or enhance the filtering process in chemical reactions. It was only after they had the new material that applications began to pop up.

In a pull situation things are reversed. There is a recognized need for a material with specific properties, and scientists try to find it. There are many examples of this kind of research, since what we call materials science usually operates in this mode. Some examples of materials that scientists would like to develop include the following:

- High-temperature superconductors (see page 64)
- Biodegradable plastics for packaging
- Filters that can be used in the desalination process
- Materials that can increase the efficiency of batteries
- High-efficiency (and low-cost) solar cells
- Materials that can remove carbon dioxide from the atmosphere for long periods of time

The list can go on, but the point is clear. At any given moment there are problems that people would like to solve, and often a new material can be part or all of the solution. ■

Solar cells may someday supply much of the world's energy.

▷ ca 620 B.C.

It's Just a Phase

The Phases of Matter

The fact that matter comes in many forms was known to the ancient Greeks—in fact, Thales of Miletus (ca 624–ca 546 B.C.) observed that water can exist in many states (ice, liquid, steam) and suggested that water was the basic constituent of which the universe was made. Today we recognize four basic phases of matter: solid, liquid, gas, and plasma.

Above: A modern engraving of Thales of Miletus. The Greek philosopher first noted the phases of water: liquid, ice, and steam.

Solid

In the solid phase, matter retains both its volume and its shape. The best way to picture this state of matter is to think of an array of atoms held together by a rigid grid, rather like a Tinkertoy construction. Ice is the solid phase of water.

Liquid

A liquid maintains its volume but can change its shape. One way to picture a liquid is to imagine a jar partially filled with marbles. Tilt the jar and the shape of the collection of marbles changes, but the number of marbles, and hence the volume occupied, does not.

> ⊕ Although **solids, liquids, gases, and plasmas are the most common forms of matter,** scientists have found many other forms.

Gas

A gas can change both its shape and its volume, depending on the container in which it finds itself. Gases can be visualized as a collection of atoms or molecules whizzing around, changing direction only when they collide with each other or the walls of the container.

Plasma

Although the plasma state of matter is common in the universe, it is probably the least familiar to most people. If a gas is heated, the atoms or molecules that make it up will move faster and faster, and consequently their collisions become more violent. Eventually they become sufficiently violent to tear electrons out of their normal orbits, leaving the atoms or molecules with an unbalanced positive charge. This state, in which negatively and positively charged particles are free to move independently of each other, is called a plasma. Matter in stars is primarily in this state, but a partial plasma, with only a few electrons pulled loose from each atom, can also be seen in an ordinary fluorescent lightbulb. □

MATERIALS

Although every material is made from atoms, the actual form the material takes depends on things like temperature and pressure.

It's a Gas!

The Ideal Gas Law

There aren't many situations in the history of science in which several people contributed to an important final result while each one's contribution can be precisely stated, but the so-called ideal gas law is just such a situation. It specifies the reaction of a gas to changes in temperature, pressure, and concentration, with each piece of the puzzle having been contributed by a different scientist.

Robert Boyle (1627–1691) showed that increasing the pressure on a gas reduced its volume by an amount proportional to the pressure change—double the pressure and you cut the volume in half. This is known as Boyle's law.

Jacques Charles (1746–1823) showed that increasing the temperature of a gas while keeping the volume fixed increased the pressure—double the temperature and you double the pressure. This is known as Charles's law. Charles was apparently motivated by the Montgolfier brothers' hot air balloon flights (see page 222).

Amedeo Avogadro (1776–1856) showed that increasing the amount of a gas—essentially adding more atoms or molecules—increased the pressure if the volume was held fixed.

In 1834, Émile Clapeyron (1799–1864) put all of this together into the ideal gas law, which is usually written as $PV = nRT$, where P, V, and T are the pressure, volume, and temperature of a gas; n is the amount of gas (measured in a chemical unit called a mole); and R is a universal constant.

> 🔍 In 2015 the New England Patriots football team was **accused of deflating balls** during a championship game.

As the name implies, the ideal gas law describes the behavior of a perfect gas, whose atoms are geometrical points without internal structure. It is, however, a useful (and simple) approximation in many situations. □

Right: The ideal gas law explains why a soda can sometimes erupts when it's opened.

▷ 1849

Brrrrr!

Absolute Zero

How cold can it get? This turns out to be a deep question in every sense of the word. It occupied many scientists throughout the 18th and 19th centuries, but it was William Thomson (Lord Kelvin) (1824–1907) who put it on a firm mathematical footing in 1849.

Here's the way a 19th-century physicist might have thought about the question: We know that temperature is related to the motions of atoms in a gas. The faster the atoms move, the higher the temperature. Similarly, if a gas is cooled, the atoms slow down. Keep cooling, and the atoms move more slowly. You can, in fact, imagine a situation in which the atoms stop moving altogether.

This would represent a limit—the gas can't get any colder than this. In the classical view of things, this is absolute zero—the coldest possible temperature. It is minus 459.67 degrees Fahrenheit.

With the advent of quantum mechanics (see page 74) this picture of absolute zero has to be modified slightly. The Heisenberg uncertainty principle says that an atom cannot be located in a specific spot and be stationary at the same time. Consequently, absolute zero is now defined as the temperature at which no more energy can be extracted from a system rather than as the point at which all motion stops. The change of definition does not, however, change the numerical value of the temperature. □

Above: A rubber ball, which has been cooled almost to absolute zero, shatters when it hits the floor, rather than bounce.

Some Like It Hot

Steel

Throughout human history, steel has been a rare commodity. The reason is simple: Steel is a combination of iron and carbon, and to produce it in quantity you need to heat iron to 2,700 degrees Fahrenheit. Until the 19th century, no one could build a furnace capable of achieving that temperature.

⊕ In some specialty steels there are **more atoms of other materials** than there are atoms of iron.

Iron is held together by the metallic bond (see page 35), with positive iron ions floating in a sea of free electrons. Pure iron is not a particularly strong material. Adding a little carbon, in effect, pins down some points in the iron and makes the resulting material stronger. This is steel.

In the 17th century the first step was taken toward steel by heating iron ore until the impurities—sulfur and silicon, for example—burned to form a slag, some of which was then removed by hand. The temperature was again raised until carbon impurities started to burn as well. This material, with the iron and slag mixed together but not combined chemically, was wrought iron. It is mainly used for decoration today, but it can be used in structures—the Eiffel Tower, for example, is built from wrought iron.

In 1856 the English industrialist Sir Henry Bessemer (1813–1898) introduced the first technique for mass producing steel. Iron ore was heated in a cauldron and air was blown through. This had the effect of burning off the impurities and raising the temperature inside the cauldron to 2,900 degrees Fahrenheit—more than enough to melt the iron. A single 15-minute "blow" in Bessemer's device could produce over ten tons of steel—probably more of the metal than existed in the entire Roman Empire.

Modern steels involve adding different materials to the steel to produce desired qualities. Ordinary "mild" steel—the kind used in I beams and construction—has about 0.25 percent carbon added to the iron. At about 1 percent carbon we get "high carbon steel," which is often used in

Above: The Eiffel Tower, despite its height, is not made from steel but from wrought iron.

Opposite: The incredibly hard steel needed for the railroad tracks shown on the left is produced by adding manganese to molten iron.

kitchen knives. Push the carbon content above a few percent and you get cast iron—strong but brittle.

Add other atoms and you get different qualities. Chrome and nickel added to iron produce "stainless steel," which will not corrode. Add manganese and you get the incredibly hard metal used in railroad tracks. Add vanadium and you get a steel that retains its edge at high temperatures and is used for cutting tools. There are literally thousands of recipes for making different kinds of specialty steels. ☐

Baby It's Cold Inside

Liquefaction of Gases

There are few phase changes in matter that have been more productive in terms of both commerce and science than the ability to turn gases into liquids. Liquefied natural gas is becoming an important factor in world energy commerce, and liquid oxygen is a standard feature in hospitals. Liquefying gases is a process involving both increased pressure and lower temperatures. The Dutch physicist Heike Kamerlingh Onnes (1853–1926) was the first to liquefy helium in 1908, a process that led to the discovery of superconductivity (see page 59). He received the Nobel Prize for this work in 1913. □

Above: Liquid natural gas, stored under pressure in containers like these, is an important source of energy in world markets.

▷ **1985**

Strange Carbon
Buckyballs

Scientists have known about two states of pure carbon for a long time. These states are diamond and graphite (pencil lead), with the differences between the materials being due to the differences in the chemical bonds that appear in the two substances. Then, in 1985, British astronomer Sir Harold Walter Kroto (b 1939) noticed a strange new material in the outer atmosphere of a type of star called a red giant—a material that seemed to consist of long chains of pure carbon. He began collaborating with American scientists Richard Smalley (1943–2005) and Robert Curl, Jr. (b 1933), and the three were able to reproduce the stellar conditions in their laboratory by heating gases with a laser. When they did, they discovered a totally new form of pure carbon.

> 🔍 **The only other forms of pure carbon known are graphite (pencil "lead") and diamond.**

This particular structure contains 60 carbon atoms arrayed in a sphere. Because its structure calls to mind the geodesic domes invented by American architect Buckminster Fuller (1895–1983), the sphere was dubbed buckminsterfullerene, or buckyball for short. The discovery caused quite a stir in the chemical community, and other ways of producing it were quickly found. Even passing an electric arc between carbon electrodes—the basis of old-fashioned arc lighting—produced them. One potentially important variation of the buckyball is the carbon nanotube, which is basically a microscopic cylinder with half a buckyball closing each end.

In 1996 Curl, Kroto, and Smalley shared a Nobel Prize for the discovery of buckminsterfullerene. □

Left: In this model of a buckyball, the black spheres are carbon atoms and the gray struts are the chemical bonds holding them together.

On the Horizon

▷ Carbon Nanotubes

Despite the widespread interest in buckyballs since their discovery, there have been surprisingly few commercial applications of the new material. Research continues in their use in electronic equipment and as filters in chemical reactions. One of the more interesting possible applications is for carbon nanotubes—hollow cylinders of carbon with half a buckyball closing off each end. The idea is that, because the tubes are hollow, they could be filled with drugs or other chemicals and used as a sort of microscopic delivery system.

▷ Bose–Einstein Condensates

In 1924 the Indian physicist Satyendra Nath Bose (1894–1974) and Albert Einstein predicted that certain types of particles—those that are not spinning, for example—would display some unusual behaviors. A gas of these particles, when cooled to a temperature near absolute zero, would condense into a situation in which all of the particles would be together in the system's lowest energy state. This so-called Bose–Einstein condensate was first seen in 1998, when scientists in Boulder, Colorado, cooled a gas made of 2,000 rubidium atoms to within 170 nanokelvins (that is, 170 billionths of a degree) above absolute zero. For this spectacular feat of experimental physics, Eric Cornell (b 1961), Carl Wieman (b 1951), and Wolfgang Ketterle (b 1957) shared the Nobel Prize in 2001.

The Bose–Einstein condensate is an entirely new phase of matter, one in which the laws of quantum mechanics (see page 74) play an important role. It is not clear what the consequences of this new frontier in the properties of matter will be, but they will surely sharpen our understanding of the subatomic world. ■

Artist's conception of a carbon nanotube.

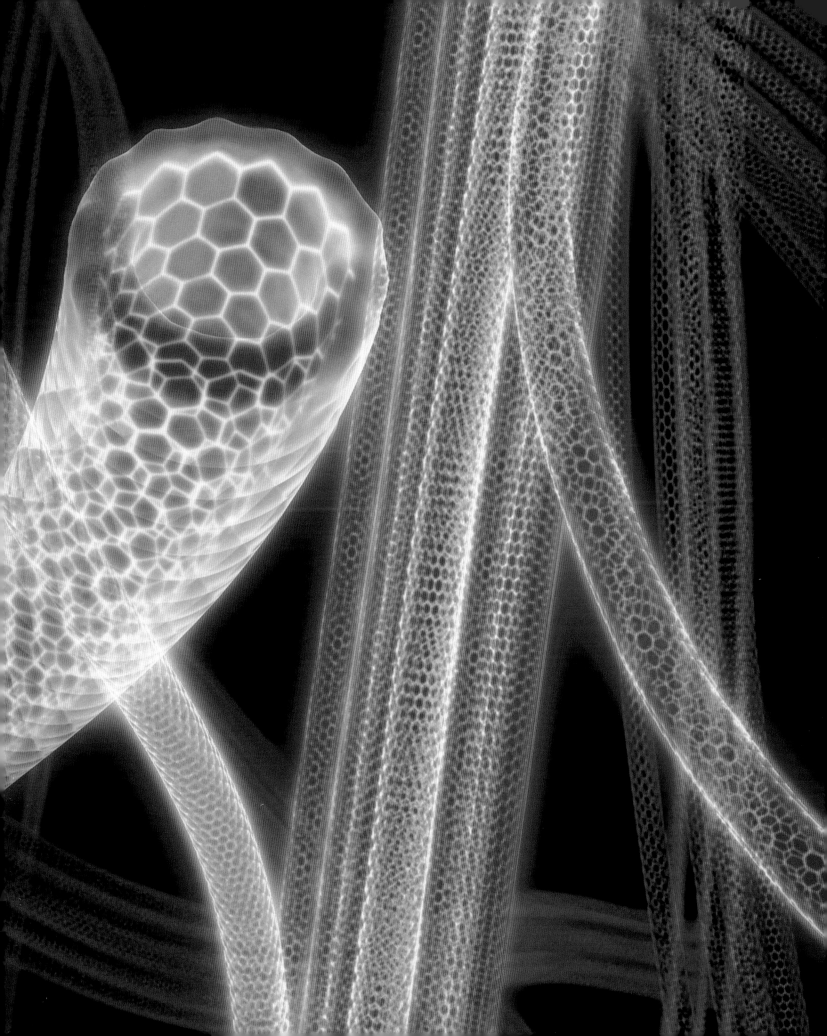

WAVES & OPTICS

▷ Middle Ages

It's All Bent

Lenses and Eyeglasses

The ability of glass to bend light beams led to the development of lenses. Perhaps the most ubiquitous use of lenses is in eyeglasses. We know that the use of eyeglasses to assist in reading was present in the Middle Ages. Eyeglasses were not common in those days, but then, neither was the ability to read. The development of the bifocal lens, allowing the user to shift easily from distance vision to reading, was due to the American statesman, scientist, and inventor Benjamin Franklin (1706–1790), who simply got tired of having to change glasses every time he wanted to look at something else. ▢

⊕ It was Galileo Galilei (1564–1642) who first used lenses in a **telescope to look at heavenly bodies**.

Above: Eyeglasses are one of the most common implements making use of the ability of glass to bend light rays.

By using the properties of light to build instruments like the microscope and telescope, scientists opened the worlds of the very small and the very large.

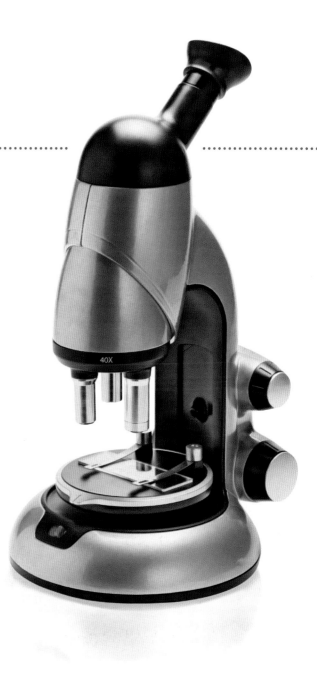

▷ ca 1590

It's So Small

The Microscope

As with many important discoveries, the invention of the microscope is clouded in conflicting claims and counter-claims. The general consensus is that the Dutch lens maker Zacharias Janssen (1585?–1632), possibly with his father Hans, is supposed to have developed the first microscope sometime in the 1590s. This claim is clouded, however, by the fact that Janssen's son

> 🔍 Galileo's name for the microscope was **occhiolino** (the "little eye").

published several dates for the discovery—some as late as 1620—in an effort to establish his own priority. It is also not helped by the fact that Janssen was convicted of counterfeiting several times in his life.

In any case, the microscope opened a new world for scientists, allowing them to see things too small to be seen with the unaided eye. The most famous early user of the microscope was the Dutch scientist Antoni van Leeuwenhoek (1631–1723). Unlike most of the people we've discussed in this book, van Leeuwenhoek did not regard himself as a scientist but as a businessman—he was a cloth merchant. It was his desire to inspect the threads in cloth that led him to develop a high-quality microscope lens by drawing glass rods through a flame to produce small spheres. His instruments were small— only a few inches long—but quite powerful. It was his 1676 observations of what he called animalcules in a

Right: The modern optical microscope is a far cry from the earliest instruments made. But even as far back as 1676, van Leeuwenhoek was able to observe microorganisms in a drop of pond water.

drop of pond water that brought the existence of micro-organisms to the attention of scientists and led eventually to important results like the germ theory of disease (see page 128). Since those early days the optical microscope has been improved by advances in optics and the availability of artificial light sources for illumination, until it is now a standard instrument in schools and laboratories around the world. ☐

Above: A typical modern telescope observatory, this one at 2400 meters above sea level in the Canary Islands.

Below: A commemorative coin, minted in 2014, showing Galileo Galilei.

▷ 1608

Seeing Far

The Telescope

As is the case with the microscope, the invention of the telescope is clouded in claims and counterclaims. The Dutch lensmaker Hans Lippershey (1570–1619) is the first to have applied for a patent, but that application was denied as other lensmakers were making the same claim. From the point of view of science, the most important development took place in Italy in 1609 when Galileo Galilei heard about the Dutch invention and set about

> ⊕ For the last century, the world's **largest telescope** has always **cost about as much as the world's largest traffic interchange**.

building an improved telescope himself. He presented one of his instruments to the doge in Venice and was rewarded with a lifetime appointment (as well as a doubling of his salary). Eventually, he was able to build an instrument with the capability of magnifying 32 times.

Galileo was the first person to point a telescope at the sky. What he saw (and reported in his book *The Starry Messenger*) began the process of undermining the theory of the universe that had reigned since the Greeks. He saw mountains on the moon and sunspots (which weren't supposed to be there) and the moons of Jupiter (while all celestial objects were supposed to be circling Earth).

Galileo's telescope is called a refractor, since light is focused by a series of lenses. In 1668 Isaac Newton introduced a new design, which has been used in all major telescopes since then. Called a reflector, these telescopes bring light into a large mirror, which focuses the light on a device that brings the focused beam to an observation point.

Major telescopes are located on mountaintops to place them as far above atmospheric disturbances as possible—major locations today are the summit of Mauna Kea on the Island of Hawaii and the Atacama Desert in Chile. The size of the mirrors has increased from 100 inches on Mount Wilson in the 1920s to tens of meters today. □

▷ 1704

Wave or Particle?

Theories of Light

In 1704 Sir Isaac Newton (1642–1727) published his second great book on the physical sciences. Titled *Opticks: A Treatise on the Reflexion, Refraction, Inflexion, and Colour of Light*, it put the study of light on a firm experimental footing. (Incidentally, "inflexion" is an old-fashioned word for what we would call diffraction today.) He showed, for example, that, contrary to the teachings of Aristotle, white light is actually a mixture of all the colors of the rainbow. He also argued that light was "corpuscular" in nature—today we would say that it is composed of particles. This picture of light was popular because it was consistent with the mechanical view of the universe. For a while it dominated over the notion that light was a wave, which had been put forth by the Dutch scientist Christian Huygens (1629–1695).

But waves behave in ways that particles do not. Most important, they exhibit a property known as interference. If two particles (two baseballs, for example) arrive at the same point in space, there will always be two particles at that point. If two waves arrive at the same point they can reinforce each other or cancel each other out—something particles can never do. As the 19th century progressed and more data on the behavior of light became available, the prevailing scientific view began to shift, despite Newton's enormous prestige, and scientists began to regard light as a wave.

With the development of quantum mechanics in the 20th century (see page 74), thinking about the nature of light shifted again. Experiments showed that light could exhibit properties of a wave or properties of a particle, depending on the experimental setup. This so-called wave–particle duality is a feature of the quantum world, and it implies that the correct answer to the question Is light a wave or a particle? is yes. □

Above: Light shining on soap bubbles. The multicolored display is a classical argument for the wave nature of light. Sir Isaac Newton first showed that light is a mixture of all colors of the rainbow.

▷ 1931

Did You See That?

The Electron Microscope

The ability of a microscope to see small objects depends on the size of those objects. Light waves typically have a wavelength several thousand atoms across, so an ordinary light microscope really can't resolve features smaller than this. It would be like trying to determine the structure of a cork bobbing in the ocean by looking at surf coming into a beach—the wavelength of the surf is much larger than the size of the cork, so the cork is basically invisible.

One of the features of quantum mechanics (see page 74) is that all quantum objects have the characteristics of both particles and waves. This includes electrons, of course. The fact of the matter is that it is easy to produce electrons with wavelengths much shorter than those of visible light. It is not unusual, for example, for the electron wavelengths to be 100,000 shorter than the wavelengths of visible light. This is the basic physics behind the electron microscope.

In 1931 physicist Ernst Ruska (1906–1988) and engineer Max Knoll (1897–1969) built the first microscope that used electrons rather than light. In the following decades, a lot of nickel-and-dime engineering took place. Electron beams were intensified, guidance systems were improved, and so on. Today electron microscopes can achieve magnifications in the range of ten million, as opposed to light microscopes, which magnify only a few thousand times. Ruska was awarded the Nobel Prize in 1986 (the prize wasn't given to Knoll because it is never awarded posthumously).

There are many types of electron microscopes in use. Some look at the transmitted electron beam, some scan surfaces and look at various secondary particles. All, however, use the short wavelength of the electron to achieve their ends. ☐

Above: The electron microscope uses the wave nature of matter to produce images. Today's electron microscopes can achieve magnifications around ten million.

The Ultimate Microscope
Scanning Tunneling Microscope

There are lots of weird effects in quantum mechanics (see page 72), and one of the weirdest is tunneling. In the Newtonian world, if you walk toward a wall, you have to stop when you get there. In the quantum world, there is a chance that you will pass through and wind up on the other side—you will "tunnel" through. In 1981 Gerd Binnig (b 1947) and Heinrich Rohrer (1933–2013) at IBM Zurich found a way to use this fact to build a microscope capable of seeing individual atoms, a device called a scanning tunneling microscope (STM). They shared the Nobel Prize in 1986.

It works this way: If you look at the surface of a material in enough detail, you will see that it is not smooth. The lumpiness comes from the fact that the surface consists of individual atoms, each surrounded by its own cloud of electrons. As you move across the surface, these electron clouds are thickest at the location of atoms, thinnest between them.

The STM moves a small probe across the surface. At places where there are atoms, the distance between the electron clouds and the probe is smallest and tunneling is easiest. Consequently, a current will flow from the probe to the surface. Between atoms the distance will be greater and tunneling will be more difficult. The result will be the creation of a picture of the atom-by-atom structure of the surface.

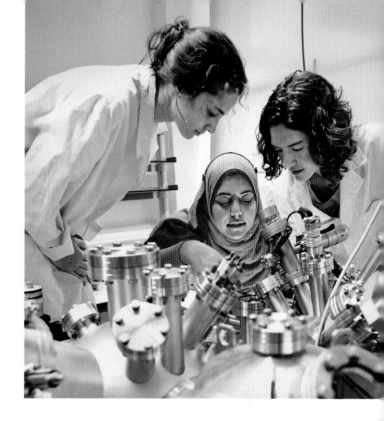

Above: Scientists adjust the setting on a scanning tunneling microscope, which proved incontrovertibly that atoms exist.

In a sense, the STM is the final answer to a question that bedeviled scientists in the 19th century—the question of whether atoms are real or whether matter simply behaves as if it were made from atoms. STM photos are incontrovertible proof of the reality of atoms. ☐

Living with the Atmosphere
Adaptive Optics

The main disadvantage of operating a telescope on the ground (as opposed to in orbit) is that light has to come to the telescope through a turbulent atmosphere. This problem began to be dealt with in the 1990s with the development of adaptive optics. The basic idea is that a laser beam is shot up through the atmosphere to keep track of air movements. The mirror in the telescope is built in segments, each of which has actuators that can change its orientation. Thus the shape of the mirror can be adjusted in real time to compensate for changes in the atmosphere. ☐

Left: This telescope in Hawaii uses a laser to adjust its mirror to changes in the atmosphere.

On the Horizon

▷ The European Extremely Large Telescope

The European Southern Observatory is in the process of building the world's largest telescope on a mountaintop in the Atacama Desert in Chile—one of the best locations for telescope operation in the world. Called the E-ELT (European Extremely Large Telescope), it will have a mirror 39 meters across—a little less than half a football field. It will cost over a billion euros. Construction started in 2014, and first light is expected in 2024. ■

A technician adjusts the machine and polishes the mirrors of a modern telescope.

Left: Because its electrons are tightly bound, glass is a good insulator, which is why it was used in these old pieces of electrical equipment.

Any material that has electrical charges that can respond to an external voltage will be a conductor. Water, for example, usually contains dissolved ions, and can therefore conduct current.

Insulators

In some materials, electrons will be tightly locked in to ionic or covalent bonds (see page 34). These electrons will not be able to respond to an external voltage, and the material will therefore not be able to conduct electrical current. Such materials are called insulators. Glass, rubber, and plastics are examples of insulators.

> ⊕ Electrical outlets and switches are usually **made of insulating plastic** to protect you from electrical current.

Semiconductors

Most of the modern electronics industry is based on the use of semiconductors. We can consider how semiconductors work by thinking about silicon, the most commonly used material of this type.

▷ **Late 19th Century**

Simply Shocking

Electrical Properties of Materials

As soon as physicists had batteries to supply a reliable source of electrical current, they began to investigate the electrical behavior of different kinds of materials. We can look at three important classes of materials: conductors, insulators, and semiconductors.

Conductors

In materials held together by a metallic bond (see page 35), heavy positive ions are seen in a sea of loosely bound electrons. If a voltage is applied to the materials (for example, by putting it between the poles of a battery) the electrons will move. The movement of electrons, of course, constitutes an electrical current. We say that the material is a conductor. Common conductors include copper and other metals.

MAGNETISM

Electricity and magnetism are such an integral part of our modern world, it's nearly impossible to imagine our lives without them.

Silicon has four electrons in its outermost shell, and under normal circumstances each of those would be used to form covalent bonds with a different neighboring atom. You would expect, therefore, that silicon would be an insulator. It happens, however, that the covalent bonds are relatively weak, so that the normal jiggling of the atoms at room temperature is enough to shake a few electrons loose. These electrons will be able to conduct electricity, but as there are so few of them, silicon will not be a very good conductor—hence "semiconductor."

Below: Modern electronic devices like integrated circuits are typically fabricated on silicon wafers like this.

Doped Semiconductors—a Special Case

If a little bit of phosphorous (five electrons in the outermost orbit) is added to molten silicon, a phosphorous atom will take the place of silicon here and there when the melt crystallizes. Four of its electrons will form bonds, like the silicon, and the extra electron will wander off, leaving behind a positively charged ion in the semiconductor. Similarly, adding aluminum (three outer electrons) will leave behind a negatively charged ion.

Thus this process, called doping, can produce semiconductors that have positive or negative charges locked into them. These charges can affect the flow of electrons in the material. □

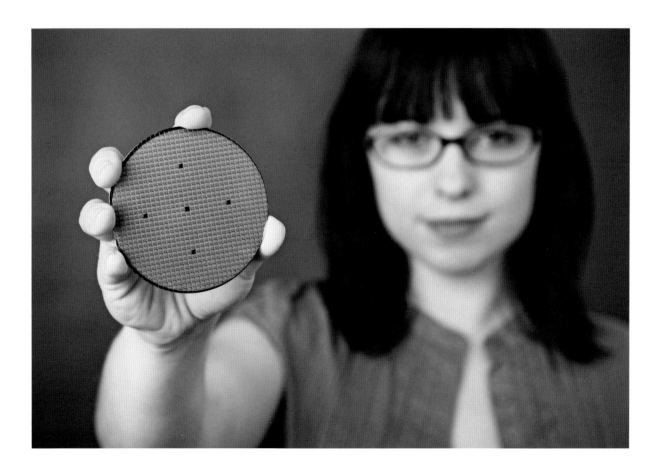

▷ 1894

Magnetic Attraction

Permanent Magnets

People have known about permanent magnets for millennia, but it wasn't until the French scientist Pierre Curie (1859–1906) began working on the subject that people understood what they were. Our modern understanding is this: Every atom has electrons in orbit, and hence can produce a magnetic field. In a few substances, like iron, the interatomic forces are such that these atomic fields will line up and reinforce each other over a region called a domain, a few thousand atoms across. In normal iron, the orientation of these domains is random, so the magnetic fields cancel each other out. If, on the other hand, we arrange things so that the domains line up, then the fields will reinforce each other, and the material will produce a strong field. This is a permanent magnet.

Pierre Curie found that if he melted iron and then allowed it to cool, it would reach a temperature where domains formed. This temperature is now known as the Curie point. Furthermore, cooling the iron in the presence of a magnetic field lines up the domains and creates a permanent magnet. ☐

🔍 Pierre Curie had **worked on magnetism** for years but never bothered to write up his results.

Above: The knives are held up against gravity by the magnetic force exerted by the horizontal metal bar.

▷ 1911

Won't It Ever Stop?

Superconductors

In 1911 the Dutch physicist Heike Kamerlingh Onnes noticed something strange. When he lowered the temperature of a sample of mercury to within a few degrees of absolute zero (see page 41), its electrical resistance seemed to vanish. In other words, it appeared that, once an electrical current started to flow through the material, it never stopped. He soon saw similar behavior in other materials. He noted that, if he connected a battery to a ring of material in this state so that current started flowing, then disconnected the battery, the current just kept right on going. This sort of material is now called a superconductor.

The phenomenon remained a well-verified experimental fact but a theoretical mystery until 1957, when the theoretical physicists John Bardeen, Leon Cooper (b 1930), and John Robert Schrieffer (b 1931) published a theory (called the BCS theory after the three authors' names) that explained it. It provides the following explanation of superconductivity: At very low temperatures, heavy ions in a metal react sluggishly to the electrons around them. As a result, the electrons form pairs (known as Cooper pairs), partnering with electrons thousands of atoms away. As a result, the electrons form an interconnected mass—think of a plate of spaghetti, in which the end of each strand is an electron and the strand represents a Cooper pair. In this situation, you cannot slow down one electron (as you would have to do if you wanted to stop the flow), but you have to stop them all. Consequently, the electrons keep moving because nothing can stop them. Raise the temperature, however, and the pairs dissolve and we're back to normal operation. Bardeen, Cooper, and Schrieffer received the Nobel Prize in 1972 for this work.

For years scientists struggled to find materials that would continue superconducting at high temperatures, but they were barely able to exceed 20 degrees above absolute zero. Then, in 1986, two scientists working in Switzerland, Georg Bednorz (b 1950) and Karl Alexander (Alex) Müller (b 1927), found a material that continued superconducting to 92 degrees above absolute zero. This is still very cold—180 degrees below zero Celsius—but it was the first major advance in this area for a long time. Bednorz and Müller received the Nobel Prize in 1987. ☐

Left: A superconducting disk floats above a magnet, illustrating a phenomenon known as magnetic levitation.

▷ 1947

A Strange Device

The Transistor

Arguably the most important invention of the 20th century, the transistor is a device that can be made from doped semiconductors and used in a variety of ways in electrical circuits. It was invented in 1947 by three physicists: William Shockley (1910–1989), Walter Brattain (1902–1987), and John Bardeen (1908–1991). They shared the Nobel Prize in 1956.

An early design for a transistor consisted of a "sandwich," with the two slices of "bread" having one type of doping (positive charges, for example) and the middle material, called the base, having the opposite type of doping (negative charges in this example). In such a device there will be two junctions that will have to be negotiated by electrons flowing through the device, one going from a positive to a negative charge, the other from negative to positive.

A good analogy to understanding how a transistor works is to think of the device as being like a valve in a water pipe. When water is flowing in a pipe, applying a small amount of energy to the valve can have a large effect on the flow—even shut it off completely. In the same way, running a negative charge onto the base can have a large effect on electrical current running through the transistor.

Perhaps the most important application of transistors is in computers, where they function as on–off switches. Computers operate in a digital mode, where information is carried in a string of 0s and 1s. In a computer, millions of transistors are either "on" (1) or "off" (0). Thus the transistor serves as the basis for the information revolution. ☐

Above: Before the invention of transistors, electronic devices depended on the functioning of vacuum tubes like these. They ran telephone networks, radio, television, and early computers. A few applications for vacuum tubes survive, most notably the magnetrons that power microwave ovens.

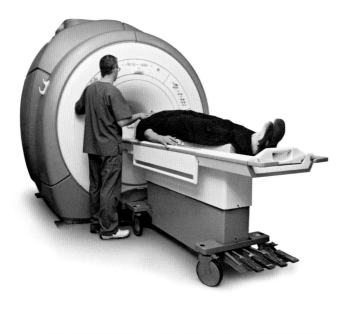

Above: The use of MRI machines containing superconducting magnets like the one shown are a standard tool in modern medicine.

▷ 1955

It Just Keeps Going

Superconducting Magnets

The idea that superconductors could be used to make magnets occurred to Heike Kamerlingh Onnes in 1911, but it was 1955 before the first one was built. A superconducting magnet is a special form of the electromagnet, which operates on the principle that an electrical current in a loop of wire will produce a magnetic field indistinguishable from that of a permanent magnet. The point, however, is that, once a current is started in a superconducting loop, the power source can be removed and the field will persist as long as the loop is kept cold.

The construction of superconducting magnets is a billion-dollar-a-year industry worldwide. Magnetic resonance imaging machines in hospitals use them, as do large-scale accelerators like the Large Hadron Collider (see page 20). Future uses might include magnetic levitation (maglev) trains (see page 220) and energy storage systems. ☐

🔍 Commercial superconducting magnets are **kept cold by being immersed in liquid helium,** a fluid that costs about as much as medium-priced Scotch.

▷ 1962

More Light, Less Heat

Light-Emitting Diode

The light-emitting diode (LED) is a device made of two pieces of doped semiconductor. When an electric current passes through the diode, some of the electrons will drop into vacancies (they're called holes) created by the doping, emitting light in the process.

The first LED to emit visible light—it was red—was produced by electrical engineer Nick Holonyak (b 1928), then at General Electric, later at the University of Illinois. Other colors of light were produced later, including green and blue. LEDs convert electrical energy to light much more efficiently than ordinary incandescent light bulbs and are now widely used in many applications. You may see them, for example, in vehicle taillights and large advertising displays. It is expected that they will soon play a major role in interior lighting as well. ☐

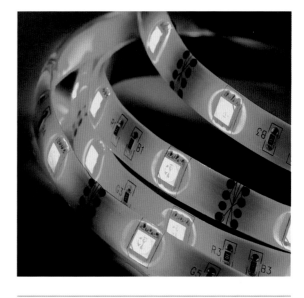

Above: These are typical light-emitting diodes—in this case they give off blue light.

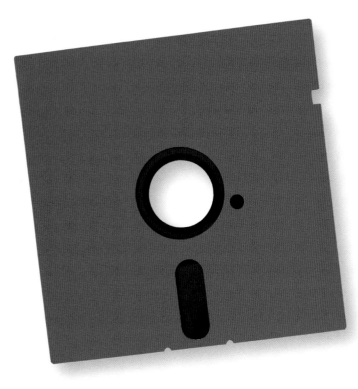

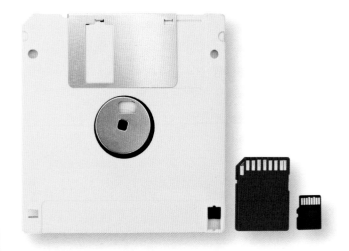

▷ 1965

Plenty of Room at the Bottom

Moore's Law

In 1965 computer scientist Gordon Moore (b 1929), one of the founders of Intel, made an interesting observation. Pick any index of computer performance, such as the number of transistors on a chip, memory capability, or speed of calculation. Moore noted that this index had been doubling every two years, and he projected this sort of advance into the future. This observation became known as Moore's law.

The amazing thing is that this "law" has held for the last 50 years, through many changes in technology and manufacturing regimens. In fact, people have even suggested that the relevant time should be 18 months rather than 2 years. One advantage of Moore's law for old-timers is that we can regale our children with stories of how limited the first personal computers we bought were—memory in kilobytes?

Moore's law is obviously not a law of nature like Newton's law of universal gravitation. Nevertheless, it seems to have worked quite well for half a century.

But it has to break down sometime—it can't go on forever. The size of a transistor, for example, can't be smaller than an atom. In 2005, Moore suggested that his law would have to break down in 10 to 20 years (though it showed no sign of doing so in 2015). Theoretical physicists, applying grand principles of entropy and thermodynamics, have established an absolute upper bound for Moore's law of about 600 years. It seems obvious that the law will collapse before then for mundane reasons, however. □

Above: Moore's law is dramatically illustrated by this series of devices for storing digital information. The devices get smaller even as their storage capacity increases.

🔍 In the 1970s, state of the art desktop computers had **memories measured in kilobytes** (thousands of bits), while today a laptop will have a memory measured in gigabytes (billions of bits of information).

Getting Straight

Liquid Crystals

A liquid crystal, as the name implies, is a state of matter midway between liquid and a solid crystal. You can visualize the liquid state by picturing a box of straws thrown randomly on the floor. Now imagine that there was an outside agent that could cause all the straws to line up. The orderly, lined-up version would correspond to the crystal state.

In a liquid crystal, long molecules play the role of the straws in our analogy. Electrical forces can cause the molecules to line up, and when they do they can often be made to emit light. Just about every numerical display you see on your various electronic devices are the result of a liquid crystal being oriented in this way. ☐

Below: Massive light displays like this one in Beijing are produced by light-emitting diodes.

On the Horizon

▷ Room Temperature Superconductors

The holy grail of superconductivity research has always been the discovery of a material that will remain superconducting at room temperature. Without the need for expensive and complex cooling, such a material could be used everywhere that electricity flows.

▷ The End of Moore's Law

Sooner or later Moore's law, which says that computer components like transistors will shrink in size by a factor of two every two years, will have to give out. Scientists are already looking for new ways to manipulate information, by using light waves, for example, or finding ways to store information in individual molecules. This sort of research will speed up as the end of Moore's law approaches. ■

Artist's conception of a machine that uses light waves instead of atoms to store information.

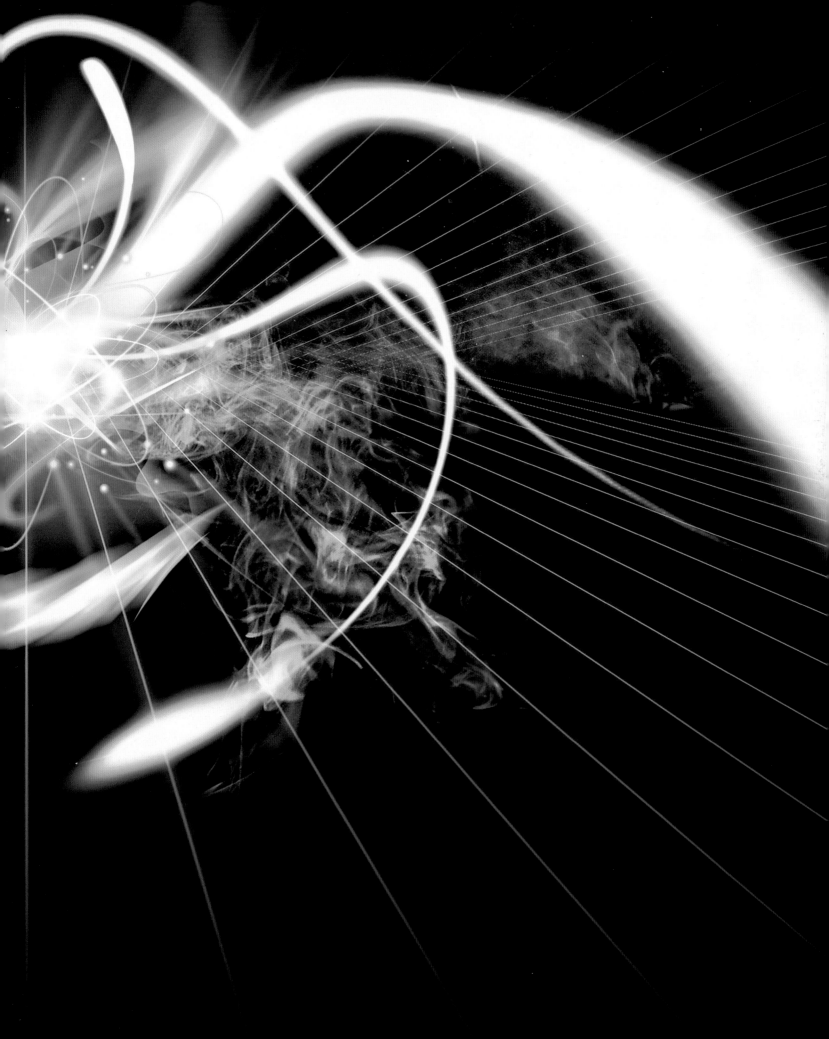

RELATIVITY

In 1905 Albert Einstein changed the way we think about space and time.

Left: Unlike most scientific theories, relativity is the result of the work of one man—Albert Einstein.

▷ 1905

It's All Relative
Special Relativity

Here's an imaginary experiment: A friend riding by as a passenger in a car throws a ball straight up and catches it when it falls. You observe this from the side of the road. Suppose I ask you each to describe the event. Your friend says the ball travels straight up and down, you say it travels in an arc. Different descriptions. But now let me ask each of you a deeper question—what are the laws of nature that govern the motion of the ball? You and your friend will give me the same answer—you will both see the same laws operating. This is an example of the principle of special relativity: *The laws of nature are the same in all inertial frames of reference* ("inertial" means frames moving at constant velocity). In 1905 Albert Einstein published a paper that would use this principle to revolutionize physics.

The problem Einstein addressed had to do with the fact that the "laws of nature" included the laws of electricity and magnetism, and these have the property that the speed of light ("c") is built into them. If the principle of relativity is correct, this implies that the speed of light is the same in all frames of reference—in fact, you often see this statement as one of the assumptions that go into the theory of relativity.

To see why this is important, let's imagine a "clock" built this way: There is a flashbulb that goes off, sending a light beam up to a mirror, which reflects the beam back into a photocell, which, in turn, triggers the flashbulb and starts the cycle over. One "tick" of this clock corresponds to the time it takes light to travel up to the mirror and back.

Now imagine a clock like this going by on a train. The light will travel on a sawtooth path, unlike light in a clock on the ground. If the speed of light is really the same in all frames, it will take the moving clock longer to "tick" than it takes a clock on the ground. The prediction that moving clocks slow down—time dilation—is one of the first results of special relativity. Other results include the following:

- Moving objects shrink in the direction of motion.
- Moving objects become more massive.
- Events that are simultaneous in one frame are not simultaneous in others.
- $E = mc^2$. □

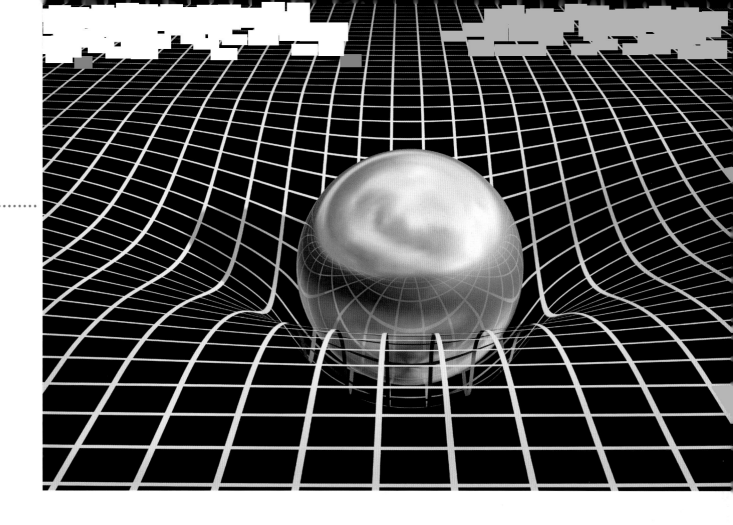

▷ 1915

Odd Man Out

General Relativity

The principle of general relativity is that the laws of nature are the same in all frames of reference, whether they are accelerating or not. The mathematics involved is considerably more difficult than that involved in special relativity—the fact that it took a man of Einstein's abilities ten years to get from one to the other attests to that.

The basic idea of general relativity can be summarized in two statements:

- The presence of matter distorts the fabric of space-time.
- Objects follow the shortest paths in that distorted space-time.

Here's a simple way to visualize how this works: Imagine a rubber sheet marked out in square Cartesian coordinates.

Now put a bowling ball on the sheet. The sheet will be distorted by the presence of the bowling ball just as the fabric of space-time is distorted by the presence of matter. A marble shot past the bowling ball will be deflected. A Newtonian would say that it was deflected by the force of gravity, whereas Einstein would say that it was traveling on the shortest path in a distorted space-time.

This, incidentally, is the source of one of the deepest puzzles in modern physics. In general relativity, gravity is basically a geometrical phenomenon—it depends on the warping of space-time coordinates. The other three forces (see page 20), on the other hand, are dynamical, depending on the interaction of fundamental particles. Gravity, at the moment, is odd man out in this game. □

Above: This artist's rendering shows how Earth makes a dent in the fabric of space-time. According to general relativity, this curvature is what we perceive as gravity.

> 🔍 At the time of Einstein's first paper on relativity, he was an **obscure patent examiner** third class in the Swiss Patent Office.

The Proof Is in the Pudding

Experimental Tests of Special and General Relativity

No theory, especially one so counterintuitive as relativity, can be accepted unless it passes the test of being compared to experimental results. There are many such successful comparisons for both special and general relativity, such as those listed here.

Special Relativity

- In 1851, the French physicist Hippolyte Fizeau (1819–1896) did an experiment measuring the speed of light in moving water. He found that the Newtonian technique of adding the velocity of light to the velocity of the water didn't work. Einstein was able to show that Fizeau's result followed from special relativity.

- In 1971, scientists put atomic clocks, accurate to 13 decimal places, on airplanes flying around the world and compared them to a clock left behind at the U.S. Naval Observatory in Washington, D.C. This was the first direct measurement of time dilation.

- Particles like muons (see page 18) are constantly being created by cosmic ray collisions in the atmosphere. Muons decay in a microsecond, so according to Newtonian notions they can travel no more than

Above: The Laser Interferometer Gravitational-Wave Observatory (LIGO) measures the distortion of space-time when a gravitational wave passes. The first such wave was detected in 2016.

300 meters before decaying. In fact, they are observed to survive all the way to sea level—another confirmation of time dilation.

- The global positioning system uses clocks in orbit to determine positions on Earth. The effect of time dilation due to this movement (seven microseconds per day) has to be accounted for if the system is to work.
- Energy is routinely generated by conversion of mass in nuclear reactors, and in machines like the Large Hadron Collider (see page 20) energy is routinely used to create massive particles—both confirmations of $E = mc^2$.

General Relativity

There are three tests that are generally referred to as the classical tests of general relativity:

- Perihelion shift of mercury—general relativity explained an old discrepancy between gravitational calculations and the orbit of the planet Mercury.
- Bending of light—measurements taken in 1919 during a solar eclipse verified predictions that light, like material objects, would be deflected if it passed near a massive body such as the sun.
- Gravitational red shift—the theory predicts that light climbing upward in a gravitational field would be shifted toward the red end of the wavelength spectrum. This effect was first seen in 1959.

In addition, there are a lot of modern confirmations of general relativity:

- In 1970, scientists began measuring the time delay on signals sent out to and reflected from planets in such a way that the signals passed near the sun. In 2003 scientists used a fortunate configuration of the Cassini spacecraft (see page 184) to verify the predictions of the theory about the effect of the sun's gravity on light to a value of 0.002 percent.
- In 1979 astronomers discovered the phenomenon of gravitational lensing (the bending of light from a distant object by a nearby object). Today this effect is routinely used to look for dark matter (see page 208) and other types of mass. □

Above: The arcs in this photograph result from the bending of light by distant masses. They are called Einstein rings.

🔍 The detection of gravitational waves constituted **the last remaining test of general relativity.** It passed with flying colors.

On the Horizon

▷ Gravitational Wave Astronomy

The detection of gravitational waves by LIGO in 2016 not only supplied the last missing confirmation of general relativity, it also opened a new window through which astronomers could learn about the universe. Strong gravitational waves are produced whenever large masses of material undergo violent changes—the wave detected in 2016, for example, was created when two black holes spiraled together and merged. Thus the ability of detectors like LIGO to detect gravitational waves gives us a way of studying the most violent events in our universe.

▷ The Theory of Everything

As we have seen, gravity is odd man out among the forces of nature. It will not always be so. Some of the best minds in the human race are trying to unify gravity with the rest of nature. We can expect that soon we will have what theorists refer to as the theory of everything (TOE).

▷ Warp Drive

Don't hold your breath on this one. The "speed of light limit" follows from the fact that moving objects become more massive as their speed increases, approaching infinity as the object approaches the speed of light. Concepts like warp drive and hyperspace were invented by science fiction writers to get around this difficulty. Here's how they work: Imagine making two marks on a piece of paper. To get from one to the other, you would have to travel along the paper at less than the speed of light. But if you could fold the paper over and step into the third dimension, you could go from one dot to the other instantly. This is the idea of hyperspace.■

An artist's conception of what hyperspace and warp drive might look like.

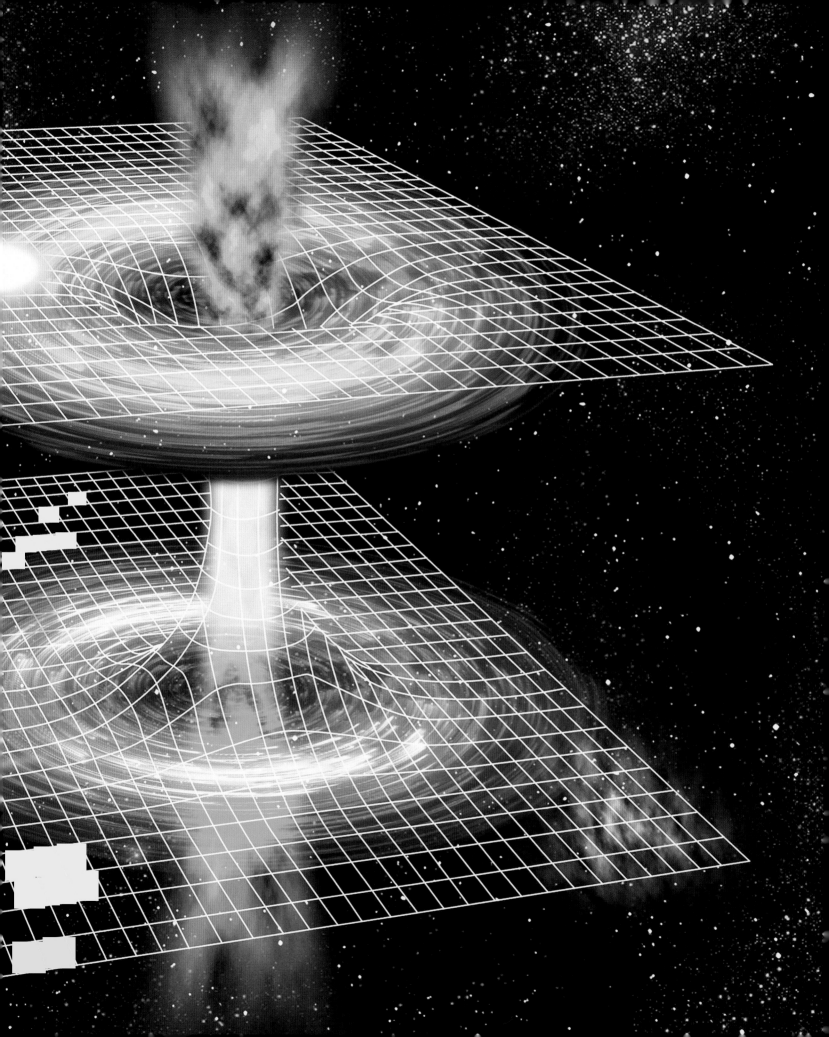

QUANTUM

> Although **quantum mechanics seems to be a strange science,** it has been estimated that as much as a third of the American GDP depends on it.

▷ 1900

It All Comes in Bundles
The Birth of Quantum Mechanics

The word "quantum" is Latin for "bundle" or "heap," and "mechanics" is the old word for the science of motion. Thus quantum mechanics is the science of the motion of things that come in bundles. Starting with the discovery of the bundle of matter called the electron (see page 14), it rapidly became obvious that everything inside the atom— mass, charge, energy, and so on—came in quanta. In 1900 the German physicist Max Planck (1858–1947) showed that certain theoretical problems involving the interaction of light and matter could be resolved if he assumed that atoms could absorb and emit light only at certain fixed (that is, quantized) energies. In 1905, in the paper that would win him a Nobel prize, Albert Einstein showed that other experimental results could be understood if light itself came in bundles (they're called photons). Then, in 1911, Niels Bohr (see page 16) showed that the spectra of light emitted and absorbed by atoms could be explained if a quantity known as angular momentum in atoms was quantized as well.

All of these developments pointed to the idea that the world inside the atom is very different from the world we're used to. Just how different it was came as something of a surprise as quantum mechanics was developed. ☐

Left: Artist's conception of a quantum mechanical wave.

MECHANICS

In the early 20th century scientists began exploring the world inside the atom. It turned out to be a very strange place.

▷ 1920s

Heisenberg May Have Slept Here

Uncertainty and the Wave Function

The modern science of quantum mechanics was developed by a group of young European physicists in the 1920s and 1930s. It is perhaps best typified by talking about the German physicist Werner Heisenberg (1901–1976). He spent a summer alone on an island in the Baltic to avoid attacks of hay fever (the island had no trees) and formulated what has come to be called the Heisenberg uncertainty principle. It works this way: Because the only way we can measure the properties of a quantum object is to bounce another quantum object off of it, every quantum measurement will change the thing being measured. This means, for example, that if we measure the position of an electron exactly we will not be able to measure its velocity and vice versa. Alternatively, we could accept some uncertainty in the measurement of the position and determine the velocity with some other uncertainty.

The key point is that, in the quantum world, our knowledge of nature will always be uncertain.

This concept was put into its modern form by the Austrian physicist Erwin Schrödinger (1887–1961). Rather than describing a particle as being in a certain place, Schrödinger described the position in terms of what is known as a wave function, which basically gives the probability that the particle will be found at each point in space. It was this probabilistic interpretation of nature that caused Einstein to get off the quantum train and generate his famous remark, "God does not play dice with the universe." ☐

> 🔍 **In the quantum world, our knowledge of nature will always be uncertain.**

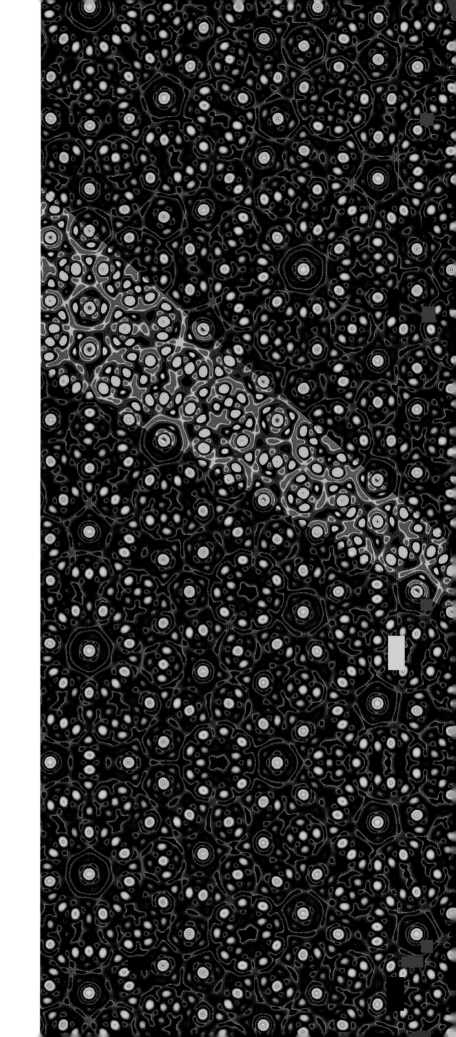

Boy, This Is Really Weird

Quantum Weirdness

The world inside the atom is very hard to visualize. The American physicist Richard Feynman (1918–1988) is supposed to have remarked, "Don't ask how nature can be that way. No one knows how it can be that way." Some examples of quantum weirdness include wave–particle duality and entanglement.

Wave–Particle Duality

In the Newtonian world, everything is either a particle or a wave, and there is a straightforward way of telling the difference—if the object displays interference (see page 51), it's a wave. If it doesn't, it's a particle. Period.

In the quantum world it's not so simple. If we shoot an electron at a target, we can set things up to measure it as a particle—we see if we get a single "ping" when it enters the detector, for example. Alternatively, we can set things up to measure interference—send the electron beam

> 🔍 **If you're not bothered by quantum mechanics, you don't understand it.**

through a screen with slits in it, for example, so that electrons arrive at the detector from different places and interfere with each other.

But what if we send the electrons through the slits one at a time? Each arrives at the detector as a single particle, but if you add up the electrons as they accumulate, you get an interference pattern characteristic of a wave. How does each individual electron know what the others are going to do?

It gets worse. You can actually set up experiments that will decide whether to measure wave or particle properties *after* the electron is on its way to the apparatus. It makes no difference: If you measure particle properties you get particle results, if you measure wave properties you get wave results.

Clearly, in the quantum world, electrons and photons are neither particle nor wave, but some unimaginable thing that has properties of both. This, of course, is completely outside of our experience in the Newtonian world.

Right: This complex array of atoms is an example of yet another state of matter known as a quasicrystal.

Entanglement

In 1935 Einstein and two of his collaborators—Nathan Rosen (1909–1995) and Boris Podolsky (1896–1966)—proposed a thought experiment which they thought would show that the probabilistic thrust of quantum mechanics had to be wrong. Called the EPR experiment, it worked this way: Suppose you have a system that emits quantum objects in opposite directions, and suppose there is a rule that governs the nature of those objects. For example, if the system emits a right-handed glove to the left, then it must emit a left-handed glove to the right. Now let those gloves get so far apart that a light beam could not travel from one to the other in the time it takes to make a measurement. Then, they argued, if you measured the handedness of the glove moving to the left, you would know the handedness of the glove moving to the right *even if you never measured it directly.*

Einstein and his collaborators took this result to mean that there were ways of describing quantum systems in a Newtonian way—the idea came to be called the hidden variable theory. In 1964, however, Irish physicist John Bell (1928–1990) discovered a theorem with a remarkable property—it showed that there were certain experiments which would give different results for standard quantum mechanics and the hidden variable theories. When the experiments were done in the 1970s, the results were clear—quantum mechanics was correct.

The explanation of the EPR situation was this: Once two systems are described by the same wave, they are always connected by that wave function. In modern jargon, they are "entangled." No matter how far apart they are, they are always connected. ☐

Above: The interlocking rings symbolize the concept of entanglement.

More Quantum Teleportation

"Teleportation" refers to a process in which an object is destroyed at one point and re-created at another—think of the transporter on *Star Trek*. Teleportation has been achieved for photons using the phenomenon of entanglement. It works this way: A pair of entangled photons is created. One goes to Alice, who, in her laboratory, allows her entangled photon to interact with another one— call it the input photon. The interaction destroys both photons, but she calls Ted on the phone and tells him what the interaction was. With this information and his entangled photon, Ted can produce another photon—call this one the output photon— identical to the input photon. Thus the input photon has been teleported.

A pixel-by-pixel application of this technique has been used to send pictures hundreds of miles over optical fibers (see page 290). The really interesting question is whether it can be used to teleport matter, because once we can send an atom, it won't be long before we can send people.

Beam me up, Scotty!

Quantum Dots

Quantum dots are small bits of semiconductor. They are small enough so that quantum mechanical effects play a role in the behavior of their electrons but not big enough to behave like large chunks of matter. Think of them as being midway between a molecule and a transistor.

Depending on its size and how it's made, the electrons in a quantum dot will emit intense light beams at different frequencies. Although there are no large-scale commercial applications of quantum dot technology, such applications are being explored. Quantum dots may be combined with light-emitting diodes (see page 257). to enhance displays, for example, or they may play a role in quantum computers (see following).

The fictional transporters in the science fiction series *Star Trek* are often cited as an example of what quantum teleportation might look like in the future.

Quantum Computers

In a standard computer, information is stored and manipulated in bits—strings of 0s and 1s. This is why the transistor (see page 60) figures so prominently in computer operation. In a quantum computer, information can be dealt with in this way, but it can also be in the form of what are called quantum bits (qubits), which are combinations of 0s and 1s.

Unfortunately (or fortunately, depending on your point of view), these machines are far in the future. Right now laboratory scientists are limited to performing operations with at most a few dozen qubits.

Our theories tell us that if we could build a machine to manipulate the qubits it could solve complex problems not accessible to ordinary computers—it could, for example, be used to crack encryption codes now considered unbreakable. Unfortunately (or fortunately, depending on your point of view), these machines are far in the future. Right now laboratory scientists are limited to performing operations with at most a few dozen qubits. ∎

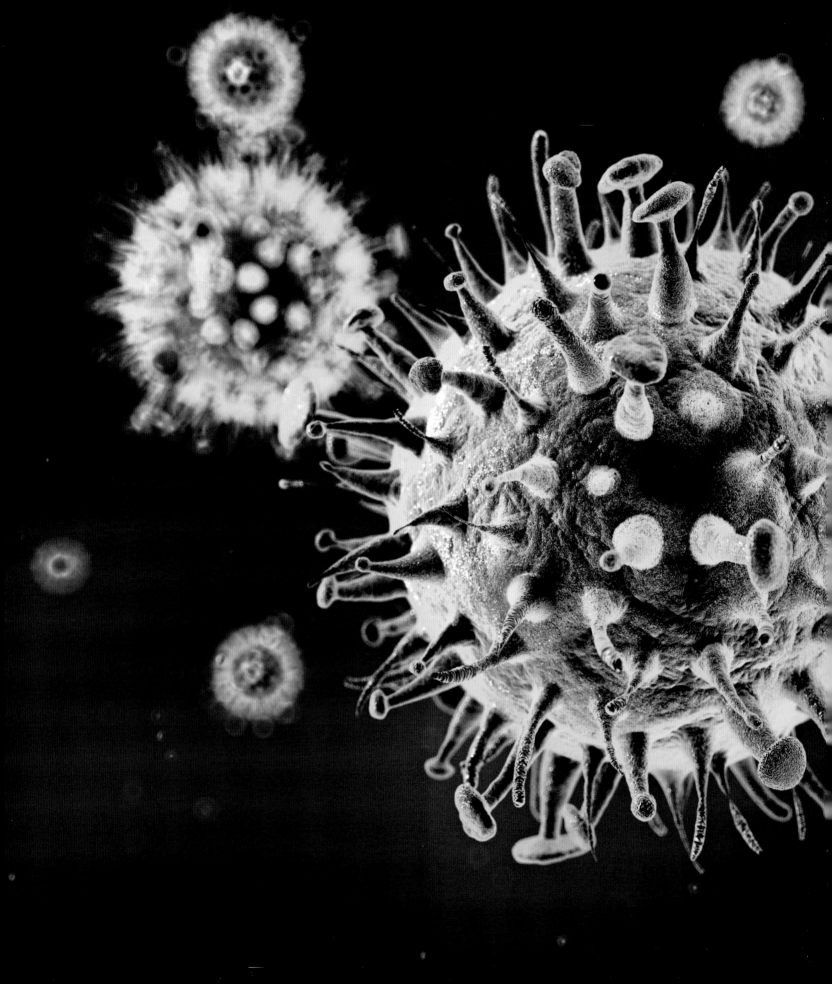

Chapter 2
LIFE
SCIENCES

ORIGIN OF LIFE

▷ ca 4,000,000,000 B.C.

It Had to Start Sometime

When Did Life Develop?

Early on, Earth was a molten, airless ball floating in space, constantly bombarded by meteorites. As the planet cooled, oceans formed, and the possibility of the development of life arose. The bombardment didn't stop, however, and we know that the impact of an Ohio-sized meteorite would have vaporized the oceans and given Earth an atmosphere made of live steam for centuries.

Thus life that survived to the present could not have arisen until the bombardment stopped, about 4 billion years ago. We know that complex single-celled life on Earth appeared about 3.5 billion years ago (see page 84), so once it was possible for life to survive, it seems to have developed quite rapidly. ☐

🔍 Life might have arisen many times on Earth, **only to be wiped out.** We are descended from the first cells that never faced this fate.

Above: Early in its history, Earth underwent a period of heavy bombardment. Large impacts would have destroyed any life that had developed.

Earth is the only planet on which we are sure that life developed. Consequently, it's important to know how that happened.

▷ 1952

In the Soup

Life's Building Blocks

The first question we can ask about the origin of life is how the basic building blocks that go into life's molecules arose. The molecules in living systems are complex, but they are complex in a specific way. Like a complex building made from simple bricks, the molecules in living systems achieve complexity by stringing simple building blocks together in complex ways. Molecules called proteins, for example, play an important role in living systems—they regulate the chemical reactions in cells. Proteins are long strings of simpler building

🔍 Understanding how life arose on Earth is an important step in **understanding how (and if) it developed elsewhere in the universe.**

blocks called amino acids. Think of the string of amino acids as being analogous to beads on a string. For a long time, scientists avoided origin of life studies because they saw no way of reproducing the observed complexity of life.

In 1952, this changed. In the basement of the chemistry building at the University of Chicago, then graduate student Stanley Miller (1930–2007) and his adviser, Nobel Laureate Harold Urey (1893–1981) did an experiment that would forever change scientific attitudes about origin of life studies. Their goal was simple: to reproduce in their laboratory the conditions of prebiotic Earth as best they could. In a glass apparatus they had water and heat (to represent the ocean and sun), electric sparks (representing lightning discharges), and an atmosphere of methane, water, hydrogen, and ammonia (the best guess people had at the time about the composition of Earth's early atmosphere). They turned the system on and waited to see what would happen. What they found was amazing. After a few weeks, they found amino acids in their apparatus! Starting with simple nonorganic materials, they had produced some of the basic building blocks of life.

A word of caution: today we think that Miller and Urey got the composition of the early atmosphere wrong, but it doesn't matter. Experiments with different atmospheres and different energy sources produce the same kinds of results. In addition, lots of simple organic molecules are found in meteorites and even in interstellar dust clouds. It appears that nature produces the basic building blocks of life by a variety of processes—they are not rare at all. Thus the real origin of life problem is not producing the building blocks, but assembling them into a functioning cell.

One of the most picturesque ideas about how that first cell might have arisen goes by the name of primordial soup. The idea is that, once the oceans formed, a Miller–Urey process (or a rain of comets and meteorites) would start dumping organic molecules into the water. Eventually their concentration would get high enough so that chemical reactions would start building complex molecules. This rich, roiling broth is what is called the primordial soup. The process by which the first cell arose from the soup is still a subject of active debate. □

Above: The basic molecular building blocks of life appeared in the primordial soup.

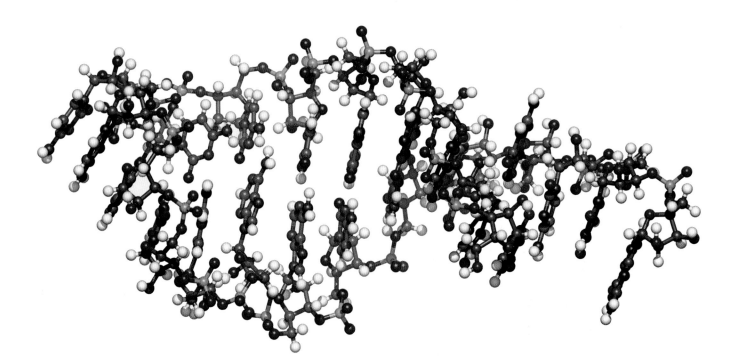

▷ 1982

Theories Duke It Out

RNA World Versus Metabolism First

Modern living systems are extremely complex. Information stored in DNA molecules is transferred, via a suite of molecules called ribonucleic acid (RNA) to the string of amino acids that make up a protein. The protein then acts as an enzyme or catalyst to run a chemical reaction in the cell. Like a modern computer-controlled automobile, the modern cell is a long way from its simple origins. Working out that simple origin is a little like trying to deduce the structure of a Model T by examining a modern car. The situation is made worse by the chicken-and-egg nature of the problem: you need the protein enzymes to make DNA and RNA, but you need DNA and RNA to make the protein enzymes.

There have been many attempts to resolve this issue. It has been suggested, for example, that the earliest guidelines for life's molecules might have been minerals or clays that used static electrical forces to bring atoms together. Here we will look at two kinds of theories being pursued by scientists today—RNA world and metabolism first.

RNA World

Today RNA molecules play an important role as mediators in the process involved in governing chemical reactions in cells. In 1982, however, it was discovered that certain types of RNA molecules can act as catalysts for chemical reactions, including the chemical reactions that produce RNA. This discovery led to the idea of RNA world, a world in which RNA molecules act both as enzymes and as carriers of information. The idea is that, once we have

Q Will life arise whenever the geological conditions are right, or does it require the chance assembly of a complex molecule?

a self-reproducing system using RNA, the current (more complex) system involving DNA will evolve by the process of natural selection (see page 86).

Metabolism First

It turns out that there is a simple chemical cycle that operates in all cells. Today it takes in large molecules, breaks them down, and produces energy. Called the Krebs cycle or the citric acid cycle, it can also run in the opposite direction, taking in energy and small molecules and producing larger molecules. In this mode it can run without enzymes. In the metabolism first theory, the Krebs cycle operates to produce a self-replicating cell by taking in energy and producing more and more complex molecules. As with the RNA world theory, once this simple system becomes operational, the current complexity follows through the effects of natural selection.

Which of these two theories (if either) will turn out to be correct is still very much an open question. The question of how the basic building blocks of life's molecules were turned into a reproducing cell remains one of the great research topics in the life sciences. □

Above: A computer model of an RNA molecule.

On the Horizon

▷ Artificial Life

With all the scientific brain power going into understanding the development of that first cell, sooner
or later (probably sooner) someone is going to produce something in a test tube that we will recognize
as being alive. This doesn't mean that that person
will have discovered what happened on early
Earth—there could well be many ways of arriving
at life. It also won't be dangerous. If a primitive cell
got loose, it would be a prime candidate for lunch
for thousands of organisms whose skills have been
sharpened by billions of years of evolution. It will,
however, generate lots of headlines. ∎

Could we produce life in a chemistry laboratory?

EVOLUTION

Charles Darwin first posited natural selection as the mechanism for evolving life, but the process has been going on for billions of years.

▷ ca 3,500,000,000 B.C.

The Rocks Talk

The Fossil Record

The preservation of ancient life in mineral form has been known from ancient times. Chinese sages called fossils dragon bones and ascribed healing powers to them. Scholars from Aristotle to Leonardo da Vinci argued that they were the remains of organisms that lived long ago. Today the study of fossils lies within the domain of paleontology, and the collection of all fossils that have been found and studied is known as the fossil record.

Here's a typical story of how a fossil might be formed: An animal dies and is buried, perhaps in a flood. Its soft parts decay quickly, but the hard parts—bones, shells, teeth—do not. Over thousands of years, mineral-laden water flowing through the ground produces an atom-by-atom

> 🔍 **Geologists name periods** in the past after the place **where rocks from that period were first studied.** Cambria is the Latin form of Cymru, the name for Wales in Welsh. **Jurassic**, of movie fame, **is named for the Jura mountains in France.**

replacement of the original hard parts until, at the end, there is a reproduction of those hard parts in stone. If this reproduction is then found and cataloged, it becomes part of the fossil record.

It used to be thought that the fossil record began about 500 million years ago, in what geologists call the Cambrian. We now recognize that life didn't suddenly appear in the Cambrian—that's just when easily fossilizable hard parts like shells appeared. Over the last several decades we have discovered that multicelled organisms without hard parts (think jellyfish) predated the Cambrian by several hundred million years, and that single-celled organisms existed at

least 3.5 billion years ago. Thus the fossil record of life on Earth goes back almost to the time when the end of giant meteorite impacts made the survival of life possible. It provides us with a chronological tree of life—a record of how complex life developed. □

Above: This fossil record contains evidence for creatures that lived at the bottom of the sea, like the ammonite.

Opposite: The fossilized *Archeopteryx* was the ancestor of modern birds.

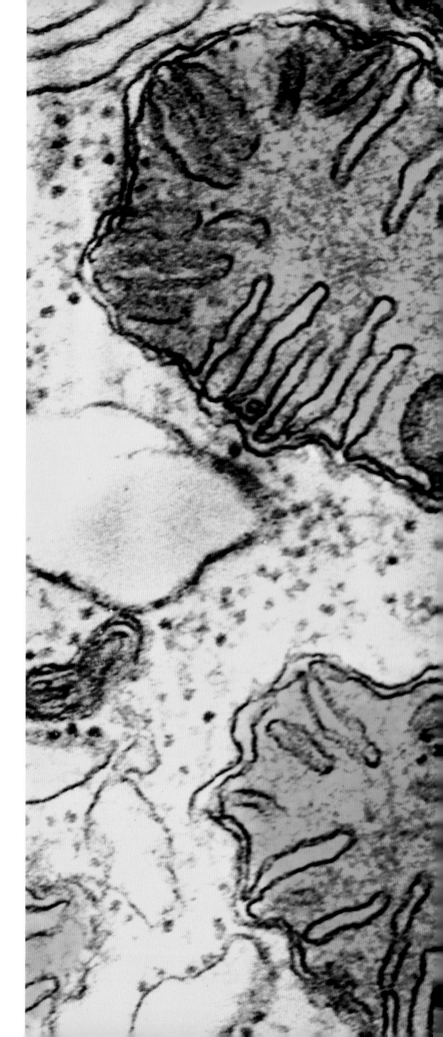

The Big Swallow

The Appearance of Eukaryotes

There are two kinds of cells in nature. The simplest (and oldest) carry their DNA loose in the cell body. These are called prokaryotes (*karys* is Greek for "nucleus," so "prokaryote" means "before the nucleus"). The second type carry their DNA in a structure called the nucleus, and hence are called eukaryotes ("true nucleus"). All cells in multicelled organisms (including you) are eukaryotes.

There is strong evidence to suggest that eukaryotes evolved through a process of symbiosis. Essentially, two prokaryotes found that they could function better as a team than individually. One prokaryote simply absorbed the other. Over evolutionary times, this process occurred many times to produce the complex modern cell.

⊕ Borrowing a turn of phrase from **big bang cosmology,** some evolutionary biologists have called this symbiotic event the **big swallow.**

For example, all of your cells have small structures called mitochondria. This is where fuel is "burned" in your cell to produce energy. Evidence that mitochondria are a product of the type of symbiosis just described is (1) mitochondria have their own small complement of DNA, and (2) mitochondria have a double wall—think of one as coming from the original absorbed prokaryote, the other from the original absorber. ☐

Right: There is strong evidence to suggest that eukaryotes, such as these, may have evolved from two prokaryotes, one absorbing the other. This process repeated over evolutionary times to produce the modern complex cell.

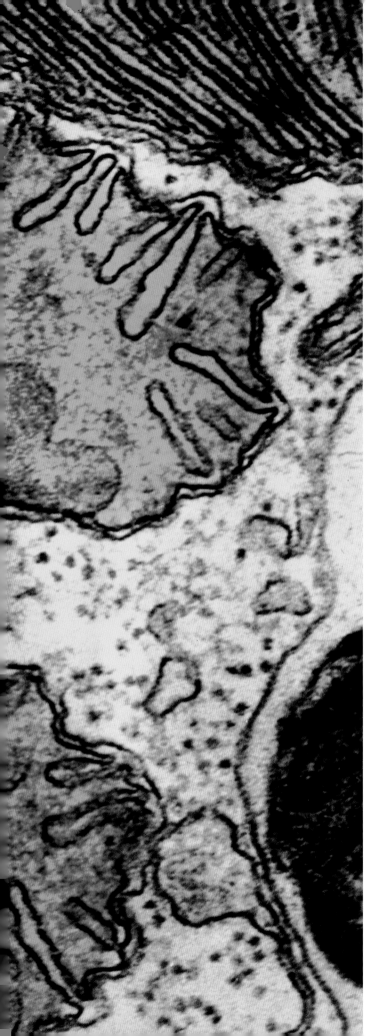

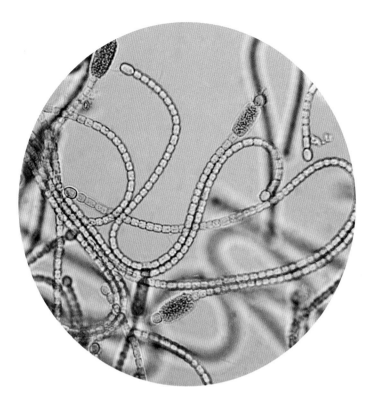

▷ 3,500,000 B.C. to the Present

How It Happened

The Story of Life

With the evidence of the fossil record and DNA, we can build a picture of the way life evolved on Earth. The basic building blocks of the molecules of life accumulated in the oceans, either brought in by meteorites or produced by processes of the Miller–Urey type (see page 81). Then, by a process we still have to learn, these blocks assembled into a primitive self-reproducing cell, absorbing energy from molecules in their surroundings. At this point, the process of evolution by natural selection took over (see page 84). Primitive cells were carried into different environments by ocean currents, environments in which different traits were valuable. By 3.5 billion years ago, Earth's oceans teemed with cyanobacteria—we can call it a pond scum planet.

Earth stayed in that rather uninteresting state for a long time. Sometime between 2 and 1.5 billion years ago eukaryotes appeared, and around 800 million years ago multicelled organisms without hard parts (think sponges

Above: Simple bacteria like these are the first living things we see in the fossil record.

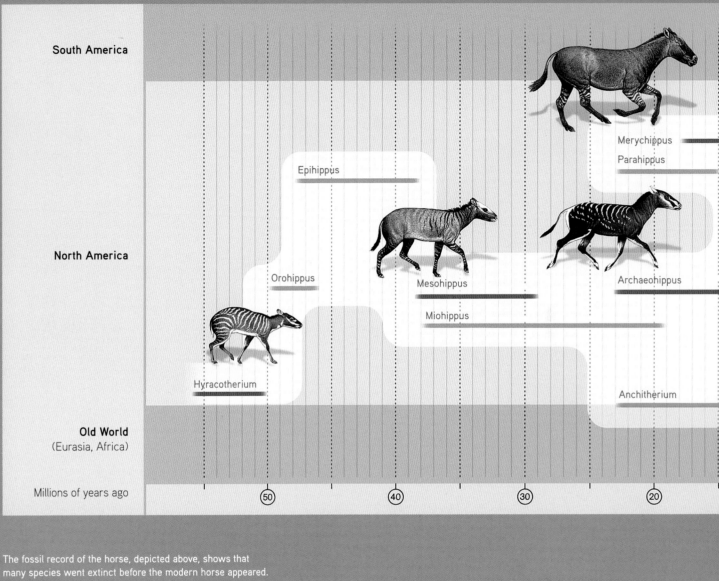

South America

North America

Old World
(Eurasia, Africa)

Millions of years ago

50   40   30   20

Merychippus

Parahippus

Epihippus

Orohippus

Mesohippus

Miohippus

Archaeohippus

Hyracotherium

Anchitherium

The fossil record of the horse, depicted above, shows that
many species went extinct before the modern horse appeared.

and jellyfish) appeared. In what geologists call the Cambrian (about 500 million years ago) organisms developed hard parts and the classical fossil record begins to contain a great deal of information about evolution. Life moved to land about 450 million years ago, mammals developed about 100 million years ago, and hominids—our ancestors—appeared about 8 million years ago.

There is one important fact that we have to understand about the story of life. Although it is true that living things have become more complex over evolutionary time, there is no overall goal to evolution. The process does not exist, for example, to produce human beings. Instead, we should think of evolution as a process that tries out every blind alley until it finds one that works. The evolution of the horse illustrates this point. In the entire evolutionary tree, involving many organisms, only one survives to the present day. This is not the result of a plan or purpose; it is characteristic of the evolutionary process itself.

Another question that is often raised concerns the rate at which evolution occurs. You can imagine two

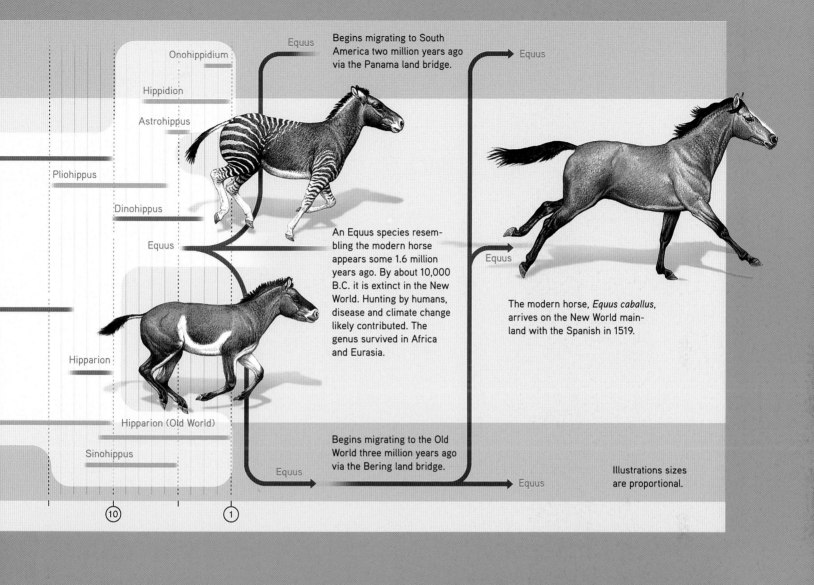

Onohippidium

Hippidion

Astrohippus

Pliohippus

Dinohippus

Equus

Hipparion

Hipparion (Old World)

Sinohippus

Equus

Equus

Begins migrating to South America two million years ago via the Panama land bridge.

An Equus species resembling the modern horse appears some 1.6 million years ago. By about 10,000 B.C. it is extinct in the New World. Hunting by humans, disease and climate change likely contributed. The genus survived in Africa and Eurasia.

Begins migrating to the Old World three million years ago via the Bering land bridge.

Equus

Equus

Equus

Equus

The modern horse, *Equus caballus*, arrives on the New World mainland with the Spanish in 1519.

Illustrations sizes are proportional.

10

1

🔍 Nature tries many blind alleys that lead to extinction before finding a **scheme that allows a species to survive.**

extremes. One, associated with Darwin, is gradualism—the idea that small changes accumulate over time. The other, most often associated with paleontologist Stephen Jay Gould (1941–2002) is that changes occur in bursts, interspersed with periods of quiescence—the so-called punctuated equilibrium model. In fact, we can find examples of both of these modes—and everything in between—in the fossil record. The correct answer to the question Is evolution gradual or punctuated? appears to be yes. ☐

There Were Some Really Bad Days

Mass Extinctions

The evolution of life was not a smooth climb from that first cell to complex creatures like us. The story of life is punctuated with events known as mass extinctions, events in which appreciable fractions of Earth's species went extinct. Depending on how you count, there are as many as a dozen or as few as five such events. The best known happened about 65 million years ago, when the dinosaurs, who had ruled the planet for over 200 million years, simply vanished at the end of what geologists called the Cretaceous period.

> 🔍 The movie should have been called *Cretaceous Park,* since all of its dinosaurs came from that period.

Although the dinosaurs capture our attention, fully two-thirds of all living species went extinct in that event. For some, such as ocean plankton, the percentage of extinctions was well over 90 percent. In 1980, the team of the Nobel Laureate physicist Luis Alvarez (1911–1988) and his son, geologist Walter Alvarez (b 1940), argued that, based on their study of rocks from the period, this particular extinction was caused by the impact of an asteroid some eight miles across. Subsequent investigations have identified a buried crater on the Yucatán Peninsula as the impact site. There is a debate among scientists about whether other mass extinctions were also caused by asteroid impact or by other events, such as massive volcanic outflows. ☐

Left: The skull of a dinosaur called a *Dinogorgon* found in the South African scrubland.

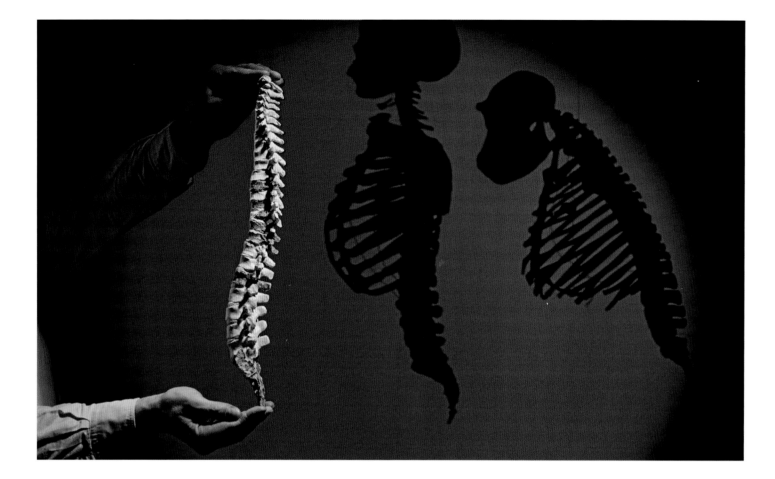

▷ ca 8,000,000 B.C.

The Story of Us

Human Evolution

Like all other species, human beings have a history in the fossil record. We shared our last common ancestor with the great apes sometime between six and eight million years ago. Since that time we have found over 20 fossil species that we could call hominids—animals who walked upright and had large brains. A partial list would include the following:

- *Australopithecus afarensis* (Southern ape from the Afar region of Ethiopia). This is the famous Lucy fossil. She walked upright, was about four feet tall, and lived in family groups—about 3.5 million years ago.
- *Homo habilis* (Man the toolmaker) one of the first members of the genus *Homo*, the remains of this species are found associated with stone tools—about 2 million years ago.
- *Homo erectus* (Man the erect). These were the first humans to leave Africa and to use fire—from about 1.9 million years ago to about 70,000 years ago.
- *Homo neanderthalensis*—our closest hominid cousin—see comments about DNA analysis below—went extinct about 35,000 years ago.

- *Homo sapiens*—us. Fossils date from about 200,000 years ago.

Note that for most of evolutionary history more than one species of hominid lived at the same time.

In what can only be described as a tour de force of genetic technology, a team at the Max Planck Institute for Evolutionary Anthropology in Leipzig, led by Svante Pääbo (b 1955) managed to sequence the Neanderthal genome, using DNA extracted from fossil bone fragments. In 2010, the group announced a surprising result: from 1 to 4 percent of the DNA carried by modern Europeans and Asians (but not Africans) comes from Neanderthals. Apparently, when modern humans entered the Neanderthal home territory in Europe and the Middle East, some limited inter-breeding took place.

Another important event took place in 2010. Working with a fragment of a finger bone found in a place called the Denisova cave in Siberia, the Leipzig group was able to identify a previously unknown member of the genus *Homo*. Called Denisovans, this group contributed some genes to some Melanesians and Australian aborigines. ☐

Above: The backbone of *Australopithecus afarensis* with shadows of a modern human and a chimpanzee on the wall.

A New View of Life

Charles Darwin

A few scientists have done work so important that their names are forever attached to an important scientific advance. Charles Darwin (1809–1882) is one of this select company. As a young man, Darwin served as the naturalist on a ship named the *Beagle* as it made a five-year voyage of exploration. One stop on that voyage—at the Galapagos Islands off the coast of Peru—he got the first glimmerings of what was to become the central theoretical framework of the life sciences.

Darwin

🔍 **Charles Darwin originally studied to be a physician, but switched when he realized he was squeamish about blood.**

A word of explanation: at the beginning of the 19th century the reigning theory held that all species had been created separately by God and had not changed during the (relatively brief) history of Earth. On the Galápagos Islands Darwin found many species of finches, obviously closely related, but filling what we would call today different ecological niches. The question, of course, is why God would have bothered to make so many closely related versions of the same bird.

On his return to England, Darwin spent many years establishing his reputation as a naturalist, studying organisms as diverse as earthworms and barnacles. He also began developing the ideas that would lead to the theory of evolution. He started by thinking about what he called artificial selection—the well-known ability of breeders to produce plants and animals with desired characteristics (Darwin himself was a pigeon breeder.) Obviously, there was a process by which the traits of parents could be passed on to offspring.

Above: Charles Darwin.

Right: The skulls of the kinds of finches Darwin saw in the Galapagos Islands.

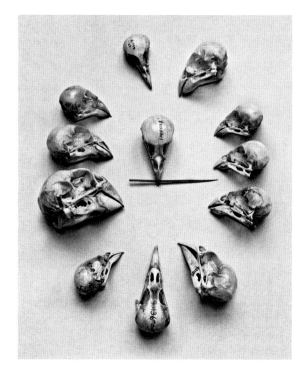

He then asked a simple question: Is there a way for nature to accomplish the same process without human intervention? This led to the idea of evolution by natural selection. To put this idea in modern language, genes that give an individual an advantage in a certain environment are likely to be passed on to offspring. Over time, those genes will come to be shared by all members of a population. Darwin published these ideas in his 1859 book *The Origin of Species*, and the publication of that book revolutionized science. ☐

▷ 1930s–1940s

Darwin Meets Mendel

The Grand Synthesis

One of the standard criticisms of Darwin's work revolved around the fact that it did not include a mechanism for the process by which traits could be inherited. It wasn't, in fact, until the third and fourth decades of the 20th century that theorists resolved this issue. The basic idea that they advanced, and which still constitutes the core of evolutionary theory, was that the mechanisms developed by geneticists from Mendel on (see page 106) explained the working of natural selection—in fact, we already used this notion in the previous entry when we described natural selection in terms of genes. The important point is that, once a new gene shows up through the process of mutation, that gene can be passed on to future generations. If it confers an advantage, by making it easier for an organism to avoid predators, for example, it will eventually come to be shared by all members of a population. □

Above: These salamander embryos live on stored food in their bodies—an unusual adaptation.

Right: Scientists study the way limbs form in embryos, as with the skates shown on the right, to understand how changes in DNA lead to changes in structure.

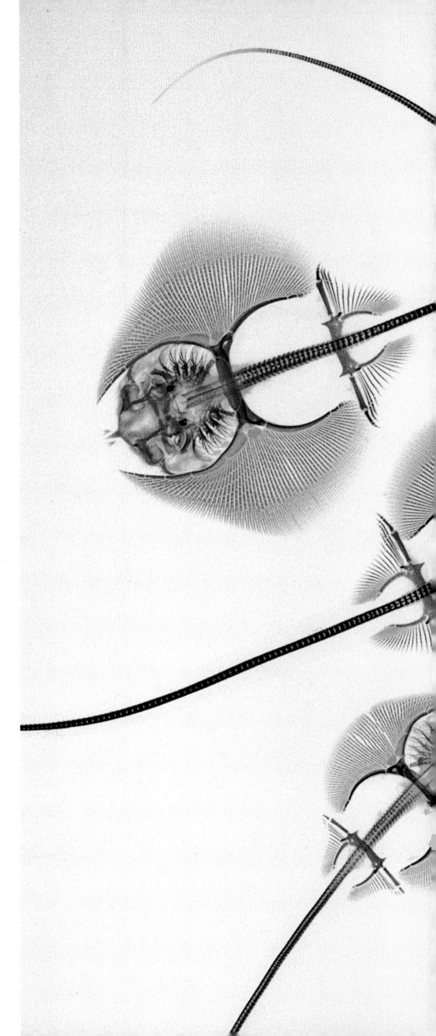

▷ Late 1900s

DNA Talks Too

DNA Evidence

The fossil record isn't our only record of the past. Each of us carries around evidence of evolutionary processes in the DNA of our cells. When sequencing DNA became a routine laboratory operation (see page 106), a story about the past could be produced by comparing the DNA of different organisms. Essentially, the idea is that the more differences there are in the DNA of two species, the longer it has been since the two shared a common ancestor. It was this type of analysis, for example, that established the fact that chimpanzees are our closest relation in the animal world.

The remarkable fact is that, when the history of life deduced from DNA is compared with the history of life deduced from the fossil record, they turn out to be the same. This remarkable result is one of the strongest pieces of evidence for evolution by natural selection. □

Above: A chimpanzee recognizes himself in a mirror— a standard way of testing animal intelligence.

On the Horizon

▷ New Humans

Our newfound ability to sequence ancient DNA will surely lead to important new discoveries about human evolution. The fact that there was some limited interbreeding between modern humans and Neanderthals, for example, caused quite a stir in both the scientific and popular cultures. The discovery of the Denisovans suggests that there are more close relatives out there waiting to be discovered.

▷ What Happened to the Neanderthals?

The disappearance of the Neanderthals has always posed a problem for scientists. After all, they were a successful species, well adapted to Ice Age Europe. They even seemed to have shared space with modern humans in places like Denisova, though they were not there at the same time. Yet, about 35,000 years ago they disappeared. Why? The evidence of limited interbreeding may tell us something about this, but there are surely surprises waiting in obscure caves in Europe and Asia. ■

A reconstruction of a female Neanderthal hunter.

GENETICS

▷ Mid-1800s

How Are We Like Two Peas in a Pod?

The Discovery of Genes

Gregor Mendel (1822–1884) worked in a monastery in what is now the Czech Republic. The region around the monastery was largely agricultural, so it's not surprising that he was interested in the way that farmers improved their stock by selective breeding. Working in a small garden plot, he carried out experiments that were to change the way that scientists thought about inheritance.

Mendel chose the pea plant as his laboratory organism. This was not because he was particularly interested in

peas, but for convenience—it is possible to raise three generations of these plants in a single growing season, a fact that makes the study of inherited traits in a limited time frame possible. We can understand his results by describing a typical experiment.

He began with true-breeding plants—that is, plants whose offspring had the same characteristics as their parents. He might have, for example, plants that always had tall offspring or plants that always had short offspring. When he crossed these plants by using the pollen from one to fertilize the other, he found that all of the offspring were tall. When he cross-fertilized these first-generation plants, however, three-fourths of the second generation were tall, whereas one-fourth were short. Similar regularities showed up when he investigated

Although heredity was long appreciated as a natural occurrence, the discovery of DNA and genetic coding revolutionized our understanding of life.

other properties, such as white versus pink flowers or smooth versus rough pea pods.

To explain these regularities, Mendel introduced something he called a unit of inheritance, or gene. He argued that each offspring receives one gene for each trait from each parent. If the two genes would produce the same outcome (for example, if both were for tallness) then the offspring would have that characteristic. If, however, the genes were different, then one would be dominant—in the experiment described above, for example, the first-generation plants all received one gene for tallness and one for shortness, and the fact that all the plants were tall indicates that the gene for tallness is dominant. The gene for shortness is said to be recessive.

What Mendel worked out is what is called classical or Mendelian genetics. Unfortunately, he published his results in the journal of the Brno Natural History Society—an obscure journal indeed. Consequently, the work remained largely unknown until it was rediscovered in the early 20th century. ☐

Opposite: Peas of the type that Mendel used to create the study of genetics.

Right: Gregor Mendel, an Augustinian monk, discovered the basic laws of inheritance by cross-fertilizing pea plants with different characteristics.

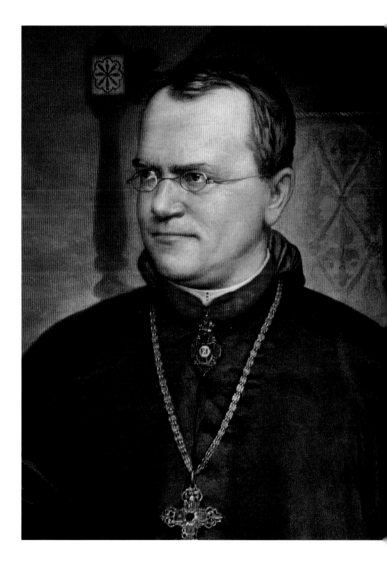

🔍 To Gregor Mendel, the gene was a **mental construct** needed to explain his data. To us, it is a physical thing—**part of a DNA molecule.**

▷ 1910

What the Fruit Flies Had to Say

Genes on DNA

In 1861 the Swiss physiologist Friedrich Miescher (1844–1895) discovered a new molecule we call DNA. At the time, no one had any idea of its importance or function. It was the American geneticist Thomas Hunt Morgan (1866–1945) and his students who finally worked out the connection between Mendel's genes and the DNA molecule.

Like Mendel, Morgan had to choose a convenient organism for his studies. He chose the fruit fly, *Drosophila melanogaster*, not because he wanted to breed bigger and better fruit flies, but because the generation time for this insect is measured in days, making it the ideal organism with which to study the transmission of inherited traits down through the generations. Morgan's team observed many traits in their flies—eye color (red or white), wing texture (smooth or fuzzy), and so on. They began to notice that certain traits went together through the generations—eye color and wing texture, for example. They knew that part of reproduction was a process called recombination, in which chunks of DNA are exchanged between the mother's and father's chromosomes. They realized that the fact that the traits went together meant that the genes producing them had to be close to each other so that they would remain together during recombination.

With this insight they assembled the first genetic map of a living organism, showing the location of genes. They also established an important fact about genetics: genes are arrayed linearly on the DNA molecule. For this work, Morgan received the Nobel Prize in 1933. □

Above: The common fruit fly has played a major role in the development of modern genetics.

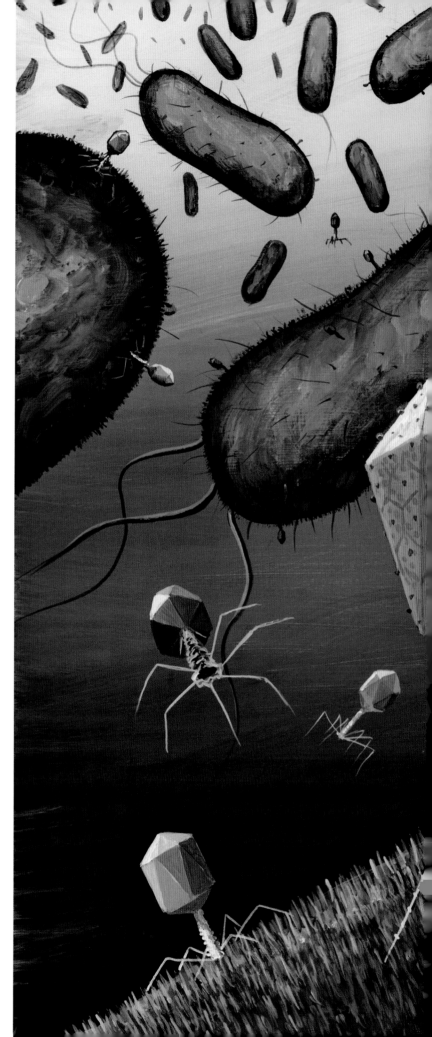

▷ 1952

Is It Really DNA?

Proving That DNA Carries Hereditary Information

Despite Morgan's work, many scientists in the early 20th century had a hard time believing that a single molecule like DNA could carry life's entire genetic message. Scientists who thought this way often suggested proteins as a possible genetic messenger. This issue was finally laid to rest in 1952, in a cleverly designed experiment done by Alfred Hershey (1908–1997) and Martha Chase (1927–2003).

🔍 Morgan was the great-grandson of Francis Scott Key (1779–1843), **who composed "The Star-Spangled Banner."**

They worked with viruses (see page 120) known as bacteriophages ("bacterium eaters"). They grew bacteria to feed their viruses in two different environments: one containing radioactive phosphorus (which is found in DNA), the other radioactive sulfur (which is found in the viruses' protein coating). When viruses attacked these bacteria, two separate populations of viruses were created—one with their DNA marked, the other with their protein coat marked. When these two groups of viruses were then allowed to attack other neutral bacteria, the radioactive tracers told a clear story. The DNA molecules clearly were taken into the body of the bacteria (where, presumably, reproduction occurs) and the proteins stayed outside.

The result was clear: DNA is the molecule that carries genetic information. For this work, Chase received the Nobel Prize in 1969. ☐

Left: An artist's conception of a bacteriophage (orange-red) attacking a bacterium (brown).

The Double Helix

The Structure of DNA

The American biochemist James Watson (b 1928) and the British theoretical physicist Francis Crick (1916–2004) are usually credited with discovering the structure of the DNA molecule. Before their 1953 breakthrough, however, scientists had spent decades learning things about DNA. We knew, for example, that the molecule contained a sugar (the *D* in *DNA* stands for the five-carbon sugar deoxyribose), a group consisting of a phosphorus atom attached to four oxygens, and four molecules know as bases. The bases are called adenine, thymine, guanine, and cytosine, but are usually referred to by the letters *A, T, C,* and *G*. We also knew that the molecule always contained equal parts of A and T as well as equal parts of C and G.

Below: Sketch of the DNA double helix. Watson and Crick discovered the structure of the DNA molecule in 1953, paving the way for today's genetics revolution.

A good way to picture the DNA structure that Watson and Crick discovered is to think of a ladder. The sides of the ladder are the sugar and phosphate groups, but it is the rungs that are most interesting. One of the base molecules sticks out from each side of the ladder and binds to a base sticking out from the other side. Because of their shape, A binds only to T, and C binds only to G—a fact that explains why we always find equal amounts of A and T and equal amounts of C and G, but not necessarily the same amounts of C and T.

Now twist the top and bottom of the ladder in opposite directions in your mind. The result is the famous double helix structure of DNA. Watson and Crick received the Nobel Prize in 1962.

There is one issue about the discovery of the structure of DNA that remains unsettled, and that is the role of British crystallographer Rosalind Franklin (1920–1958). She had taken x-ray photographs of DNA that the director of her London laboratory shared with Watson without her knowledge. We do not know the role this disclosure played in the discovery of the double helix, and unfortunately Franklin died of ovarian cancer before the Nobel Prize (which is never awarded posthumously) for the discovery of DNA structure was announced. ☐

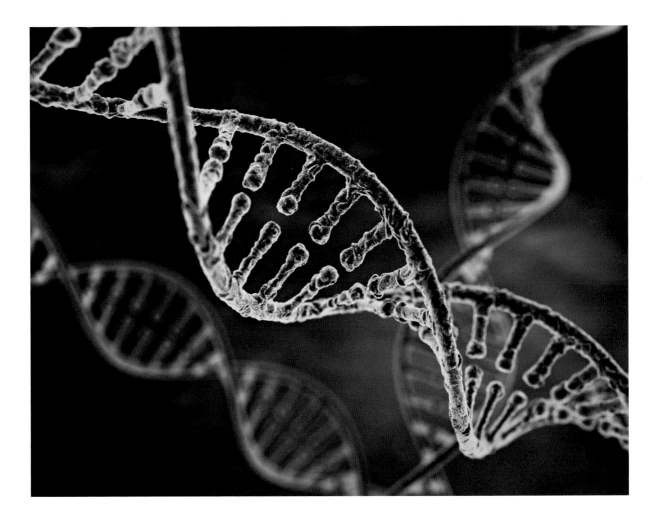

▷ 1961
DNA Unraveled
The Genetic Code

Once the structure of the DNA molecule was known, the next task was to figure out how information in DNA was used to run a cell's chemistry. We know that the cell's chemistry is run by molecules called proteins, which are themselves made from building blocks called amino acids (see page 81).

The process starts with another molecule called RNA (for "ribonucleic acid"), a kind of a cousin to DNA. RNA is just like DNA except that (1) it is only one side of the ladder, (2) it has a different sugar (the *R* stands for "ribose," which is the name of the sugar), and (3) a different base—uracil (U)—takes the place of thymine.

Different kinds of RNA perform three essential functions in running life's chemistry. First, a molecule called messenger RNA (mRNA) copies the sequence of bases on a stretch of DNA and moves out into the body of the cell. Second, a molecule called transfer RNA (tRNA) attaches to the mRNA at one end and an amino acid on the other. A protein is just a set of amino acids fastened together like beads on a string, and this final assembly takes place on a third kind of RNA that provides a kind of "workbench."

The unraveling of this rather complex process began in 1961 at the National Institutes of Health outside of Washington, D.C. Marshall Nirenberg (1927–2010) constructed an artificial version of RNA in which all of the base pairs were the same—CCC, for example. This artificial RNA was put into a series of media, each containing a different amino acid. He found that each of his artificial sequences bound to only one kind of amino acid.

The picture that emerged from Nirenberg's work was this: Three base pairs in the DNA—what is called a codon—determined the type of amino acid that goes into the protein being assembled. The string of base pairs that carries the information needed to assemble one protein (and hence to run one chemical reaction) is a gene. With the work of Nirenberg and those who followed him, the gene passed from being Mendel's mental construct to being a physical object—part of a DNA molecule. Nirenberg received the Nobel Prize in 1968.

The most important statement we can make about our current understanding of DNA is this: Every living thing on our planet uses the same genetic code. This is a profound proof of the theory of evolution (see page 86) as well as the basis for the new technique of genetic engineering (see page 108). □

Above: Marshall Nirenberg, who pioneered the understating of the genetic code. He was awarded the Nobel Prize in 1968 for his work explaining how genetic information is coded in sequences of paired amino acids.

🔍 Only about **5 percent of our DNA is made up of genes.** Some of the rest controls when genes are turned on and off, some has functions we don't yet understand, and some may just be "junk."

▷ 1987

Reading the Past

Mitochondrial DNA

It is generally accepted that certain organelles inside our cells resulted from the absorption of one cell by another in a symbiotic relationship (see page 86). The organelles known as mitochondria, where the cell generates its energy, result from one such event. In fact, mitochondria have their own complement of DNA—molecules independent of the DNA found in the nuclei of cells. Mitochondrial DNA contains 37 genes. Mitochondria are brought into the fertilization process by the egg, so everyone's mitochondria come from his or her mother. In the language of genealogists, mitochondrial DNA descends in the maternal line.

In the 1980s, scientists at the University of California at Berkeley began sequencing mitochondrial DNA and using it to construct a family tree for human beings, much as you would construct a family tree by using family names (which pass in the paternal line). To their surprise, many of their family trees seemed to go back to a single woman who lived between 100,000 and 200,000 years ago. This woman was dubbed mitochondrial Eve. Since that time, similar analyses have been done to trace the mitochondrial ancestry of different populations—there appear to have been several women who are ancestral to modern Europeans, for example. □

Opposite: If indeed there was a mitochondrial Eve, as some scientists believe, she would likely have lived in Africa where human beings first evolved.

Q Attempts have been made to use nuclear **DNA to find a "chromosomal Adam"**—a hypothetical male ancestor—by tracing the Y chromosome. But it's **unlikely that a chromosomal Adam** would have known chromosomal Eve.

▷ 1997

Hello, Dolly!

Cloning

In 1997 the world was introduced to Dolly the sheep, the first cloned mammal. The procedure that led to Dolly is easy to describe, if not so easy to put into practice. First, the nucleus with its cargo of DNA is removed from the egg of an adult sheep—in this case, a Scottish Blackface ewe. Using a small electric shock, this denucleated egg is fused with an adult cell from another sheep (in this case, a Finn Dorset ewe). By a process we still don't understand, the egg was able to turn on all the genes that had been turned off in the maturation of the Finn Dorset ewe. The egg, with its cargo of newly renovated DNA was then planted in the uterus of still a third sheep and Dolly was born. In 1998, Dolly had lambs through the normal procedure, and she died at age six, about half the natural life of sheep. She suffered from lung disease, not uncommon in older sheep, and was euthanized in 2003. Since then, many mammals have been cloned—monkeys, rats, cows, pigs, and horses, to name a few.

When Dolly was born, there were all sorts of alarms in the press. Overheated journalists conjured up visions of cloned humans being created to supply replacement organs for their DNA donors. A moment's thought should relieve your mind on this topic. A human clone is simply a human being whose DNA is identical to another's. We have millennia of experience in dealing with people like this—we call them twins. □

Right: Dolly the sheep, the first cloned mammal.

▷ 2000

Know Thyself

Sequencing the Human Genome

There are approximately three billion base pairs in the human DNA molecule. Reading them in order is called the process of sequencing the genome. Sequencing the human genome became a topic of conversation among scientists in the 1980s, but it took some time before the goal was met. The main obstacle was the requirement that automatic sequencing machines be developed. As this process moved forward in the 1990s, progress took the form of sequencing the genome of more and more complex organisms. In 1995 the genome of a bacterium was sequenced—the first genome sequenced anywhere. In 1998 the genome of a flatworm was sequenced—the first multicelled organism to be decoded.

The scientists responsible for the rapid advance of sequencing in the 1990s were Craig Venter (b 1946), head of a private company he founded, and Francis Collins (b 1950), head of the genome project at the National Institutes of Health. Venter developed a process known as the shotgun technique. Basically, a stretch of DNA is broken up into small pieces, each of which is fed into an automatic sequencing machine, and the results are then reassembled by computers. It would be like tearing this book into many pieces, giving each piece to a different reader, and then having computers reassemble the book from the readers' pieces.

In 2000, at a White House ceremony, Venter and Collins announced the first assembly of the human genome. At the time there was an enormous hope that this would lead to major advances in medicine. That these advances have been slow in coming is due to the unexpected complexity that scientists encountered as they began investigating the genome in detail. □

Above: Craig Venter invented a process known as the "shotgun technique" that enabled the sequencing of the human genome.

Right: A DNA sequence in which different fluorescent molecules are attached to segments of the DNA.

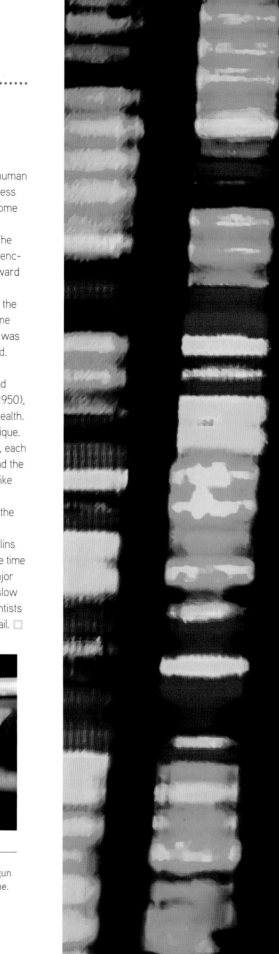
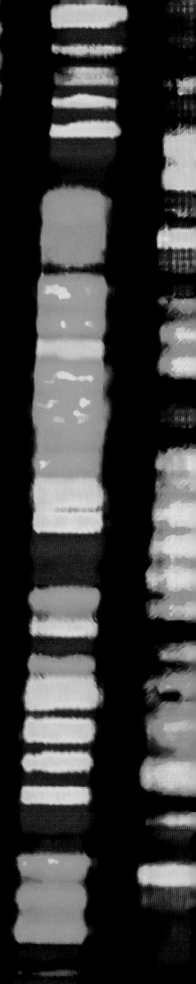

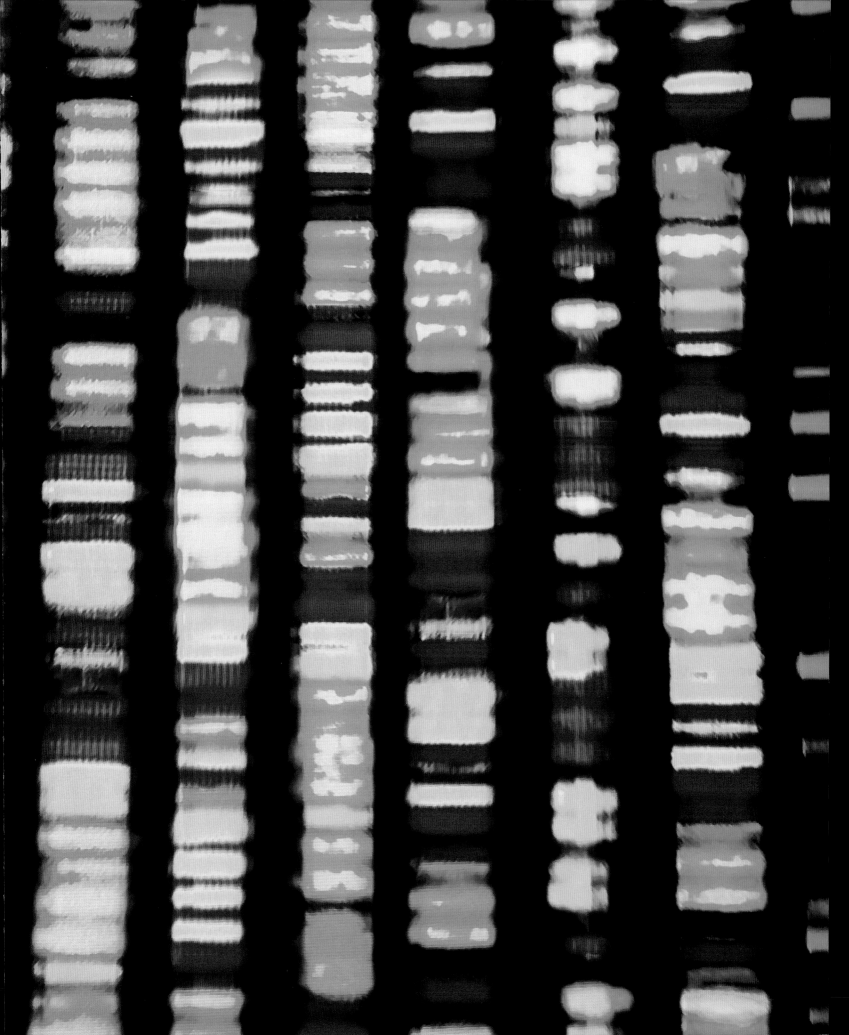

On the Horizon

▷ Advanced Genetic Engineering

The fact that all living things use the same genetic code means that it is possible to transfer genes from one organism to another. Indeed, most of the major agricultural crops grown in the United States have been modified in this way. A new technique known as CRISPR (it's pronounced crisper) is going to take this process to a whole new level. In essence, it is a technique that allows scientists to "edit" DNA, not just putting in or removing genes, but changing the code itself.

To give just one example of the impact this new technology will have, ethicists and scientists are already discussing the moral issues involved in using CRISPR to modify the DNA of fetuses in utero. This is a perfect example of a technological advance moving past our moral and legal codes.

▷ Synthetic Biology

Modifying living things by switching genes between organisms is one thing, creating a living cell from scratch, using "off the shelf" chemicals is another. Building new organisms is the goal of an emerging field of science known as synthetic biology. The advantages of being able to manufacture living things to specifications are far reaching. You can imagine, for example, artificial cells built to manufacture specific drugs, or to turn atmospheric carbon dioxide into gasoline.

The field is in its infancy. In 2010, Craig Venter (who was involved in the sequencing of the human genome) removed the DNA from a cell and replaced it with DNA that had been fabricated in a laboratory. The cell began running the chemical reactions coded for in its new DNA. This is, of course, only a first small step toward synthetic life, but an important one.■

Bacteria that have been genetically engineered to glow pink are seen in this laboratory photo. The test tube contains bacteria modified to glow green.

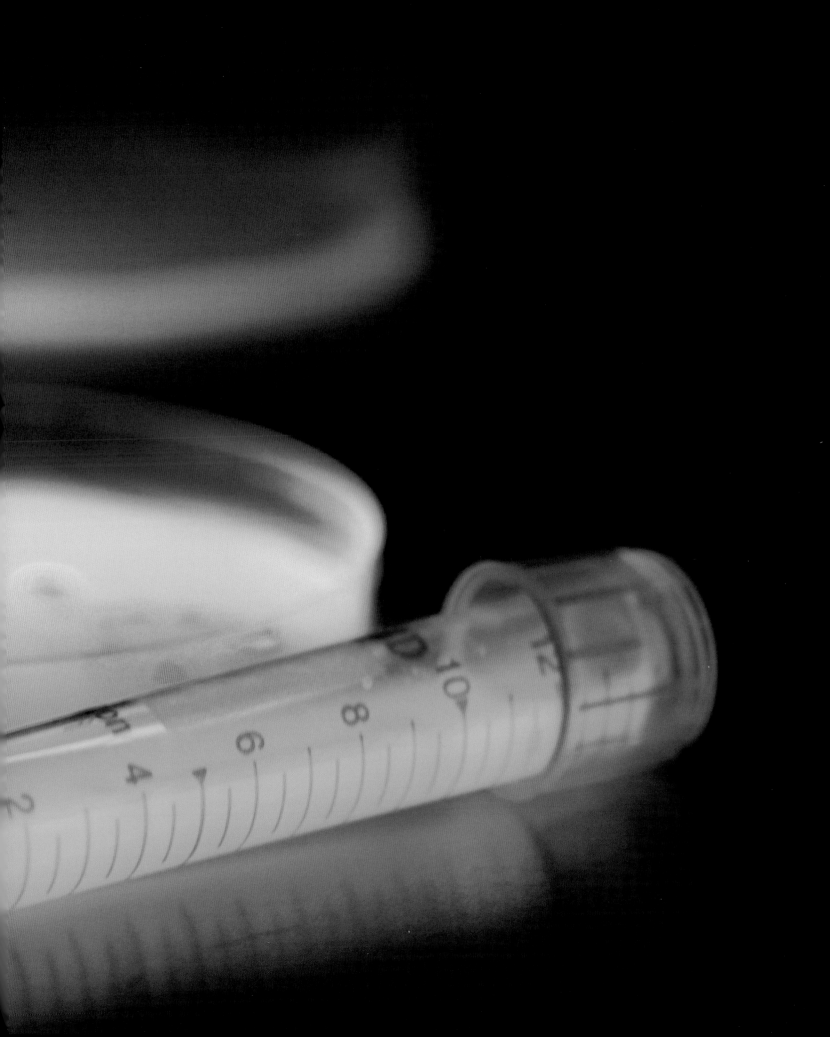

CELL THEORY

▷ 1837

A Fateful Dinner

Cells

The term "cell" to describe the basic constituent of living things was coined by the British scientist Robert Hooke (1635–1703), a contemporary of Isaac Newton. He was examining a piece of cork with a microscope and noticed that it seemed to be divided into compartments. They reminded him of the small rooms that monks occupied in monasteries, so he called them cells—the name the monks used for their quarters.

In 1837, two young men sat down to dinner in a German restaurant. Both would go on to distinguished scientific careers. Matthias Schleiden (1804–1881) was a lawyer with an intense interest in botany, Theodor Schwann (1810–1882) was an assistant in a physiology laboratory. Both had made extensive microscopic studies of the cellular structure of living things—Schleiden of plant cells, Schwann of animal cells. As their dinner conversation progressed, they realized that there were significant similarities between the two kinds of cells. Eventually that conversation led to one of the central tenets of biology— the idea that all living things are composed of cells. Later, the German biologist Rudolf Virchow (1821–1902) expanded this idea to include the statement that all cells are produced from preexisting cells. With this, the cellular theory of life was complete. □

Above right: A full-size replica of Robert Hooke's compound microscope reconstructed from his 1665 book, *Micrographia.*

⊕ Matthias Schleiden was **one of the first German biologists** to accept and teach Darwin's theory of evolution.

Cells are the basic constituent of living things—from cork to pluripotence.

▷ Early 20th Century
The Factory
Cell Structure

It used to be thought that cells were just inert blobs of living stuff—an idea that led to the term "protoplasm," which was supposed to be what was inside the blob. As biologists got better at using their microscopes, however, this view changed. It was a gradual process, but eventually we began to realize that cells—especially those in multicelled organisms like humans—are actually complex structures, more like factories or oil refineries than inert blobs.

In 1886, for example, microscopists discovered the structure called the mitochondrion. This is one example of what is called an organelle—a structure inside the cell that carries out a specific function (the mitochondrion is where the cell's energy is generated, for example). Many of these organelles are thought to be the result of

symbiotic events in the past. Other examples of organelles are the nucleus, where DNA is stored, ribosomes, where protein enzymes are assembled, and chloroplasts, where the process of photosynthesis is carried out in plants. As you can see from the diagram, there are many more of these specialized structures in cells. The bottom line: A living cell is itself a complex structure containing many specialized organelles, each carrying out a specific function. □

Above: As this drawing of a typical animal cell illustrates, the cell has a complex structure with many different parts. Every living cell is complex structure akin to a sophisticated factory.

🔍 All advanced organisms, like human beings, **have many organelles in their cells** and have their DNA in an organelle called a nucleus.

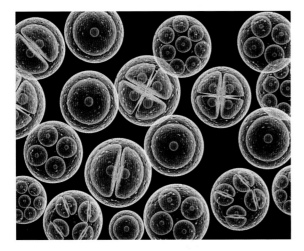

After this initial period, genes start to be turned off as cells start to specialize. Some cells retain a limited ability to produce different kinds of tissue—for example, there are skin stem cells capable of producing the different cells that compose the skin. These are called somatic stem cells.

In 1998, researchers at the University of Wisconsin showed that it was possible to keep stem cells "undecided" for long periods of time, which means that as they divide they do not switch off genes as they normally would. Such a collection of stem cells is called a stem cell line.

> There are over **30 trillion cells** in the human body.

Stem cells are intimately connected to regenerative medicine (see page 137) and hence are important for the future of medicine. Unfortunately, in the United States they are also connected to one of the most difficult social and political issues in the country—the abortion controversy. ☐

Above left: Cells in the process of dividing. Every cell in your body is descended from the single fertilized egg cell from which you started.

▷ 1998
Pluripotence
Stem Cells

The original fertilized egg from which every complex life form develops contains DNA in which none of the genes have been switched off. In the language of genetics, they are pluripotent. As the cell starts to divide, this property is maintained for several cell divisions—about the time it takes for the embryo to implant in the uterus for humans. During this period, there are cells in the developing embryo capable of turning into any cell in the adult. These cells are called embryonic stem cells.

▷ Late 20th Century
Growing Up and Turning Off
The Development of Cells

Every cell in your body, except for sperm and egg cells, has exactly the same DNA. They have to, because all those cells are descended from the single fertilized egg from which you started. Cell division by cell division, that original DNA was copied to produce the adult organism that you have become.

This means, for example, that every cell in your body contains the gene for producing insulin, a protein involved in metabolism. Yet only a relatively few cells in your pancreas actually manufacture insulin. This fact gives us a clue as to how cells develop specialized functions: as we mature, nothing is added to our DNA. Instead, genes like the one for insulin are turned off in all cells except the few where they are supposed to function. The study of how this process is carried out and how genes are controlled is a major task of biology today. ☐

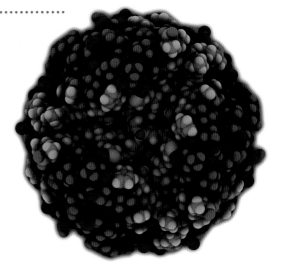

Above right: The insulin molecule, shown here, is made only in a few specialized cells in the pancreas. Diabetes is caused by the failure to produce insulin.

On the Horizon

▷ Pluripotence from Ordinary Cells

There are several snags in the production of embryonic stem cells. First, you have to have a supply of eggs, and then there is the fraught issue of abortion. It would be much better if we could produce pluripotent stem cells from somatic stem cells or even from ordinary cells. After all, they all have the same DNA. Furthermore, in the cloning process (see page 105) we know that the denucleated egg is able to reverse the switching off of genes that is part of maturation. If the egg can do it, the argument goes, why can't we?

There has been some progress in this area—scientists have been able to produce other kinds of tissue from somatic skin stem cells, for example. Expect more news in this field. ■

Early in the developmental process, the cells in the embryo are pluripotent.

CLASSIFICATION

Animal, Vegetable, or Mineral

Classifying Life

From the time that human beings first began thinking about the variety of life around them, the main task of the science we call biology could be stated quite simply: What kinds of life exist on our planet? And almost as soon as they asked that question, scientists began to try to find ways to classify and organize what they observed.

Carl Linnaeus (1707–1778) was a Swedish physician and botanist who spent a good deal of his career at the University of Uppsala. He was in charge of a large botanical operation where plants from all over the world were grown, a background that gave him an interest in organizing and classifying different living things.

The Linnaean classification scheme works by grouping together organisms with similar characteristics. The largest grouping is called a kingdom, and in the modern Linnaean scheme there are five kingdoms—plants, animals, fungi, and two kingdoms of single-celled organisms. Kingdoms are broken up into phyla, phyla into classes, classes into orders, and orders into families. The final two categories are genus and species, and it is these two we normally use to refer to an organism like *Homo sapiens* (genus *Homo*, species *sapiens)*. The names of these last two groupings are meant to stand for the whole classification scheme. ☐

Above: Drawing of a tobacco plant from a book published in 1799 in Philadelphia shortly after Linnaeus's death.

Biologists have been cataloging and classifying living things for more than 300 years.

What the Molecules Say

Other Ways of Classifying

The Linnaean scheme is not the only way to classify living things. It was developed long before scientists had any idea of either evolution or the molecular basis of life. In addition, we should note that there is no "right" way to classify living things—different classification schemes are simply more or less useful.

In the late 1970s, University of Illinois microbiologist Carl Woese (1928–2012) developed a classification scheme based on ribosomal RNA sequences. In this system there are three domains—two comprising single-celled organisms without nuclei and one that comprises all cells with nuclei, from amoebas to humans.

Yet another classification scheme comes from paleontology. In this scheme, called cladistics, organisms are grouped together according to common ancestry. All organisms that share a common ancestor form what is called a clade. For example, humans and the great apes form a clade, since they shared a common ancestor about eight million years ago. ☐

Above: The gorilla is an animal whose DNA is very much like that of humans.

On the Horizon

▷ Classifying with DNA

The classification process is by no means over. As more genetic sequencing data becomes available it becomes possible to use different stretches of DNA as a classification criterion. Attempts to do this seem to produce superfamilies of organisms with similar segments of DNA, but run into situations where different segments of DNA of one organism suggest different ways of classifying it.

In any case, it is very likely that when you take your children to the zoo they will still see a sign with the old-fashioned Linnaean *Ursus arctos horribilis* introducing the grizzly bear. ■

A scientist examines the DNA fingerprint of an animal he is trying to classify.

Left: "The Pill," shown here, is thought to have initiated a major social change in developed countries.

▷ 1957

Controlled Cycles
The Birth Control Pill

Scholars have remarked that, for as long as people have been making babies, they have been trying to find ways not to make them. Some common birth control techniques, such as condoms and diaphragms, work by preventing sperm from reaching an egg, whereas others, such as the intrauterine device (IUD), apparently prevent the fertilized egg from implanting in the uterine wall. Unfortunately, these techniques require either an implantation procedure (in the case of the IUD) or clear thinking in situations that do not always lend themselves to rational planning.

The birth control pill introduced an entirely new method of birth control, one in which women can control their own fertility. By introducing specific hormones into a woman's system, they prevent ovulation and hence remove the possibility of pregnancy. The technique was the result of research and clinical trials carried out over decades. The first of what we would call birth control drugs was approved by the Food and Drug Administration in 1957, but it was supposed to be used only to treat severe menstrual cramps although it was well known that it could also be used to avoid pregnancy. Mysteriously, over the next few years millions of American women developed severe menstrual cramps. What came to be known as "the pill" was finally approved for contraceptive purposes in 1960.

The person who is generally regarded as the "father of the pill" is the Bulgarian American biochemist Carl Djerassi (1923–2015). Social scientists have written extensively about the effect that this method of birth control has had on American society, attributing everything from the sexual revolution to the massive entry of women into the workforce to it. Whether these attributions are correct is a question beyond the scope of this book. □

🔍 Carl Djerassi was an accomplished novelist who pioneered a style known as **science-in-fiction,** in which science is portrayed as part of the normal human environment.

TECHNOLOGY

Discoveries about the
basic molecular processes
of life often lead to far-
reaching social consequences.

▷ **1970s**

Cut and Paste

Genetic Engineering

The fact that all living things use the same genetic code opens the way for a completely new kind of technology called genetic engineering. (You sometimes see it referred to it as "recombinant DNA" or "gene splicing" in older publications.) It works like this: a particular type of molecule, known as a restriction enzyme, cuts a strand of DNA in such a way that several bases are left exposed at the location of the cut. In this situation, another strand of DNA can attach to the exposed bases provided that the new strand has the right sequence of bases exposed. The genome, in other words, can be spliced.

If we can make one splice, we can make two, and what this means is that we can insert a new strand of DNA into the original genome. If this new strand contains a gene, that gene will be expressed in the usual way. The important point is this: *the new gene doesn't have to be from the same organism as the original DNA.* Thus we can modify any genome by inserting genes from other organisms, or even genes created artificially, to create a desired outcome. □

Below: DNA is packaged in structures, as shown here. The bright section represents one stretch of DNA. Our understanding of these structures, known as chromosomes, is critical to the nascent field of genetic engineering.

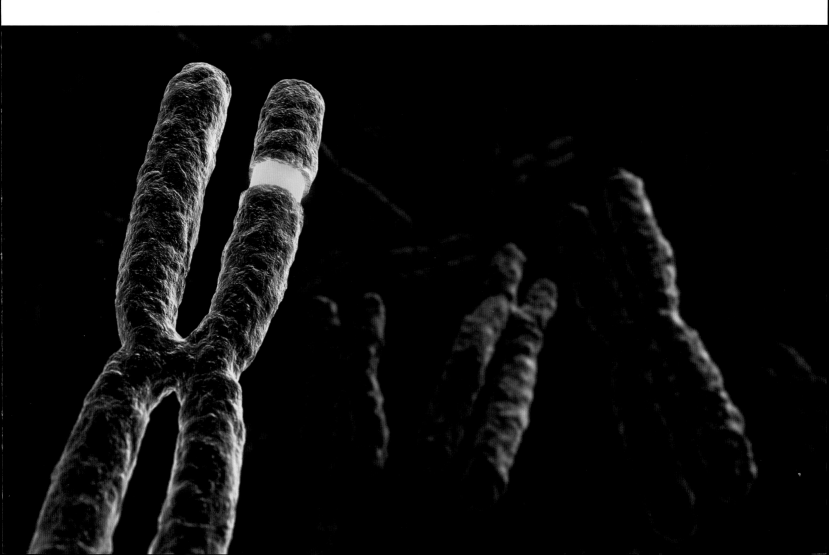

The Telltale Evidence

DNA Fingerprinting

You can hardly watch a crime show on TV these days without hearing about DNA fingerprinting. And this makes sense—every person's DNA sequence is as unique as his or her fingerprints. The problem, of course, is that sequencing an entire human genome is a lengthy and expensive process, and the procedure is not fitted to the demands of the legal system.

But you don't need to sequence an entire genome to make an identification—all you need are distinguishing landmarks. For example, if you looked out your window and saw the Washington Monument, you wouldn't need a street map of Washington, D.C., to tell you that you were in the nation's capital.

For modern DNA fingerprinting, such landmarks are short pieces of repeating nonsense DNA—something like CGTCGTCGT. These sorts of sequences are scattered around our DNA and are called short tandem repeats (STRs pronounced "stars"). We don't know where they came from—one theory suggests that they were deposited in our DNA by long-forgotten viruses. What we do know is that the number of repeats in a given location in our DNA varies from one person to the next. A given STR, for example, might have five repeats in your DNA and seven repeats in the DNA of the person sitting next to you.

The actual process of fingerprinting works like this: The DNA to be tested is cut up at specific places, so that each stretch of DNA contains a STR. These stretches of DNA are tagged and sent through a fluid, a process that separates the shorter strands (which move more quickly) from the longer strands (which move more slowly). At the end, the length of each STR is recorded. In practice, we know that getting data on 12 to 15 STRs is enough to make an unambiguous identification of the DNA. This is what DNA fingerprinting is all about. ☐

⊕ Scientists believe that **obtaining the entire DNA sequence** for an individual human being will soon cost less than $1,000.

Right: An artist's interpretation of a DNA fingerprint.

VIRUSES

▷ Late 20th Century

It's Different

What Is a Virus?

Viruses are strange and scary things. Unlike everything else we know about, they are not composed of cells. The best way to describe a virus is this: It is a package of nucleic acid—either RNA or DNA—wrapped in a protein coating.

The protein coating of a virus plays an important role in its life cycle. The proteins in a virus's coating have a shape that fools a cell's normal recognition system. In essence, the protein in a particular virus will have a "lock and key" relationship with receptor molecules in a cell's outer membrane. The virus thus is allowed to insert its nucleic acid (RNA or DNA) into the interior of a cell. It's important to realize that the shape of a virus's coating allows it access only into certain specific cells in the body of its host. Thus, for example, the rhinoviruses, which cause the common cold, can gain access only to cells in the mucous membranes of the nasal passage, whereas the viruses that cause hepatitis are recognized only by cells in the liver.

Once it has gained entrance to a cell, the virus will either implant its cargo of DNA into the DNA of its host or use its RNA to trigger the host's protein assembly system. In either case, the virus takes over the cell's reproductive machinery to make more copies of itself. Thus, unlike other life forms, a virus cannot reproduce on its own.

This method of reproduction, incidentally, explains why viruses cannot be controlled by ordinary antibiotics. Penicillin works, for example, by clogging up the molecular processes a cell needs to expand—think of it as putting bubble gum on a Lego block. Since the virus doesn't need its host cell to expand, the penicillin will not affect it. In fact, the main weapon we have to combat viral disease is our own immune system. □

Above: Artist's conception of a group of viruses. The main weapon we have against viral disease is our own immune systems.

A virus is either the most complicated nonliving thing on the planet or the simplest living thing. You decide.

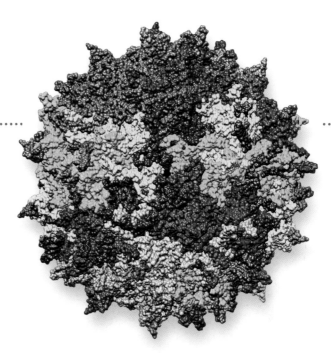

▷ 1990s

Can Viruses Be Useful?

Use of Viruses in Gene Therapy

There is one property of viruses that may turn out to be very important in a developing medical procedure known as gene therapy. This is the ability of a virus to seek out and be recognized by specific cells in the body. One goal of gene therapy is to find a way to replace or repair malfunctioning DNA in specific cells. As we have seen, viruses have the ability to deliver DNA to specific cells. The goal of developing so-called therapeutic viruses is precisely that—to deliver specific segments of DNA to specific cells and insert that DNA into the cell's own DNA.

The main problem in this field right now is finding a way to be certain that when the therapeutic DNA is inserted into a cell's DNA it is inserted in a way that does not damage the normal operation of the cell (for example, by being inserted into the middle of a functioning gene). ☐

Above right: Sketch of the surface of a typical virus. The complex shape facilitates the "lock and key" method of gaining entry to cells.

Most viruses **do not respond to antibiotics**, which makes treating viral diseases difficult.

On the Horizon

▷ Search for an AIDS Vaccine

Perhaps the most devastating viral disease we have encountered so far is acquired immunodeficiency syndrome (AIDS), which is caused by a virus known as the human immunodeficiency virus (HIV). This virus is transmitted via bodily fluids, such as blood, semen, and saliva, and attacks cells in the human immune system. There is a major worldwide effort to find a vaccine that would prevent infection, but to date we have not found one that is effective. Efforts continue, however, and you may see headlines about success in this area in the near future. ■

Dr. Maria Papathanasopoulos, one of the many scientists worldwide who is trying to find a cure for AIDS.

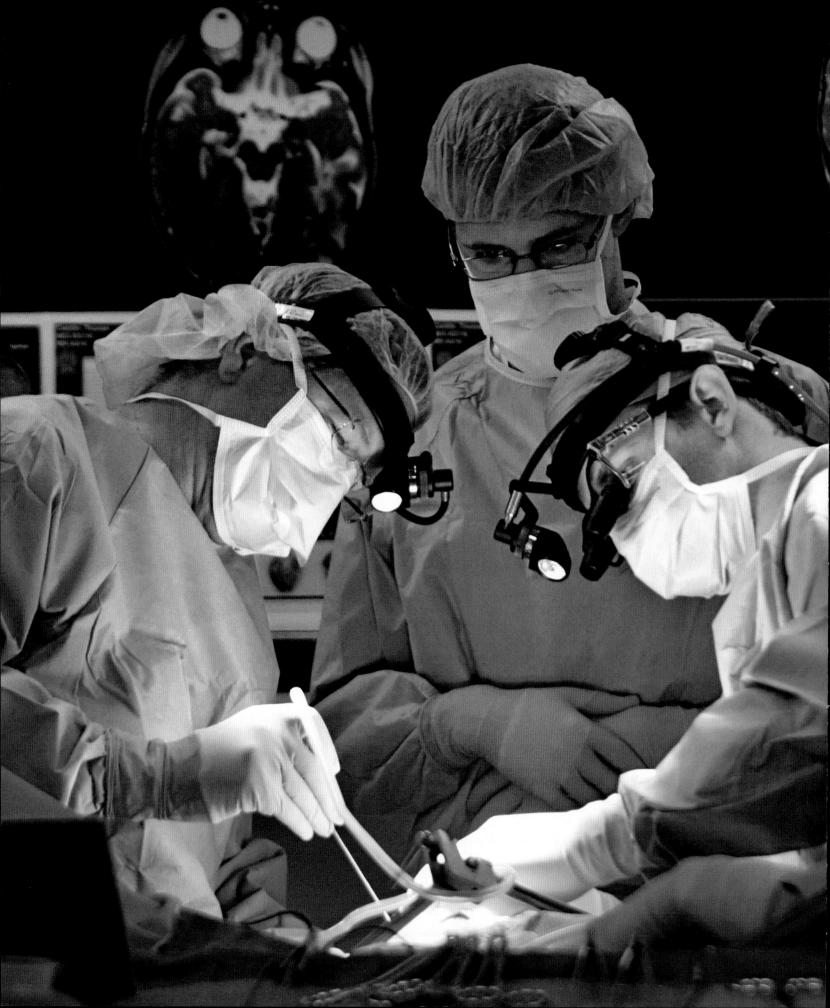

Chapter 3
MEDICINE

For as long as people have been getting sick, other people have been trying to figure out how to cure them.

HISTORY OF

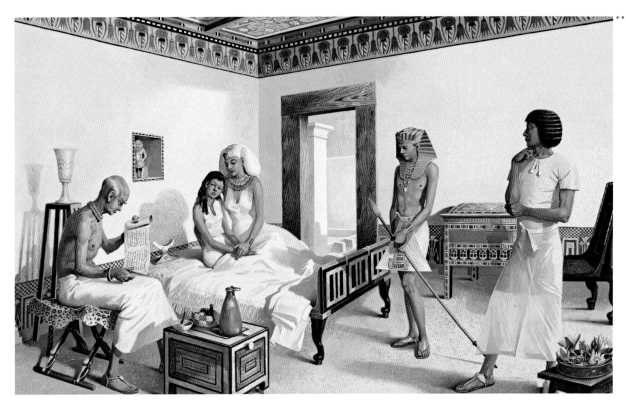

Above: While an ill princess's family waits, an ancient Egyptian physician consults a medical papyrus.

▷ ca 2500 B.C.

In the Shadow of the Pyramids

Egyptian Medicine

The Egyptians were known as the best doctors in the ancient world—a status some scholars have suggested may be related to their practice of mummification. In any case, we have letters from the kings of neighboring countries asking the Egyptian pharaohs to send physicians to help members of their courts.

As often happens, we know a good deal about Egyptian practices because of the survival of a papyrus manuscript. The so-called Edwin Smith Papyrus is named after the man who bought the papyrus in 1862 (the document was eventually donated to the New York Historical Society). The papyrus is basically a medical textbook containing 48 cases, along with instructions to the physician. The document we have was written about 1600 B.C., but it is clearly a copy of an older text. It may have been written by the legendary Imhotep, architect to the pharaohs and builder of the pyramid at Saqqara, around 2500 B.C.

You can get some sense of the document by considering case 6.

Case 6: Instructions concerning a gaping wound in his head, penetrating to the bone, smashing his skull, and rending open the brain of his skull

After giving diagnostic instruction, the entry concludes as follows:

Thou shouldst say concerning him "An ailment not to be treated."

Needless to say, most of the other 47 cases are more hopeful. □

MEDICINE

▷ ca 300 B.C.

First, Do No Harm

Hippocratic Medicine

Anyone who has ever attended a medical school graduation has heard the students take the Hippocratic oath, arguably one of the oldest ceremonies we have. The oath refers to the Greek physician Hippocrates (ca 460–ca 377 B.C.), a man often referred to as the Father of Modern Medicine. Living on the island of Kos, off the coast of what is now western Turkey, he founded a school of medicine whose influence would extend well into modern times.

The most important contribution that Hippocrates made to medicine (and to science in general, for that matter) was the notion that diseases have natural causes. You aren't sick, in other words, because the gods are punishing you, but because of some natural effect that we can study and understand. In fact, Hippocrates taught that the body is governed by four "humors," and that disease resulted in an imbalance in these humors.

⊕ The instruction **"First, do no harm"** is the most famous part of the Hippocratic oath, which is still taken by new doctors.

For reference, the four humors were blood, black bile, phlegm, and yellow bile. The practice of bleeding patients, which seems so bizarre to the modern observer, makes sense in this scheme, since it was administered when physicians thought the humor associated with blood had become too strong and needed to be brought back into balance. The notion of humors survives in our language today, when we speak of people being sanguine, bilious, or phlegmatic.

It was the Roman physician Galen (A.D. 129–ca 199) who codified the Hippocratic corpus for future generations. Perhaps because he served as a physician to gladiators, he seems to have developed a more detailed knowledge of human anatomy than most of his contemporaries. His main influence came from his anatomy books, which were used in Europe well into the 17th century. Unfortunately, this means that his mistakes—he taught that venous blood originated in the liver, for example—were propagated as well. As happened with so much of ancient knowledge, Galen's works were translated first into Arabic and then into Latin.

At about the same time as these developments, an independent but similar process was going on in China. Again, we know something about Chinese medicine because of the survival of an ancient text—in this case a text titled *The Inner Canon of the Yellow Emperor* written about 500 B.C. but obviously a copy of something older. The central thesis of the text is that different organs in the body controlled each of the five elements that the Chinese thought constituted the universe—wood, fire, earth, metal, and water. As with the Greeks, the goal of Chinese medicine was to establish harmony among these elements. ☐

Above: Hippocrates, considered to be the father of modern medicine.

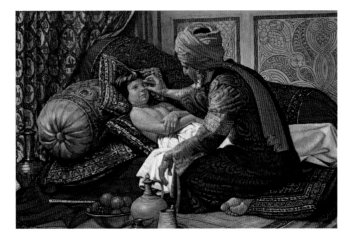

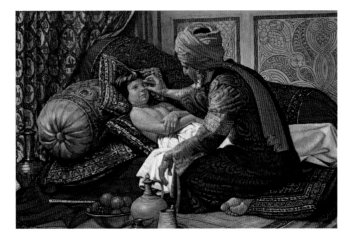 removed duplicate

A.D. 8th–13th Centuries
The Golden Age
Islamic Medicine

The period from the 8th to the 13th century is often referred to as the Golden Age of Islamic culture. The newly formed Islamic caliphate became the world's major center of learning, and advances were made in fields like mathematics (for example, the invention of algebra) as well as medicine. We can list the medical advances made in the Islamic world as the development of hospitals, the communicability of disease, and advances in surgery.

Development of Hospitals
There have always been places where the ill could go for treatment, but until the Islamic Golden Age, these places always had a religious affiliation, something like modern-day Lourdes. It seems that the first European hospitals, in Paris, were established by Europeans who had seen these institutions in the Islamic world.

Communicability of Disease
Although the Hippocratic tradition on which Islamic medicine was based operated on the assumption that disease, an imbalance of the humors, was internal to the body, Islamic physicians established that some diseases were caused by agents external to the body. In a sense, this is a precursor to Louis Pasteur's (1822–1895) germ theory of disease (see page 128).

Advances in Surgery
Islamic surgeons routinely removed cataracts and performed other kinds of surgery.

Perhaps the most important contribution of the Islamic world to medicine wasn't a specific advance but a questioning, empirical, data-driven approach to problems. One good example of this was the technique Muhammad ibn Zakariya al-Razi (865–925), known as Rhazes, used to find a building site for a new hospital in Baghdad. He put chunks of meat out in various locations around the city, and he built the hospital in the spot where the meat spoiled most slowly. ☐

▷ 1543
The Cutups
The Birth of Modern Anatomy

By the end of the Middle Ages, religious objections to performing autopsies were relaxed, and dissection of corpses became a routine part of physicians' training. The procedure that was introduced, however, looks a little strange to modern eyes. Students would look on while a technician performed the autopsy and a professor read from Galen. And if what they were seeing didn't match what Galen said, well, most students knew enough to keep quiet.

Not, however, a young Belgian named Andreas Vesalius (1514–1564). Raised near the gallows in Brussels, Vesalius had had a lot of experience watching bodies decompose. Unlike Galen, who was allowed to dissect animals but not humans, Vesalius stressed direct hands-on experience in his teaching at the University of Padua. In the course of this work he discovered many mistakes in Galen's writings.

> ⊕ The Islamic physician Zakariya al-Razi chose the site for a hospital by laying out pieces of meat, then **building where the meat decayed most slowly.**

In 1543, assisted by artist Jan Stephan van Calcar (1499–1546, a student of Titian), Vesalius published his monumental work *On the Fabric of the Human Body*. Most scholars regard his book as the foundation of the modern science of anatomy. From this point forward, medical scientists no longer had to accept what was written in ancient texts—they could examine the data for themselves.

An example of this new spirit can be found in the work of the Italian anatomist Giovanni Morgagni (1682–1771). He performed over 600 autopsies and in 1761 published a collection of letters summarizing his findings. His main result: diseases are caused by the malfunctioning of specific organs in the body, not by global imbalances of humors, as had been believed for centuries. ☐

Above left: An Islamic physician examines a boy who needs eye surgery. Islamic surgeons were skilled at removing cataracts.

Opposite: Vesalius produced the first detailed, accurate drawings of human anatomy.

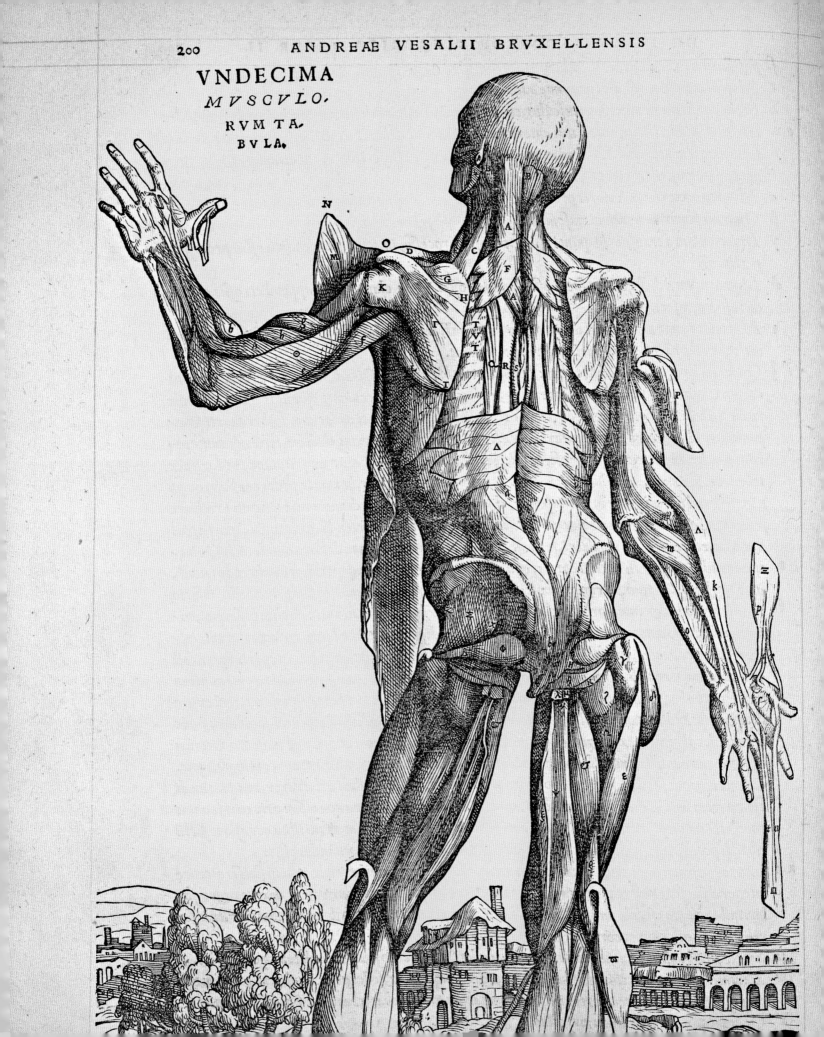

GERM THEORY

The French scientist Louis Pasteur conducted experiments that not only ended the reign of spontaneous generation but pointed the way toward the germ theory of disease, arguably the most important medical advance ever made. His experiments were quite simple. He boiled broth, then put the broth into containers that were either sealed off from the air or exposed to it. Molds quickly contaminated the broth exposed to air, whereas nothing grew in the sealed containers. Obviously, the contamination came from something in the air, not something in the broth. From there, of course, it was a short step to arguing that infections and diseases were also caused by microorganisms too small to be seen with the naked eye.

> **Q** One of the spaceships in the *Star Trek* series was the **USS *Pasteur,*** **named in fitting tribute to** a man who contributed so much to humanity.

▷ 1862

Discovering the Microbial World

Louis Pasteur

The question of where living things come from is an old one. People observed that if meat is left exposed to the air it is soon crawling with maggots, and observations like this led to the theory of spontaneous generation—the idea that life would appear from nothing if the conditions were right. Even though the Italian physician Francesco Redi (1626–1697) had demonstrated that using gauze to keep flies away from the meat prevented the appearance of maggots, the evidence against spontaneous generation was fragmentary and not very well understood, so the theory survived into modern times.

In 1862, with colleagues, Pasteur demonstrated that heating milk killed harmful microbes—a universally applied procedure we now call pasteurization. His theory that human health could be improved by keeping microbes out of the body—what we call today the germ theory of disease—was picked up by surgeon Joseph Lister (1827–1912) and led to the introduction of antiseptic surgery (see page 157). ☐

Above left: French scientist Louis Pasteur's simple experiments pointed toward the germ theory of disease, arguably the most important medical advance ever made.

OF DISEASE

Diseases can be caused by organisms invisible to the naked eye.

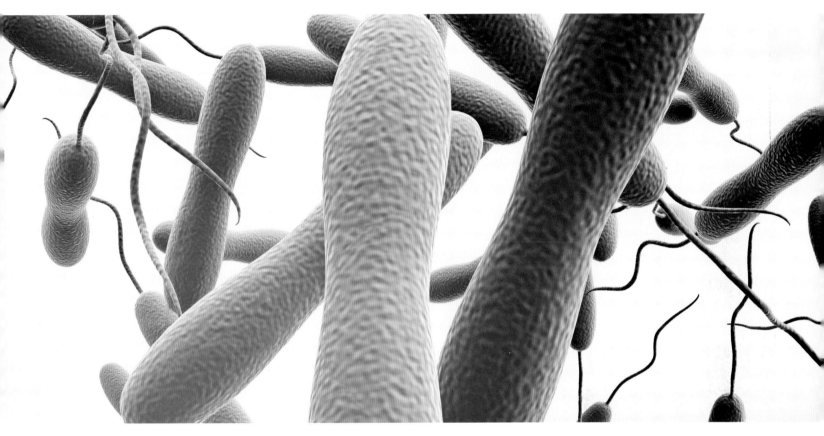

▷ **1854**

In the Time of Cholera

John Snow and the Broad Street Pump

Cholera is a nasty disease. During the 19th century periodic outbreaks occurred in cities, and no one understood what caused them. That changed when John Snow (1813–1858), a distinguished London physician, began to suspect that the appearance of cholera was connected in some way to the city's water supply. Gathering data on London's water was no easy task since centuries of building had left the delivery system hopelessly complicated.

London drew its water from the Thames, where it also dumped its waste. In addition, Snow had to deal with the prevailing view that, if water looked clear, it had to be safe to drink. In 1854, Snow was able to show that an outbreak of cholera was concentrated in a neighborhood where people got their water from a single pump, known

as the Broad Street pump. He convinced authorities to remove the pump's handle, a move that ended the outbreak because people were no longer able to drink from that source. While the cause of the disease was still unknown, Snow's work was the beginning of the public health movement.

The discovery of the cause of cholera, a bacterium known as *Vibrio cholerae*, involves one of those priority arguments so common in science. It now appears that Italian anatomist Filippo Pacini (1812–1883) identified the bacterium when he was doing autopsies in 1854. Although he published his results, it appears that most scientists (including John Snow) were unaware of them. It wasn't until 1884 that German scientist Robert Koch (1843–1910) identified the bacterium that the microbial source of this particular disease became well known. □

Above: Artist's conception of the bacteria that cause cholera.

▷ 1928

An Important Accident

Antibiotics

"When I woke up just after dawn on September 28, 1928, I certainly didn't plan to revolutionize all medicine by discovering the world's first antibiotic," Scottish biologist Sir Alexander Fleming (1881–1955) said, "but I suppose that was exactly what I did."

Fleming had been away on vacation, and when he returned to his laboratory he noticed something strange. He had been growing colonies of bacteria in petri dishes, and a few of the dishes had become contaminated by a fungus. Around each spot where the fungus had landed in a dish was a dark, bacterium-free region. Fleming realized that something in the fungus had killed the bacteria around it. Subsequent chemical analysis showed that the "something" was, in fact, penicillin, the first antibiotic.

Below: Sir Alexander Fleming discovered the antibiotic effects of penicillin when he observed how a particular fungus killed bacteria in a petri dish.

🔍 When antibiotics were first introduced in the 1930s, they were **very dangerous, and many patients died** before the drugs were perfected.

Penicillin was not an immediate medical success. It turned out to be hard to isolate, and Fleming believed it could never be produced in quantity. It wasn't, in fact, until the pressures of World War II brought significant funding to the problem that Sir Howard Walter Florey (1898–1968) and Ernst Chain (1906–1979), working at Oxford, found a way to purify and mass produce the drug. It saved countless lives, and Fleming, Florey, and Chain shared the Nobel Prize in 1945.

Penicillin was the first of many antibiotics to be discovered. However, as we shall discuss next, the economics of the drug industry are such that there are no new antibiotics in the research pipeline at this time. □

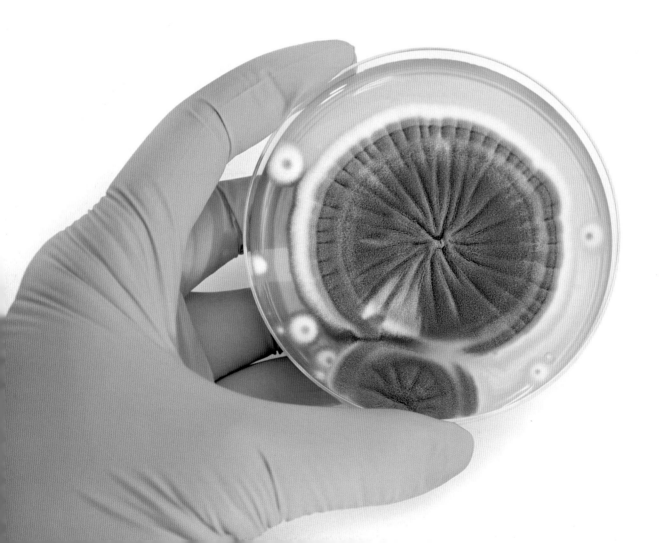

On the Horizon

▷ Antibiotic Resistance

At first, the introduction of antibiotics was seen as an unalloyed blessing. Eventually, however, unexpected strains of bacteria began to appear—strains that were resistant to certain drugs.

We can understand the appearance of antibiotic resistance by noting that antibiotics work by interfering with specific bacterial functions. Penicillin, for example, is a member of a group of antibiotics that function by blocking the growth of cell walls or cell membranes. The point is this: In any population of bacteria, there will be a few whose cell walls have a slightly different shape and which are therefore less susceptible to the drug. When the antibiotic is administered, the normal bacteria will die, but some of the different ones will survive, and these survivors have an open field with no competition. It's not hard to see that in several generations this process will lead to antibiotic-resistant strains of bacteria.

The way to deal with this phenomenon, of course, is to keep developing new kinds of antibiotics that attack different bacterial functions. Unfortunately, the cost of bringing a new drug to market makes the development of new antibiotics an unprofitable venture. Consequently, at the moment the pipeline for new drugs is largely empty. ■

A white blood cell (shown in purple) absorbs two antibiotic-resistant microbes (yellow).

MODERN

▷ 1628

What Goes Around Comes Around
Circulation of the Blood

William Harvey (1578–1657) was a prominent surgeon in London. Like other physicians of his time, he had been taught about the movement of the blood as it had been expounded by Galen. In this system, venous blood started in the liver and arterial blood in the heart, and there was no connection between the two systems. In addition, blood flowed out from the heart and liver to be consumed, as needed, by organs in the body. There was little attention paid to the possible return of blood to its source.

Using hearts obtained in autopsies, Harvey quickly saw that this system just couldn't work. Here was his reasoning: The heart contains about two ounces of fluid and beats, on average, 72 times a minute, which implies that the organ pumps about nine pounds of blood every minute. There are 1440 minutes in a day (60 × 24 = 1440), which means that the average heart pumps over half a ton of blood every day. It is simply impossible for that much blood to be created and consumed in that time frame. The only way to reconcile these numbers with physical possibility is to have the blood circulate—to have the heart pumping the same blood repeatedly. This was Harvey's great insight.

Harvey therefore predicted that a connection between the two systems would be found, and, indeed, capillaries connecting arteries and veins were found 32 years later. He also did some simple experiments in which a tourniquet was put on a patient's arm to make a vein "pop" (you may have had this done when you've had blood drawn). Then Harvey pressed down on the vein and released it to show that the blood exited toward the heart—it wasn't coming from the liver at all. ☐

Left: Our modern understanding is that blood flows outward from the heart in arteries and returns in veins.

MEDICINE

The modern system of medical care required advances both in basic science and in administrative and delivery systems.

▷ 1752

Specialization Made Hospitals Places of Healing

The Development of Modern Hospitals

There have always been places where sick people go for care. For most of history these places have been religious institutions, from Egyptian and Greek temples to places associated with medieval monasteries. In Europe, hospitals were often places to care for the poor and aged as well as the sick. The first institutions that we would recognize as hospitals arose in the Islamic world during the Golden Age (see page 126). These were basically secular institutions, devoted only to care of the sick and the training of physicians. They probably served as a model for hospitals that began to be built by Europeans returning from the Crusades, although the caregivers in these institutions were monks and priests.

It took a while for fully secularized hospitals to appear in Europe. In England the advent of Protestantism gave rise to institutions that resembled modern hospitals and medical schools. Private organizations and individuals founded a number of hospitals in London, and it was at one of these (Guy's Hospital, founded by the wealthy merchant Thomas Guy [1644–1724]) that William Harvey discovered the circulation of the blood. This model of the foundation of hospitals spread to the North American colonies.

Up until the late 19th century, hospitals were primarily places for the poor. Persons of means were cared for at home, and many medical procedures (including childbirth) were routinely carried out in that environment. It wasn't until the latter part of the 19th century that medical specialization produced the modern hospital as a place where everyone goes for care. Oddly enough, it wasn't a

Above: The Pennsylvania Hospital in Philadelphia, as it appears today, was the first hospital in the United States.

physician who drove that change, but Florence Nightingale (1820–1910), who elevated nursing to a specialized profession and drove the system that converted hospitals from places where the poor went to die to places of healing and recovery. ☐

⊕ The first hospital in America was founded in 1752 by **Benjamin Franklin** (1706–1790) and his colleagues. The Pennsylvania Hospital is still operating in Philadelphia.

A Little Shot
Vaccinations

The human immune system is a marvelously complex system that is designed to protect the human body from invaders. The process of vaccination is a way of enlisting the natural properties of the immune system to protect a person from a specific disease. You can understand how vaccines work by thinking about a simplified explanation of the immune system.

One of the most important categories of cells in the immune system are the leukocytes, or white blood cells. They are produced and stored throughout the body and are constantly on patrol, searching for invaders. Two important categories of leukocytes are called phagocytes and

Below: A boy gets a vaccination.

🔍 **We have to get flu shots every year because the flu virus mutates very rapidly; thus the immune system has to be primed.**

lymphocytes. The former cells destroy invading cells that have been marked for elimination by having specific molecules attached to their surfaces—essentially they are the "search and destroy" cells in the immune system. Lymphocytes originate in the bone marrow. Those that mature there are called B cells (*B* for "bone marrow"), whereas those that migrate and mature in the thymus gland are called T cells (*T* for "thymus").

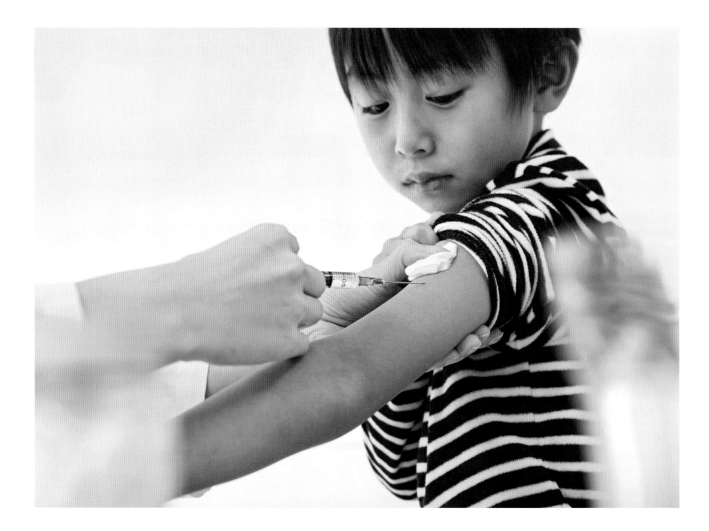

Here's how the system works: When an invader enters the body, various helper cells attract B cells to the site of the invasion. The B cells produce Y-shaped molecules, called antibodies, that lock on to the specific molecular shape of the invader and summon T cells to destroy it. The antibodies remain in the system as a kind of memory— think of them as a molecular filing cabinet—that can be called upon to combat the same invader should it reappear. This molecular filing cabinet is the basis for the success of vaccination.

In 1796, the British surgeon Edward Jenner (1749–1823), intrigued by the common knowledge that milkmaids who had had a mild disease known as cowpox were immune from the much more serous scourge of smallpox, inoculated a boy with a small amount of cowpox material and then, a few weeks later, exposed him to smallpox. When the boy showed no signs of the disease, he concluded that his procedure had conferred immunity.

Today in the United States children are routinely vaccinated to prevent an entire constellation of diseases. The fact that most of these diseases have essentially disappeared from our consciousness is a testament to the efficacy of the procedure. Unfortunately, some parents are refusing to have their children vaccinated, and as a result some of these diseases are starting to reappear. ▢

⬢⬢⬢⬢⬢⬢⬢⬢⬢⬢⬢⬢⬢⬢⬢⬢⬢⬢⬢⬢⬢⬢⬢⬢⬢⬢⬢⬢⬢⬢⬢⬢

▷ **Modern Times**

Does It Work?

Clinical Trials

In order to see if a new drug or treatment works, and to make sure we understand possible side effects, clinical trials are carried out. These trials proceed in stages.

- **Phase 0:** 10–15 subjects—what does the drug do?
- **Phase I:** 20–80 subjects—is the drug safe? What are the side effects?
- **Phase II:** 100–300 subjects—is the drug effective? Are there uncommon side effects?
- **Phase III:** 1,000–3,000 subjects—final confirmation of efficacy and safety
- **Phase IV:** continued monitoring during sales

The "gold standard" for clinical trials is the double-blind study, in which neither the subjects nor the physicians know which subjects have been given a drug and which have been given a placebo. ▢

Right: Before medications like this can be used, they must be tested for safety and efficacy.

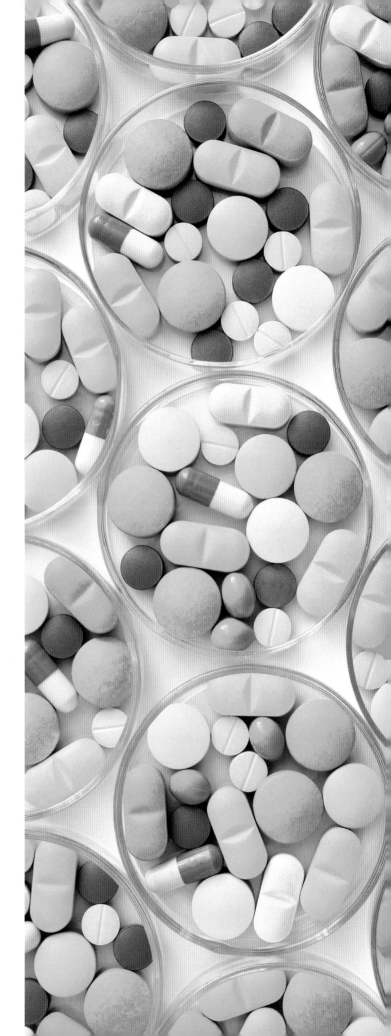

▷ 1905

Used Parts

Organ Transplants

The idea that we can replace worn-out body parts with new ones, the way we replace parts in an old car, has been around for a long time. To have a successful organ transplant, however, we have to overcome two separate difficulties. The first is purely mechanical—making sure that the proper connections are made between the new organ and the patient's body. Overcoming this difficulty is largely a

> 🔍 Today the most **common transplant** operation is the **kidney transplant.**

matter of the surgeon's skill and is not fundamental. The second difficulty is more serious, for it has to do with the nature of the immune system. If new tissue or a new organ is introduced into the body, it will be attacked like any other invader. Consequently, transplant recipients must take drugs to suppress their own immune system to keep the transplant from being rejected.

The history of organ and tissue transplants is a story of increasing ability to deal with increasingly complex systems. The first successful transplant was a skin graft done in Germany in 1823. Since the transplanted skin was taken from another location on the patient's body, the problem of the immune response just discussed didn't arise. Modern "firsts" include the following:

- **1905**—first cornea transplant in what is now the Czech Republic
- **1950**—first kidney transplant in the United States
- **1967**—first heart transplant in South Africa
- **1998**—first hand transplant in France
- **2006**—first successful penis transplant in China. Unfortunately, the transplant had to be removed when the patient's wife developed what was described as a "severe psychological rejection" of the transplanted organ.

Today the most common transplant operation is the kidney transplant, with almost 400,000 such operations having been performed in the United States since 1998. ☐

Right: The heart of a donor is readied for transplant.

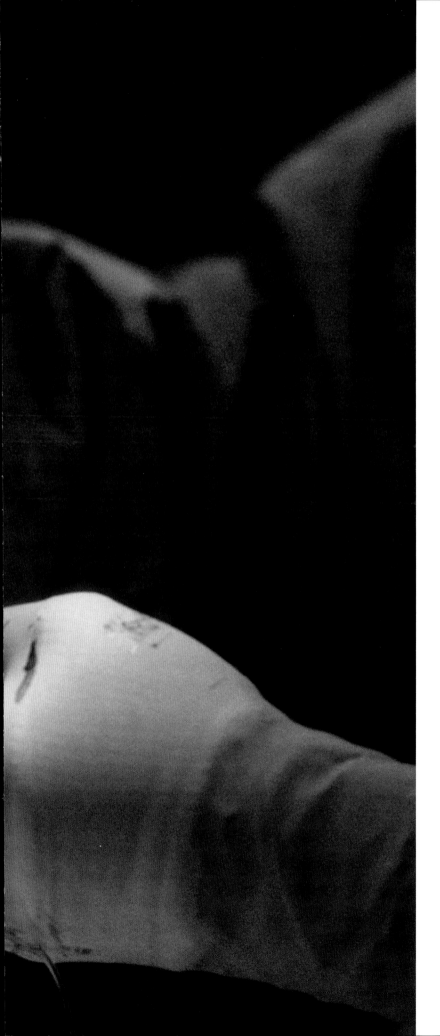

Building from Scratch

Tissue Engineering and
Regenerative Medicine

The problem of having a patient's immune system reject a transplanted organ would not arise if the organ were made from cells containing the patient's own DNA. On the other hand, we know that embryonic stem cell lines (see page 112) can be produced that have the patient's own DNA. If we could use those stem cells to grow new organs, then those organs could be transplanted without the risk that they would be rejected. This is the dream of a new field known as regenerative medicine.

The main roadblock on the way to realizing this dream is taking the step from having the right sort of cells to building organs and tissue from them. In your body, cells are surrounded by an intracellular matrix that acts both as a kind of scaffolding to keep the cells in place and as a medium through which chemical messages can be passed from cell to cell. Experimental efforts at the moment are concentrated on finding ways to replicate that structure with stem cells, producing organs that will not be rejected when implanted. □

Above: Engineered tissue is prepared for transplantation.

On the Horizon

▷ Engineering Replacement Tissues

Although at the moment tissue engineering and regenerative medicine play a relatively small role in patient care, we can expect this to change in the future. Most likely, the first advances will be in introducing engineered tissues to replace worn-out materials, such as cartilage, with research continuing to be aimed at producing engineered pancreatic tissue to deal with diabetes and neural tissue to deal with diseases like Alzheimer's and Parkinson's. ■

A synthetic ear is growing in a fluid containing cartilage cells. The cartilage cells have been coaxed to grow on an ear-shaped lattice framework.

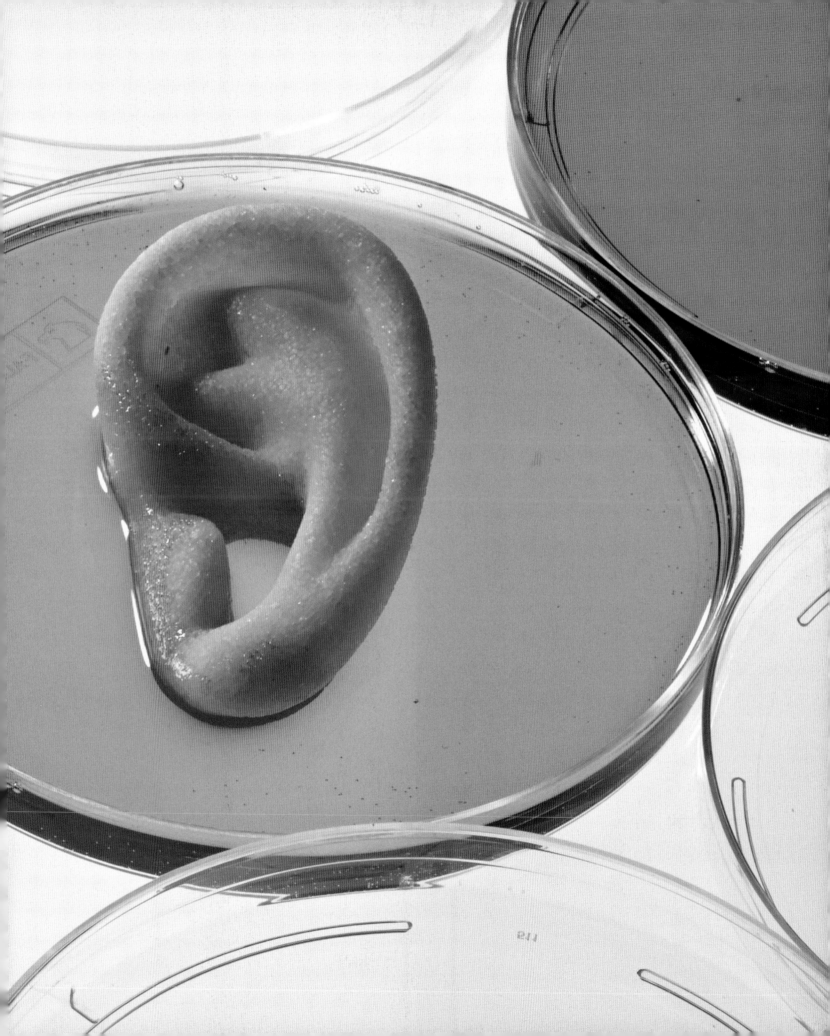

CANCER

Cancer is not a single disease, but a constellation of diseases, each with its own cause, treatment, and prognosis.

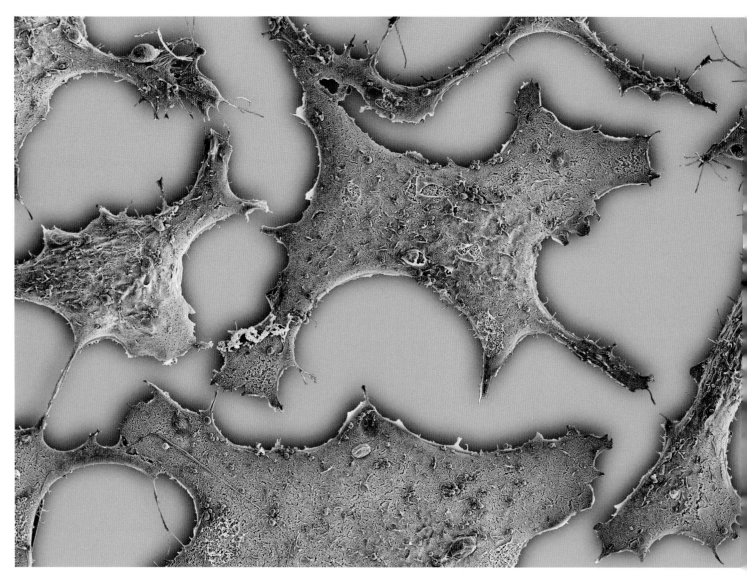

▷ From Ancient Times

The Big C

Overview of Cancer

Cancer is the second-leading cause of death in the United States, resulting in over half a million fatalities per year. It is not an overstatement to say, however, that it is the most feared disease in our experience. As stated above, the term "cancer" does not refer to a single disease but to a collection of different diseases—there are, for example, over 100 different cancers that can afflict humans.

Cancers have been observed and described since the beginning of medicine. In the Edwin Smith Papyrus (see page 124), for example, there is a description of a breast cancer by an Egyptian physician several millennia ago. Hippocrates (see page 125) used the term "cancer" ("crab") to describe the appearance of a solid tumor.

Under normal circumstances, cell division in the body is strictly controlled. Cells will divide as organs grow but

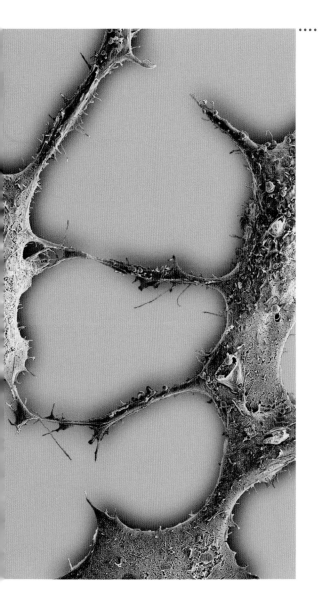

will slow down or stop dividing once the organ is formed. We don't really understand this control mechanism, but it seems to involve both signals generated inside the cell and signals received from neighbors. If these signaling mechanisms fail, a cell can escape from the normal controls and begin multiplying without restraint. This, in essence, is the way that cancer starts. Releasing a cell from the normal control mechanisms is not a particularly easy task, and it normally takes multiple "hits" for the process to start. Colon cancer, for example, requires four different mutations to occur on four different chromosomes. Nor is escaping cellular control enough to produce a true cancer. The new cells must manage to evade the immune system (a process we'll discuss later in this section) and generate their own blood supply to develop into a true cancer.

As befits such a diverse collection of diseases, there are many causes for cancer. Some are external, such as environmental chemicals and radiation, whereas others are internal, related to genetic factors or by-products of normal cell chemistry.

Perhaps the most serious development in the growth of a tumor is the process of metastasis. In this situation, cancer cells break off from their original location and are carried around the body to take root and grow elsewhere. This dispersal, of course, greatly complicates treatment strategies. ☐

Left and above: All cancer cells start as ordinary cells that for various reasons begin to divide uncontrollably

🔍 The **most common form of cancer in the United States is breast cancer,** with over a quarter of a million cases reported annually.

Getting Rid of It

Conventional Cancer Treatments

Conventional cancer therapy is built around one goal—getting rid of the cancerous cells. This can be accomplished through surgery, chemotherapy, radiation, and immunotherapy.

Surgery

The most straightforward treatment involves the physical removal of the cancer through surgery. This is particularly effective for solid tumors that are not intensely intermixed with normal organs. In surgical procedures, the surgeon has to worry about leaving cancerous cells behind, perhaps at the margins of the incisions, since those cells would eventually grow into a new tumor. It is common, therefore, to send incised material to a pathologist during the surgery to check, in real time, that the tumor boundaries have been exceeded and the margin is clear of cancer cells.

Chemotherapy

The efficacy of the first kinds of chemotherapy that were used depended on the fact that cancerous cells tend to divide and reproduce more rapidly than normal cells. Therefore agents that kill cells by interfering with the process of cell division will kill more tumor cells than normal cells. The physician's skill lies in his or her ability to adjust chemical doses such that minimal damage is done to normal tissue while, at the same time, eliminating a tumor. Chemotherapy is often used in conjunction with other treatment modes.

Modern chemotherapies are much more selective in the kinds of cells they attack, specifically targeting proteins

Below: Chemotherapeutic agents are often delivered by injection.

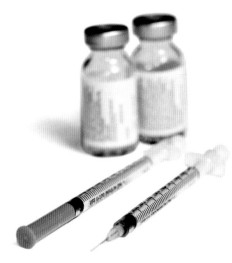

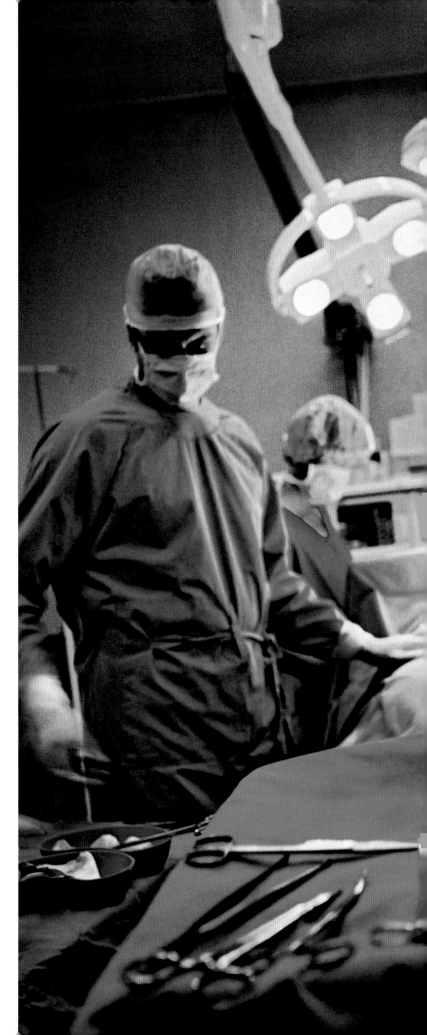

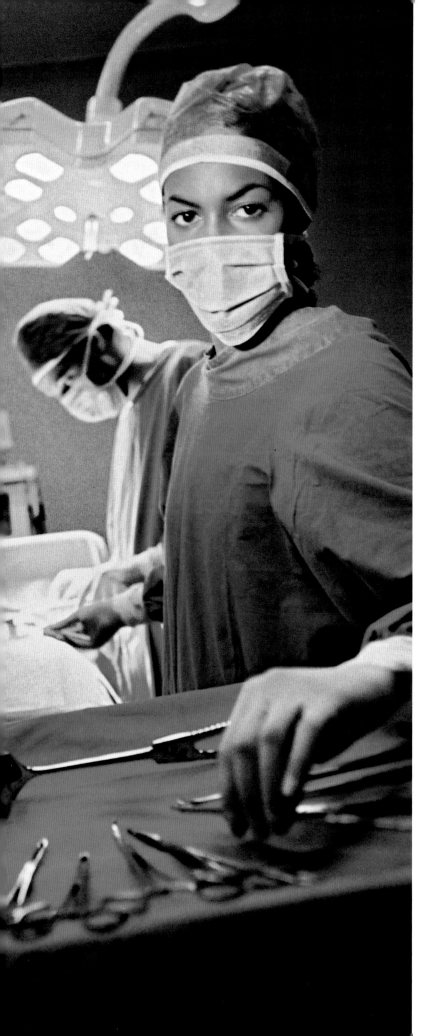

that are used by the cancer cells to block the mechanism that controls the growth of normal cells. This technique is most commonly used to treat certain types of leukemia. Because the treatment involves only cancer cells, this sort of chemotherapy does not produce the kind of side effects associated with the older drugs.

Radiation

Like the older chemotherapeutic agents, radiation affects all the cells that it encounters. It does so by disrupting the complex molecules, like DNA, that are necessary for the cell's survival.

The basic idea behind radiation therapy is to deliver a maximum radiation dose to a tumor while delivering a minimal dose to the surrounding healthy tissue. This is usually accomplished by directing beams of radiation in such a

> ⊕ There are almost
> **15 million cancer survivors**
> living in the United States.

way that every beam crosses the tumor but takes a different path through healthy tissue. In this way, radiation damage to healthy tissue is reduced.

Immunotherapy

It seems we can date attempts to use the immune system to fight cancer to 1891, when a New York surgeon injected bacteria into a patient's tumor in the hope that the immune system would attack both the bacteria and the tumor. It wasn't until a century later that the Food and Drug Administration approved a drug, interleukin-2, as the first immunotherapeutic agent. Basically, the drug fires up the T cells in the immune system (see page 134) so that they will attack tumor cells more readily. Unfortunately, for reasons discussed below, this kind of treatment has a rather low rate of success.

The most common kind of immunotherapy involves the use of molecules called antibodies that bind to specific proteins on the surface of cancer cells. Once there, they can trigger the immune system to destroy the cell or eliminate it by other means. Immunotherapy remains a major research area in cancer treatment. ☐

Left: Surgery remains an important tool in the battle against cancer.

On the Horizon

▷ Overcoming Tumor Resistance to the Immune System

One reason for the relatively low effectiveness of immunotherapeutic drugs is the ability of tumors to evade the attention of the T cells in the immune system. One way they can do this is to use the so-called checkpoint cells whose normal function is to protect healthy tissue from T cells. Scientists used molecules called checkpoint inhibitors to reduce the effect of the checkpoint cells, a procedure that, in turn, allows the T cells to attack the tumor. The first drug of this type was approved by the Food and Drug Administration in 2011. One of the main problems these drugs pose is that they sometimes allow T cells to attack healthy tissue, leading to serious side effects.

▷ Using the Genome

As the sequencing of DNA becomes cheaper and easier to do (see page 118) we can expect the new techniques to begin to play a role in cancer treatment. One such use would be screening for susceptibility to specific cancers. The idea is this: We inherent two copies of each gene in our genome—one from each parent. If one of these copies is damaged, the other can function, but there is no backup, and the person is susceptible to whatever cancer is associated with that gene. Searching genomes for these kinds of defects (we all have them) will become routine in the future.

Another technique, already being pursued in academic laboratories, involves the sequencing of tumor DNA itself, with an eye toward discovering the molecules that act as growth factors and inhibitors (think of them as the molecular "gas pedal" and "brake" for the tumor, respectively). Once these are known, individualized treatments for specific tumors can be sought. ∎

An artist's rendering of a DNA genome sequence.

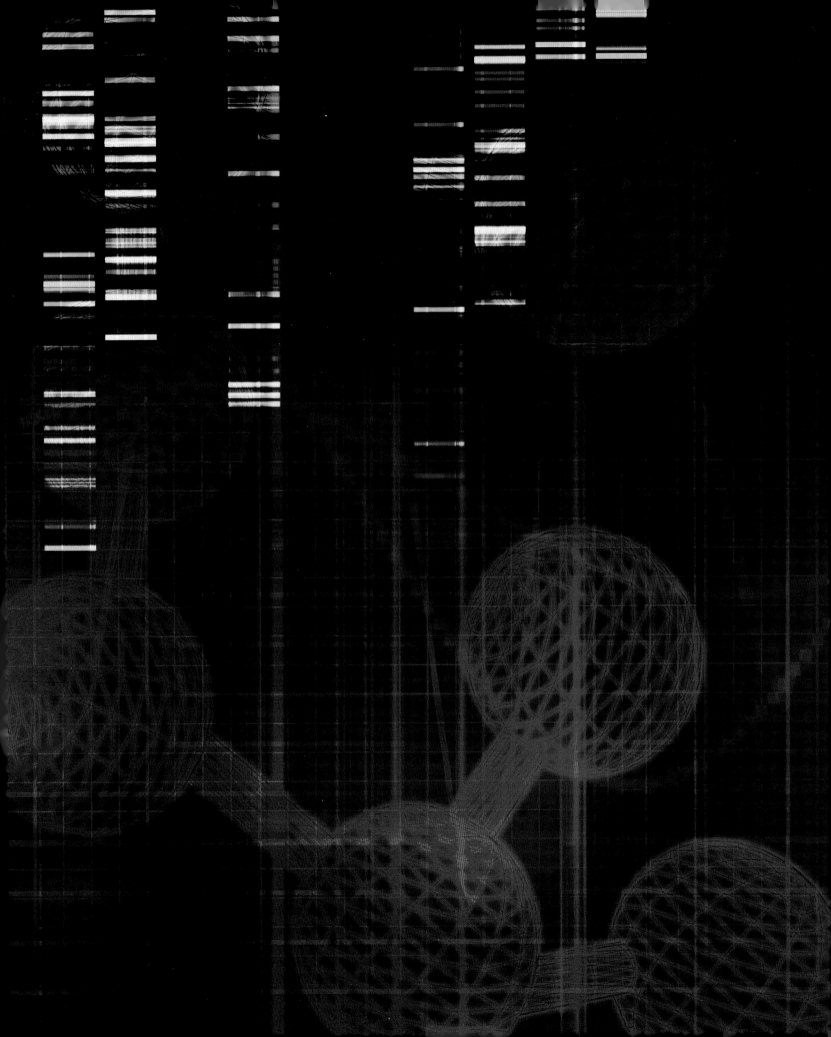

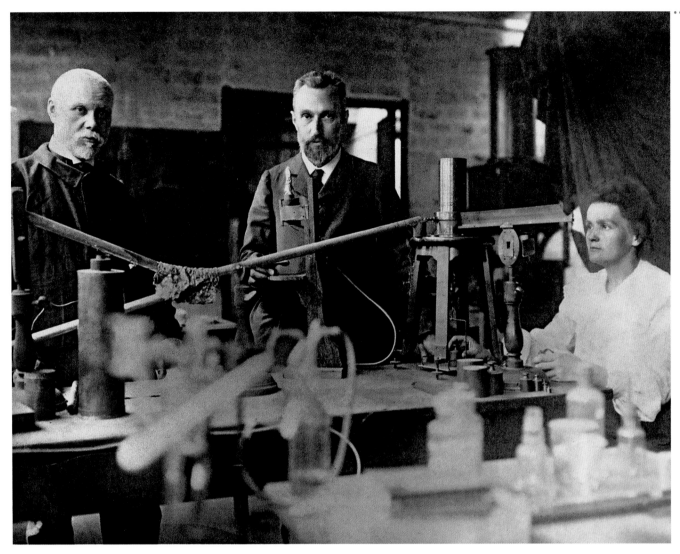

▷ 1895

The Accidental Look

X-rays

When the German physicist Wilhelm Roentgen (1845–1923) accidentally discovered x-rays (see page 24), it quickly became clear that they had the ability to penetrate ordinary materials. In fact, the first x-ray photograph of a human being was of his wife's hand, complete with wedding ring. The medical utility of x-rays for imaging body parts like bones and teeth became obvious quickly, and the technique remains the most widely used medical diagnostic imaging procedure. During World War I Nobel Laureate Marie Curie (1867–1934) created and operated a mobile x-ray unit for the French army. □

Above: This circa 1900 photograph shows Marie and Pierre Curie (center) with an unidentified man, using equipment in their Paris laboratory.

DIAGNOSIS

There are many ways of seeing what's going on inside the body without actually cutting a person open.

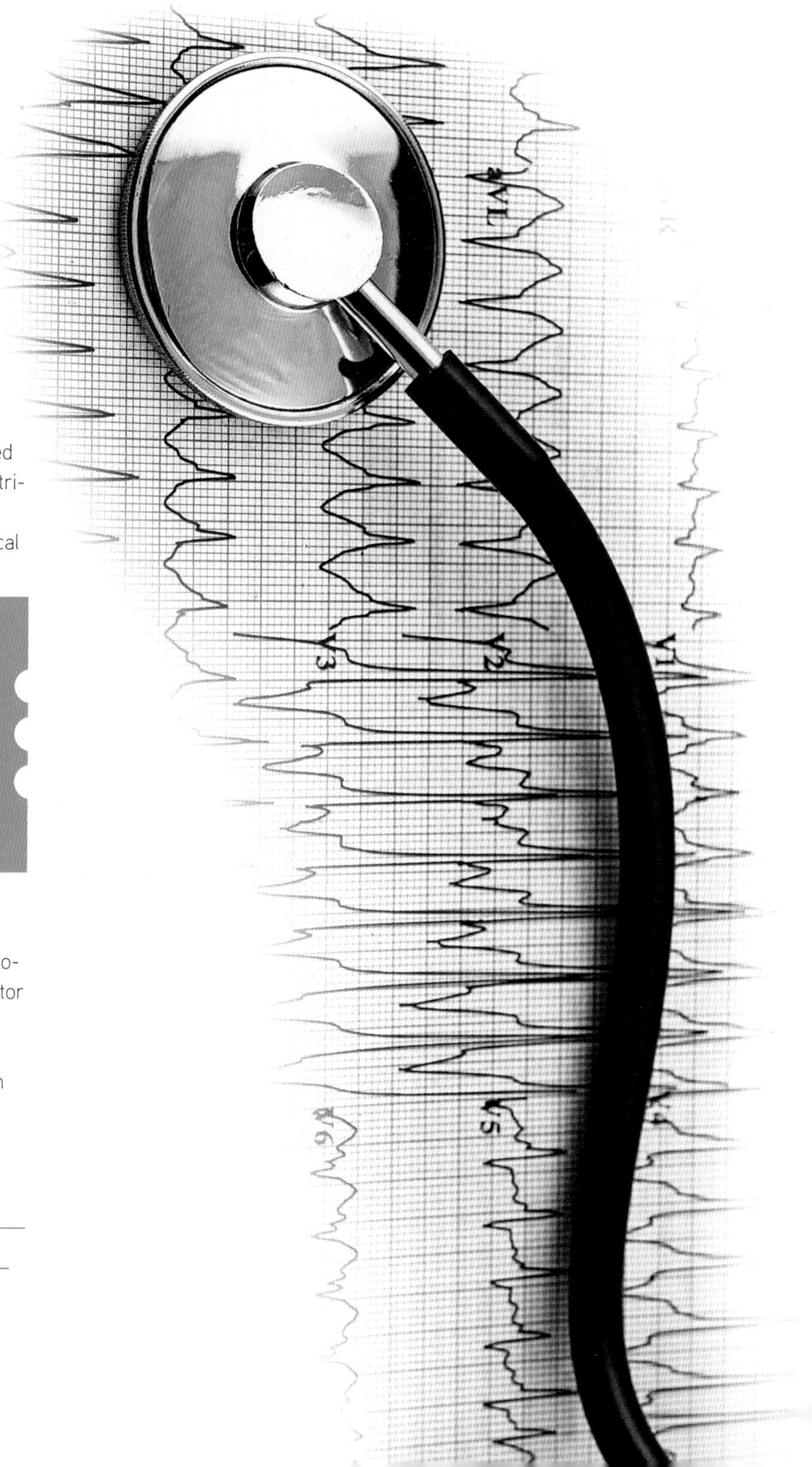

▷ 1901

The Telltale Heart

Electrocardiograph

The electrocardiograph (abbreviated as EKG in the United States and ECG in Britain) is a device that monitors electrical activity in the muscles of the heart. Electrodes are attached to the patient's chest and arms, and the electrical

> 🔍 The first stethoscope was actually **a hollow wooden tube** that the doctor held against a patient's chest.

pulses are recorded on paper by a stylus, typically for about ten seconds. The resulting trace is called an electrocardiogram. A skilled physician can use the EKG to monitor normal heart functions, screen for possible developing difficulties, and detect damage to the heart muscles.

The first modern EKG was used by Willem Einthoven (1860–1927) in the Netherlands in 1901, and Einthoven received the Nobel Prize for his work in 1924. The technique is now a routine part of physical examinations. □

Right: A stethoscope lies above the record of a heart beating—two ways of learning about the functioning of a heart.

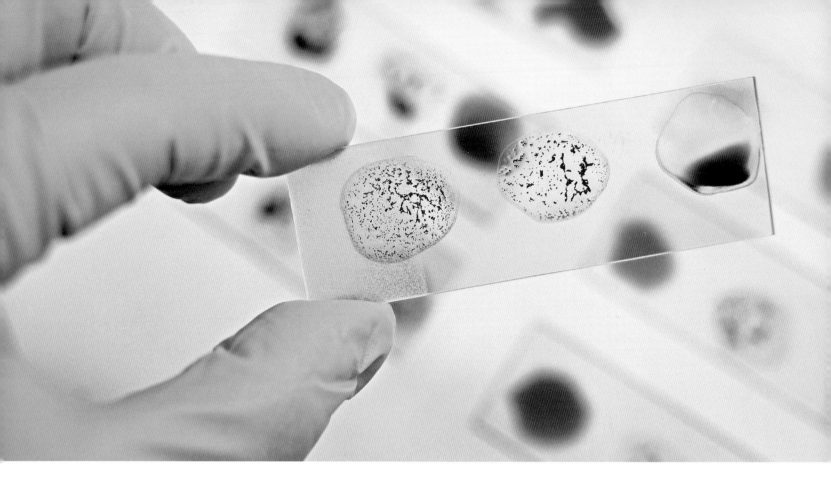

▷ 1901

Stories in the Blood

Blood Tests

Whenever something happens in your body, there will be evidence of the event in your blood. This is why your doctor almost always asks that blood be drawn as part of a routine exam. Although blood looks like an ordinary fluid, it is actually a very complex substance, containing many kinds of materials in solution. The most important components of blood are red blood cells, which carry oxygen, white blood cells, which fight infection, and platelets, which are involved in clotting.

In the 19th century, the idea that different people's blood might be different was unknown, and transfusions often involved nothing more than attaching a tube to carry blood from one person to another. In 1901, however, the Austrian physiologist Karl Landsteiner (1868–1943) discovered that some types of blood could produce immune reactions in laboratory animals. This led to the first classification of blood types—A, B, and what is now called O (type AB was added later). In essence, the red blood cells carry antigens on their surfaces. If the antigens are different from those on the red blood cells of the recipient, the recipient's immune system will attack the transfused cells, leading to serious (and sometimes fatal) medical consequences. Landsteiner received the Nobel Prize in 1930.

In 1937 Landsteiner and his colleagues discovered another important distinction between the blood of different individuals. Called the Rh factor (after the rhesus macaques that were used in the laboratory experiments), this factor involves a separate set of antigens that can trigger immune reactions. One of the most serious complications involving the Rh factor can occur during pregnancy if the mother exhibits an immune reaction to the blood of the fetus she is carrying. Today, hematologists recognize over 30 different blood "systems" (some quite rare) based on the different types of antigens carried on red blood cells.

Blood for tests is usually obtained by inserting a needle into a vein in the arm—an experience most of us remember. Once drawn, many tests can be made (similar tests are referred to as a panel). We can distinguish three important kinds of tests:

- Biochemical tests look at the presence and amount of certain chemicals in the blood and are used to measure basic metabolism and things like cholesterol levels.
- Molecular tests look at complex molecules in the blood and are used for things like monitoring liver function and detecting sexually transmitted diseases.
- Cellular tests are used for blood typing and for counting the abundance of different types of blood cells. ☐

Above: After blood is drawn from your arm, it may be put on microscope slides like this for analysis.

▷1929

Brain Waves

Electroencephalograph

In its normal mode of operation the brain is crisscrossed by electrical currents running through neurons (see page 162). The purpose of the electroencephalograph (EEG) is to detect those electrical currents.

When the EEG is in use, metal electrodes are attached to the patient's skull, and the electrical signals they detect are amplified and displayed on a graph.

Below: This student's brain waves are being recorded in a study of the effects of sleep deprivation.

🔍 EEG is still widely used today in the treatment of epilepsy.

Depending on what the patient is doing, different frequencies of waves are seen, with characteristic frequencies being denoted by letters of the Greek alphabet. The so-called beta waves, for example, are seen during intense mental activity, delta waves during dreamless sleep.

The MRI machine (see page 154) has largely replaced the EEG as a diagnostic tool for neurological problems, although the EEG is still widely used in cases of epilepsy. ☐

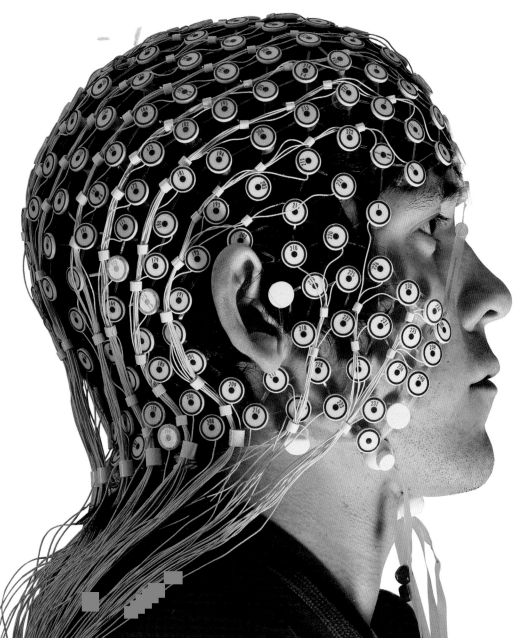

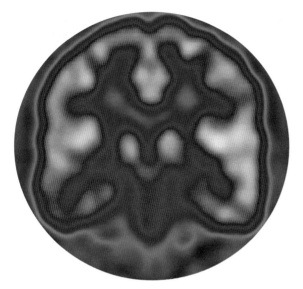

▷ 1935

Isotopes to the Rescue

Radioactive Tracers

The ability to use radioactive tracers depends on the fact that an atom's electrons, which determine its chemistry, and the radioactive properties of the atom's nucleus are largely independent of each other. In other words, whether or not a nucleus is unstable does not affect how it behaves in the body.

If an atom of a radioactive isotope (see page 25) of a particular element is introduced into the body, the electrons will guarantee that that atom will move to wherever in the body that element accumulates. Once there, the nucleus will decay, sending the decay products out of the body, where they can be detected. The first medical use of this technique occurred in 1935, when Hungarian chemist George de Hevesy (1885–1966) used radioactive phosphorous to study the metabolism of laboratory rats. □

Above: A scan of the brain using radioactive tracers.

Right: The radioactive tracers in this illustration trace out the bones in the patient's hands.

▷ 1940s

Noisy

Ultrasound

As the name suggests, ultrasound technology involved using sound waves to produce images of internal structures. In the 1920s, ultrasonography entered the medical world as a therapeutic tool, useful for breaking up unwanted masses of tissue. In the 1940s, however, it began to be used for diagnosis.

The basic idea behind ultrasound diagnostics is this: As sound waves move through the body, they encounter areas of different density (like the boundary of an internal organ, for example). At these points, some of the wave will be reflected. A computer can take measurements of these reflected waves and create an image of the region through which the wave moves.

Although ultrasonography is still used in a variety of diagnostic settings, such as detecting gallstones, the best-known use of the technology is in the field of obstetrics. Pregnant women routinely are given ultrasound images of the developing fetus, and many couples actually frame these pictures as their first baby pictures. ☐

Left: An expectant mother examines the ultrasound image of her unborn child.

🔍 Historians claim that the idea of using ultrasonography as a diagnostic tool came from scientists who had developed radar. They saw the connection between sound waves (used in ultrasound) and radio waves (used in radar).

▷ 1972

Slice and Dice

CAT scan

Computerized axial tomography (CAT) is basically a technique for forming three-dimensional images of internal organs. "Tomography" comes from the Greek word *tomos* ("slice"). CAT scans work this way: x-rays are sent on different paths and directions through a slice of the body. A computer then takes the data on how many x-rays are absorbed along each path and uses it to construct a picture of the density of tissue at each point in the slice. This done, the machine moves on to the next slice and the next after that until the entire three-dimensional image is obtained. ☐

Opposite: CAT scans of a patient's liver, showing successive layers of imaging. Before the advent of this type of imaging, exploratory surgery was the only way to confirm an internal soft-tissue diagnosis.

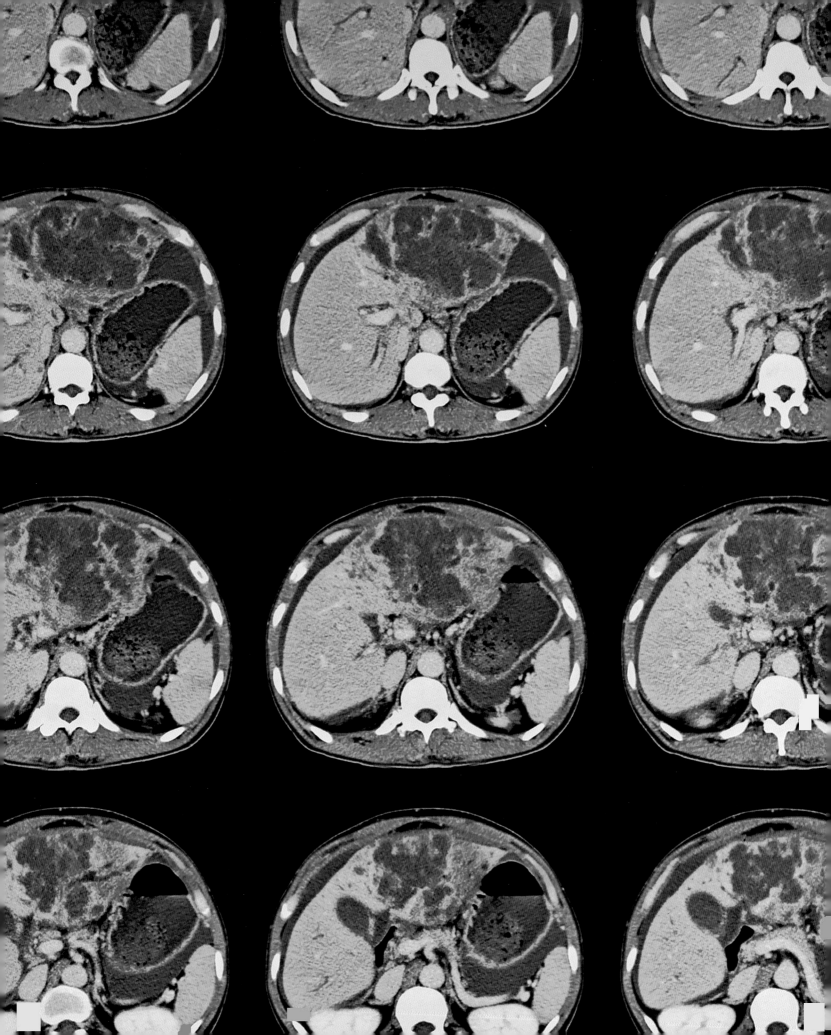

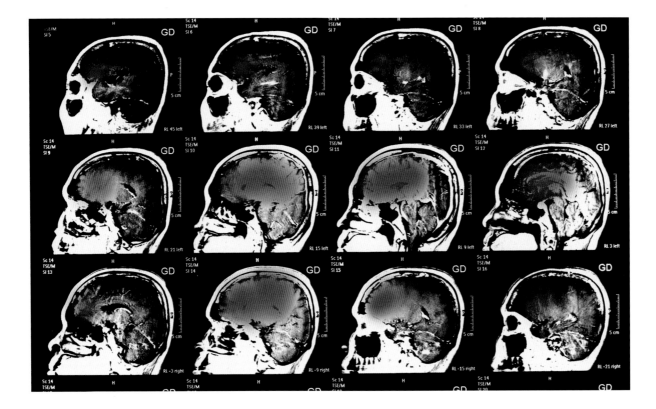

▷ 1977

Spinning Around

Magnetic Resonance Imaging

Like the CAT scan, magnetic resonance imaging (MRI) is a technique for producing three-dimensional images of internal organs. Unlike the CAT scan, however, it does not use x-rays to achieve this result.

The MRI technique depends on the fact that the nuclei of atoms behave like small magnets (hydrogen is the most commonly used atom for this purpose). If an external magnetic field is imposed on a material, the nuclear magnets will tend to line up with that field—essentially,

the north pole of the nuclear magnet will point toward the south pole of the external magnet. If we now send in radio waves of just the right energy, we can flip those nuclear magnets. When the radio waves are switched off, the nuclear magnets go back to being aligned, emitting their own radio waves when they do so. By measuring those radio waves, we can tell how much hydrogen is at a certain spot and hence construct the desired three-dimensional image. ☐

Above: Magnetic resonance imaging (MRI) of a human brain. While CAT scans use x-rays to produce images, MRI relies on magnetism and radio waves.

🔍 Magnetic resonance imaging machines use **superconducting magnets** (see page 61) to produce the external magnetic field needed for imaging. This is the **major use of these magnets** worldwide.

On the Horizon

▷ Better Testing Techniques

Although standard blood tests are a routine part of modern medicine and are relatively cheap, ways of improving them are always being sought. For example, saliva contains about 20 percent of the proteins found in blood, and having a saliva test might eliminate the necessity of the uncomfortable process of having blood drawn.

Perhaps the most exciting development now under way is the microchip. This is a postage stamp–sized chip on which an array of molecules is attached. Each molecule on the chip has a shape that will attach to one and only one molecule in the blood. If a small amount of blood is washed over the chip, each molecule in the blood will attach to one molecule on the chip. Using radioactive tagging or some other technique, the checkerboard pattern of attached molecules is visualized, giving an instant readout of the chemicals in the blood sample. This microchip technique holds the promise of faster and cheaper blood testing.

▷ Personalized Medicine

The first sequencing of the human genome cost billions of dollars and took many years to complete (see page 118). Today, scientists talk confidently of the "$1,000 genome," a genome the cost of whose sequencing is comparable to other routine but complex medical procedures. This kind of process opens a new window on the working of the human body, producing a chemical rather than a visual image. In addition to regenerative medicine and cancer therapy (see page 137), we can expect that physicians will be able to examine individual genomes for hints about susceptibility to diseases and conditions—hints that would not otherwise be available. This will be the start of the era of personalized medicine. ■

A scientist examines genetic sequences. Each black mark represents a different length of DNA, and the entire "bar code" contains information about the organism's genome.

SURGERY

British chemist Joseph Priestley (1733–1804), who isolated many gases, including nitrous oxide ("laughing gas").

A medical student named Crawford Long (1815–1878), apparently a frequent participant in ether frolics, noticed that his friends would get serious bruises from their antics but have no memory of sustaining any injury. In 1842, he removed a neck tumor from a patient who had been given ether, and later used ether in various medical procedures. Because he did not publish his results until 1849, however, he allowed questions of who deserved the title of "first user of anesthetic" to become murky.

That title is generally bestowed on dentist William T. G. Morton (1819–1868) who, in 1846, supervised the administering of ether as a general anesthetic in a public event in what is now called the Ether Dome at Massachusetts General Hospital. After a surgeon removed a tumor from the neck of an anesthetized patient, he is supposed to have told the audience "Gentlemen, this is no humbug."

Since that time many anesthetic agents have been developed, and anesthesiology has become an important medical specialty. Modern anesthetics can be separated into local and general anesthetics. Local anesthetics, like the ones you get at the dentist's office, block nerves in a specific area. One local anesthetic, widely used to alleviate the pain of childbirth, is the epidural block, in which medications are injected into the spinal column. General anesthetics are often administered intravenously and are intended to induce unconsciousness. □

▷ 1846

Ether Way
Anesthetic Surgery

Every ancient society whose medical skill had advanced to the point of having surgery tried to find ways of keeping the patient from feeling the pain attendant on the procedure. Alcohol is one of the oldest drugs used this way, and the Sumerians (among others) used opium. The modern use of anesthetics can be said to have started with the

Above left: Inhalers like this were used to administer ether in the 19th century. The sponges in the jar were soaked with ether.

🔍 During the 19th century lecturers would travel around the country hosting "ether frolics"—parties where people would **inhale nitrous oxide** and ether and, to use a modern term, **"get high."**

As long as we have understood about internal organs, humans have invented ways to repair, adjust, and even remove troublesome body parts.

▷ 1865

A Germ of an Idea

Antiseptic Surgery

It's really hard to overemphasize the importance of Pasteur's germ theory of disease. Its impacts reach into all corners of our lives, from pasteurized milk to food storage. But perhaps its greatest impact is played out in thousands of hospitals around the world every day, where surgeons work in antiseptic operating rooms—environments built around Pasteur's discovery.

⊕ In 1871, during the Franco-Prussian War, 10,006 of 13,173 military surgery patients died of postoperative infection.

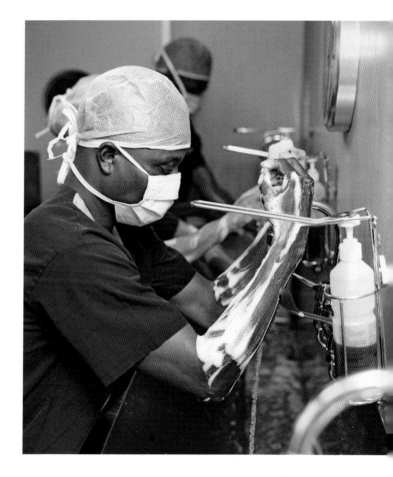

In the early 19th century the danger of postoperative infection was well recognized, but people thought that it was caused by bad air, or "miasma," as it was known. As a result, hospital wards were routinely aired out every day, a practice that did little to curb infection. Because of the miasma theory, surgeons were not even required to wash their hands before operating, and it was common for a surgeon to go from one patient to another without doing so.

This began to change when the English surgeon Joseph Lister read Pasteur's papers and began to take the notion of microbe-caused infection seriously. He realized that of Pasteur's three methods for eliminating microbes (heat, filtration, and chemicals), only the last was suitable in the surgical situation. He settled on carbolic acid, a common industrial product, and began experimenting with it.

In 1865, he treated a seven-year-old boy who had suffered a compound fracture of his leg after being run over by a cart. Ordinarily, such an injury would have resulted in death from infection, but Lister's use of antiseptic surgery saved his life. After this, Lister required surgeons under his supervision to wear clean gloves and wash their hands and instruments in a dilute solution of carbolic acid before operating.

Oddly enough, antiseptic surgery was slow to be accepted by the medical community. Some scholars have suggested that this was because doctors at the time were unfamiliar with microscopes. In any case, horrendous wartime casualty figures eventually drove acceptance. By the 1890s, antiseptic surgery was widely accepted and the modern operating room was on its way to becoming a reality. ☐

Above: A surgeon scrubs before an operation.

▷ 1987
TV Guide
Laparoscopic Surgery

Laparoscopic surgery, also known as minimally Invasive, or Band-Aid surgery, was in development throughout much of the 20th century. Most physicians, however, date the modern onset of the technique to 1987, when surgeons in France first introduced the use of television monitors to guide the surgical process.

The basic idea of laparoscopic surgery is that entrance to the body is achieved by inserting thin tubes through small incisions. The internal organs can be visualized by displaying signals from miniaturized cameras on

▷ 1985
Step Away from the Patient
Robotic Surgery

The human hand is a wonderful structure—flexible, dexterous, agile—but there are places in the body it can't go, ways it can't bend. This is why robotic surgery is so important. Typically, a surgeon operates the robotic instruments being used in an operation by means of actuators—that is, instruments that sense the movement of the surgeon's hands and translate those into movements of the instruments by means of a computer. Alternatively, the surgeon can feed instructions directly into a computer that controls the instruments. As with laparoscopic surgery, surgeons can monitor their progress through images on a TV screen or directly through a microscope system. ☐

Above: Complex machines like this are already used to perform robotic surgery.

🔍 **The most common use of laparoscopic surgery worldwide is gallbladder removal; it is also used in many gynecological procedures.**

a television screen, allowing the surgeon to manipulate miniaturized surgical instruments through the use of electronic signals sent back on wires through the same tube. When the surgical procedure is finished, the instruments are withdrawn, leaving only a small incision—a fact that explains the nickname "Band-Aid surgery." This illustrates one of the most important reasons that this type of surgery is so popular—it typically requires far less recovery time than more invasive techniques.

The use of laparoscopic surgery that receives the most publicity is in the repair of athletic injuries. If you read that your favorite football player is being operated on to repair a torn ligament, for example, chances are that the only scar he'll be exhibiting could be covered by a Band-Aid. ☐

On the Horizon

▷ Remote Surgery

Robotic surgery is already being used in hospitals worldwide, but we can expect two types of advances in the future. The first, which is probably farthest off, would be the advent of computer programs capable of carrying out surgery without the direct input of a surgeon. The advantage of such a system is that the program could incorporate the skills of the best surgeons in the world, making them universally available. The disadvantage, of course, is that the computer programs would have to be enormously complex to enable the robotic surgeon to deal with all of the complications that can arise in real-world situations.

The second future advance will come from the fact that, if you look at the procedure outlined above, you realize that there is no reason for the surgeon to actually be present in the operating room. The surgeon can be in another room or halfway around the world—so long as the appropriate signals can be delivered to the robotic system, the operation can go forward. Surgery like this, with the surgeon carrying out the operation from a distance, is called remote surgery.

The first remote surgery was carried out in 2001, a procedure in which a surgeon in New York removed the gallbladder from a patient in France. Remote surgery has also been used in Canada to carry out procedures in remote Arctic locations.

Having said that, we should note that remote surgery cannot be performed without on-site medical supervision. Procedures typically require the presence of an anesthesiologist, a backup surgeon, and a nursing staff. ■

A surgeon at a distant location can observe and guide an operation using a system like this.

BRAIN FUNCTION

Left: French philosopher René Descartes laid the groundwork for modern philosophy. A mathematician as well, he invented analytic geometry and was a key figure in the scientific revolution.

This is related to a problem that philosophers refer to as the problem of "qualia." Here's a simple version of the problem: Suppose that at some time in the future I am able to say with extreme precision what each cell in my brain is doing when I see the color red. How do I go from that information to an understanding of my experience of seeing the color red?

One of the first modern philosophers to try to answer this question was René Descartes (1596–1650) who imagined that the mind observed sensory stimuli in a kind

> ⊕ The human brain, with billions of interconnected neurons, is arguably **the most complex system we know about.**

▷ 1637

I Think Therefore I Am

The Problem of Consciousness

As you read these words, neurons are firing in your brain to produce images of the page and comprehension of the words. At the same time, you are aware of the fact that you exist and are reading the book. This brings us to what many consider the deepest and most difficult question in all of science: How does the firing of neurons result in our sense of our own consciousness? What is the relation between the physical processes in my brain and my awareness of my own existence?

of theater in the brain. We no longer accept the notion that the mind and body are separate as implied in this response—there are just too many connections between the two. But, although we know enough about the brain to rule out some old solutions to the problems of consciousness and qualia, no consensus has emerged in the scientific community about how to solve these problems. □

The human brain may be the most complex system in the universe.

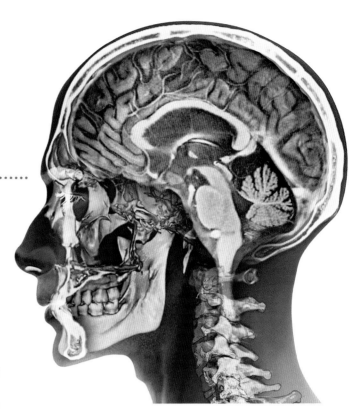

▷ 1861

It Takes a Village

Structure of the Brain

The brain is not just a collection of neurons, nor is it a factory with interchangeable parts, each capable of performing many tasks. A better picture of the brain would be to imagine a set of small villages, each performing a single specialized task, but with all the villages in constant communication with each other.

One of the first indications of this sort of specialization was the work of the French physician Paul Broca (1824–1880), who, in 1861, encountered a patient who was capable of understanding what was said to him but was unable to speak. When the man died, Broca performed an autopsy and discovered that there was a lesion in a specific spot on the left front of the brain. This is now known as Broca's area, the "village" responsible for producing

> **⊕ The human brain consumes more energy than any other organ in the body.**

speech. Shortly thereafter the Polish physiologist Carl Wernicke (1848–1905) isolated another area on the left side of the brain that governed speech comprehension. Patients with damage to the so-called Wernicke's area could talk, but their speech was meaningless. Thus there were two villages—one governing the *production* of speech, the other governing the *comprehension* of it.

For most of the 19th and 20th centuries, brain scientists were limited to the kind of melancholy studies in which they analyzed brain function by seeing what was lost after accidents or disease. Perhaps the most famous case involved a construction worker name Phineas Gage.

Above right: An MRI scan of the human brain, showing some of its large-scale structure.

In 1848 an explosion drove a steel shaft through his head, from the lower left to the upper right side. Miraculously, he survived the accident, but his personality changed completely. He had been a sober, dependable, churchgoing man, but suddenly began drinking and gambling—he even joined a circus at one point. Modern reconstructions of the accident suggest that it damaged parts of the brain involved in the ability to plan ahead.

The brain has many parts, and we can only sketch its basic structure here.

Brain Stem and Cerebellum

This is the part of the brain that connects to the spinal chord. It governs basic body functions, such as breathing, balance, and heart rate. Just above the brain stem are a series of glands that connect the brain to the endocrine system and govern things like hunger, thirst, and the sex drive.

Cerebral Hemispheres

These are the familiar bulbs that we usually think of when we picture the brain. There are two—right and left—connected by a thick bundle of nerve fibers. The cerebral hemispheres are where conscious motion is controlled, and they are involved in memory, learning, and emotion. The back part of the hemispheres is where the initial processing of visual information takes place.

Cerebral Cortex

This is the wrinkled outermost layer of the brain. It is where "higher functions," such as thought and action, reside. ☐

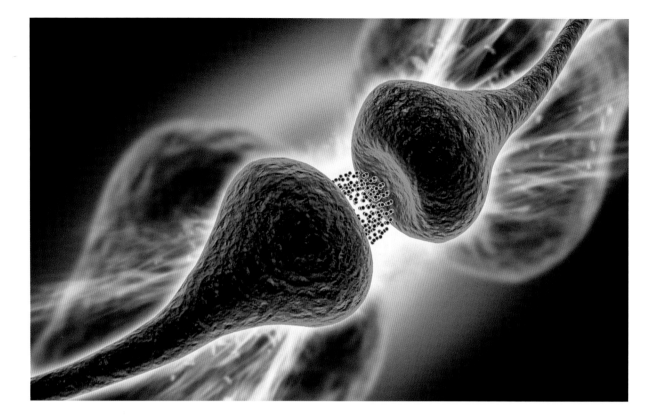

▷ 1888

Mind the Gap

How Neurons Work

In the late 19th century scientists began making microscopic studies of brain tissue, and they identified cells now known as neurons. This was a natural consequence of the cell theory that had been put forward by Schleiden and Schwann (see page 110). Originally, it was thought that the entire nervous system was connected, something like an electrical circuit. In 1888, however, the Spanish physiologist Santiago Ramón y Cajal (1852–1934) demonstrated that there was not a direct connection between neurons and initiated the modern study of the brain and the nervous system—promulgating what came to be called the neuron doctrine.

Ramón y Cajal showed that there was a gap at the point where two neurons made a connection, a gap that is called a synapse. For this discovery, he and Camillo Golgi (1843–1926) shared a Nobel Prize in 1906. (Oddly enough, despite the fact that the two men's research was so similar, the only time they met face to face was at the Nobel ceremony).

Obviously, there had to be some way for nerve signals to jump across the synapse, but for a time it was unclear whether this was an electrical or a chemical process. This question was resolved by the German pharmacologist Otto Loewi (1873–1961) in 1921. In his experiment, he removed the beating hearts from two frogs, one heart still connected to a major nerve, the other on its own. He found he could control the beating of the

disconnected heart by bathing it in a solution taken from the heart he was controlling through a nerve. This established that the process of getting a signal across a nerve synapse had to be chemical. Loewi received the Nobel Prize in 1936 for having discovered the neurotransmitter that today is called acetylcholine.

A neuron has several important parts: a central body that contains the nucleus and other organelles; a large fiber, known as an axon, that carries nerve signals outward; and many tiny branches, called dendrites, that can also carry those signals. When a nerve cell "fires," electrically charged ions move back and forth across the surfaces of the axons and dendrites, carrying the signal to the synapses. At the synapse, the neuron releases a flood of molecules, known as neurotransmitters, that cross the gap and attach to specialized receptors in the next neuron.

The key point about the brain—what makes the system so complex—is the fact that each neuron can have many connections. It is not unusual, for example, for a neuron in the brain to connect to a thousand others. It is generally accepted that there are about 100 billion neurons in your brain (although estimates go as low as 80 billion), which means that there might be as many as 100 trillion connections. (For reference, there are about 200 billion stars in the Milky Way.)

No wonder understanding the brain is so difficult! □

Above: An artist's conception of neurotransmitters being moved across the gap at the synapse of two neurons.

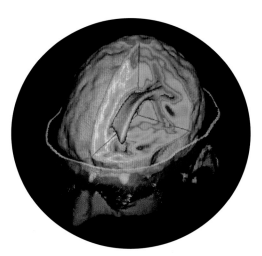

▷ 1991

Lighting Up

Functional Magnetic Resonance Imaging

We have already seen how MRI scans (see page 161) can use the magnetic properties of atomic nuclei to produce detailed images of internal organs. We can call this structural MRI. Functional MRI (fMRI) adapts this technique to give pictures of brain function in real time.

The basic idea is that if a neuron in the brain is firing it will need extra oxygen to complete its task. fMRI detects the increase in the amount of iron being carried in by hemoglobin molecules in the blood, and hence tracks the parts of the brain that are active at any given time. The resulting images are dramatic, and they corroborate the "many villages" picture of the brain. If, for example, you think about a dog, talk about a dog, and draw a picture of a dog, different parts of the brain will light up as you perform each task.

There is one fundamental limitation to the fMRI technique. It does not detect blood flow to individual neurons, but to areas about a millimeter on either side of a neuron. It is unlikely that this limitation will be eliminated soon. ☐

Above: An fMRI image of the brain. The lighted regions were receiving more oxygen when the scan was done.

On the Horizon

▷ Alzheimer's and Parkinson's Diseases

These two diseases, each named for the physician who first described it, are the most common maladies associated with the brain. Alzheimer's disease results from the accumulation of proteins called beta-amyloids in the regions of the brain responsible for memory and intellectual activity. It is the leading cause of dementia. Parkinson's disease, caused by the destruction of dopamine-producing cells in the brain, results in movement disorders. (Dopamine is a neurotransmitter.) Both diseases are incurable at the present time.

Researchers are working on finding drugs that will block the production of beta-amyloids in Alzheimer's disease, whereas Parkinson's disease researchers concentrate on finding ways to alleviate the symptoms of the disease. Both groups are concentrating on slowing the progress of the diseases rather than curing them. We can hope that someday we will understand the brain well enough to prevent and reverse their effects. ■

Alzheimer's disease is associated with the buildup of plaques (white) in the brain.

Chapter 4
PLANETARY SCIENCE & ASTRONOMY

The solar system is a marvelously complex place, full of all sorts of interesting bodies. And it is only one of thousands of solar systems we know about.

Above: Pierre-Simon Laplace gave us our first mathematical model of how the solar system formed.

▷ 19th Century

The Great Collapse

The Laplace Hypothesis

It was the Polish cleric Nicolaus Copernicus (1473–1543) who gave us the first workable model of our solar system as a collection of objects orbiting the sun, but it was the French physicist and mathematician Pierre-Simon Laplace (1749–1827) who gave us our first mathematical model of how the system formed.

It's called the nebular hypothesis and it works this way: It starts with a large cloud of dust and gas in interstellar space. We know of many such clouds—they're called nebulae (singular: nebula) from the Latin for "cloud." Under the influence of their mutual gravitational attraction, the pieces of the cloud start to collapse toward the center. Any rotation the cloud has speeds up, much as a skater's spin increases when she pulls in her arms. Most of the material in the cloud goes into a massive central object, where nuclear fusion (see page 27) ignites and produces a shining star. (Laplace, of course, didn't know about fusion, so he couldn't explain the process of star formation.)

In the meantime, the remaining material is spun out into a thin rotating disk. It is in this disk, by processes we'll describe in a moment, that the planets, moons, asteroids, and comets of our solar system formed. ☐

🔍 When Pierre-Simon Laplace presented his ideas on the formation of the solar system to Napoleon, the emperor asked him about the **place of God** in his theory. Laplace is supposed to have replied, **"Sire, I have no need of that hypothesis."**

Round and Round They Go

The Solar System—an Overview

How a planet formed depended on how far away from the sun it was. Close in, the heat from the newly forming star would vaporize materials like water and various gases, while an intense stream of particles emitted by the sun swept these volatile materials out of the inner solar system. Thus those planets closest to the sun—the so-called terrestrial planets (Mercury, Venus, Earth, and Mars)—are small and rocky. Our best models say that they formed by a process in which small grains of material came together to form objects called planetesimals—anything from boulder to mountain sized—and the planetesimals coalesced into Mars-sized protoplanets. Then, according to the models, there followed an impossible game of cosmic billiards in which the protoplanets caromed around, colliding, breaking up, coalescing, and even, in some cases, being ejected from the solar system. Earth's moon, for example, formed in the collision of a Mars-sized object with the newly formed planet.

Farther out, somewhere past the orbit of Mars, is the evocatively named "frost line," beyond which the temperatures are low enough to allow volatile materials to be taken into planets. Thus the so-called Jovian planets (Jupiter, Saturn, Uranus, and Neptune) are large and composed mainly of gases, such as hydrogen and helium. The transition between the terrestrial and Jovian planets is marked by a collection of small, rocky objects known as the asteroid belt. This debris is the remains of a planet that never formed, probably because of the gravitational pull of Jupiter. Our current best picture of the formation of the Jovian planets, for example, is called the Nice model, after the town in France where it was developed. It describes a complex shuffling around of planetary orbits until things settled down into their present state.

Beyond the Jovian planets is a disk of material known as the Kuiper (rhymes with "viper") belt. This is the part of the planetary disk that never came together to form planets and thus contains the original building materials from which the solar system formed. The planet Pluto marks the innermost object in this region, but it contains other planet-sized objects as well. Finally, the entire system is surrounded by a sphere of "dirty snowballs" known as the Oort (rhymes with "sort") cloud, which is the source of many of the comets that we see from time to time. ☐

Below: The solar system, including the planets and the asteroid belt.

On the Horizon

▷ Evolving Computer Models

Our knowledge of the formation of the solar system comes primarily from computer models. As computers become more powerful and our knowledge of the details of how the materials involved improves, we can expect these models to evolve. The general outline of the nebular hypothesis won't change, but we'll have an increasingly detailed picture of what happened. ■

The Hubble Space Telescope captures an image of stars being born in the Carina Nebula.

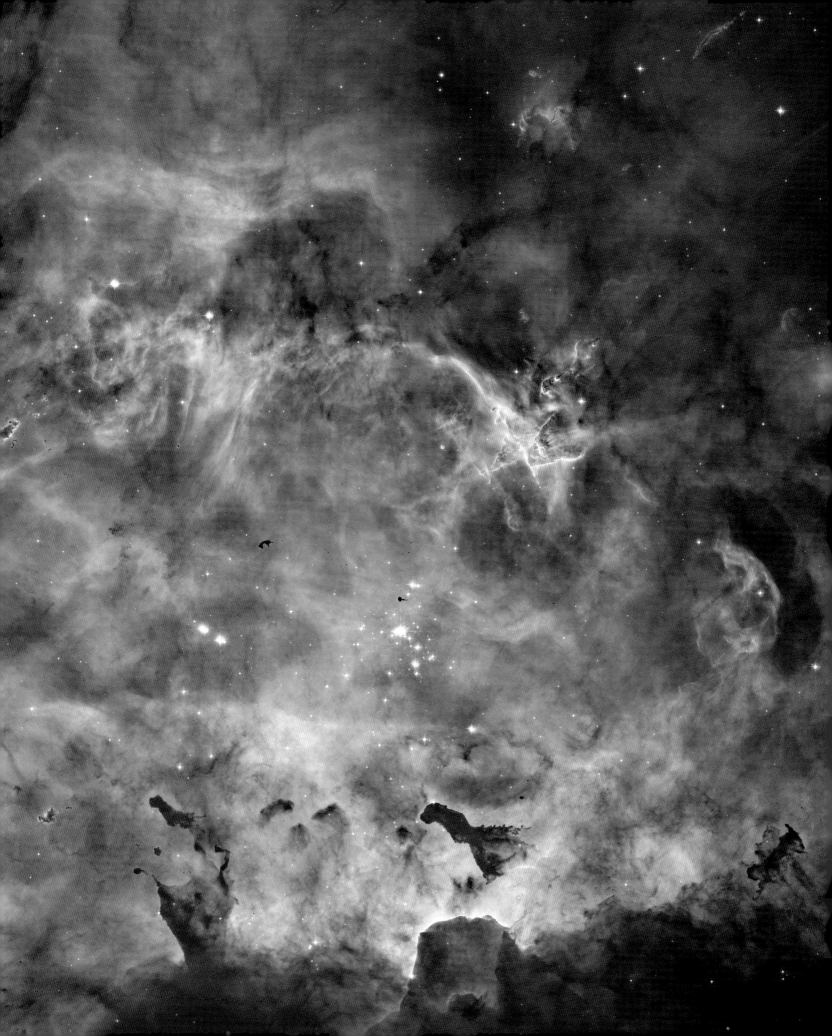

▷ 1610

A Revolutionary View of the Heavens

Galileo and His Telescope

The most dramatic telescopic discoveries about the solar system were made by the Italian scientist Galileo Galilei (1564–1642). After hearing about the invention of the telescope in Holland, he devised an improved version of the instrument. He was the first person to turn a telescope to the sky, and what he saw shook the foundations of the accepted view of the heavens.

What Galileo saw included sunspots (or, more likely, sunspot groups); mountains on the moon; the phases of Venus; and the four largest moons of Jupiter.

The reigning astronomy of the time, dating back to the Greeks, held that the heavens had to be perfect and unchanging—there couldn't be "blemishes on the sun," and the moon was supposed to be a perfect crystal sphere. It also held that Earth was the center of the universe, and that everything in the heavens revolved around it. But if this were the case, Venus wouldn't have phases and there wouldn't be those "stars" out there, perfectly happy to be revolving around Jupiter. Something was obviously wrong.

Galileo published these observations in his book *Sidereus Nuncis* (*Starry Messenger*) in 1610. Written in graceful Italian instead of scholarly Latin, it marked an important turning point in the history of discovery. ☐

Right: Artist's conception of Galileo explaining the surface of the moon to his colleagues.

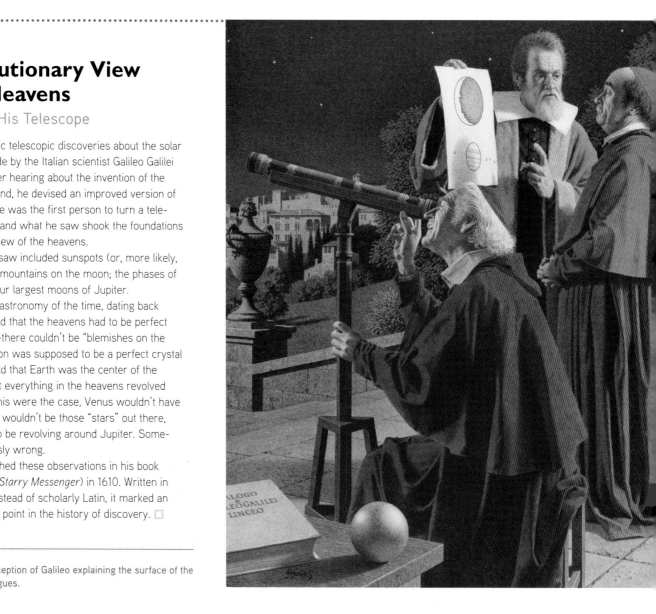

🔍 Galileo succeeded in **selling his idea for the telescope** to the Arsenal of Venice (the Pentagon of its day) for a tidy profit just before **a ship from Holland arrived with crates of telescopes** in its cargo.

▷ 1741

The Sideways Planet
Uranus Comes into View

Uranus and Neptune are not visible to the naked eye and had to wait for the development of powerful telescopes to be discovered. Uranus was discovered by the professional musician and amateur astronomer Sir William Herschel (1738–1822) using a telescope in the backyard of his home in Bath, England, in 1781. This is a reminder that, before the invention of street lighting, cities were as dark at night as the remotest farms. ☐

Below: A composite picture of the two hemispheres of Uranus.

🔍 Uranus is the only planet in the solar system whose **axis of rotation lies in the plane of its orbit,** and hence it lies "sideways."

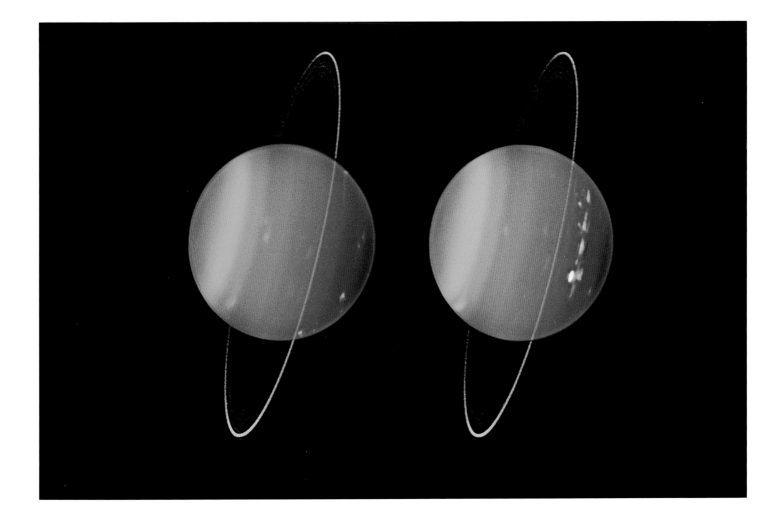

▷ 1801

The Tip of the Asteroid Belt

Spotting the Asteroid Ceres

A serendipitous discovery occurred, believe it nor not, on New Year's Day, 1801, when Italian astronomer Giuseppe Piazzi (1746–1826) spotted the asteroid Ceres. With a diameter of about 600 miles, Ceres is the largest object in the asteroid belt. It used to be thought that the asteroid belt represented the remains of a planet that disintegrated, but we now think of it as the remains of a planet that never formed, probably because of the gravitational influence of Jupiter. ☐

Left: Giuseppe Piazzi, discoverer of the asteroid belt.

Bottom: The "white spot" on Ceres was probably created by water coming to the surface and freezing.

🔍 The fictional planet Krypton, home of Superman, was modeled on the notion that the **asteroid belt was the remains of a world that disintegrated.** Superman's father, Jor-El, put him in a rocket and sent him to Earth as the planet exploded.

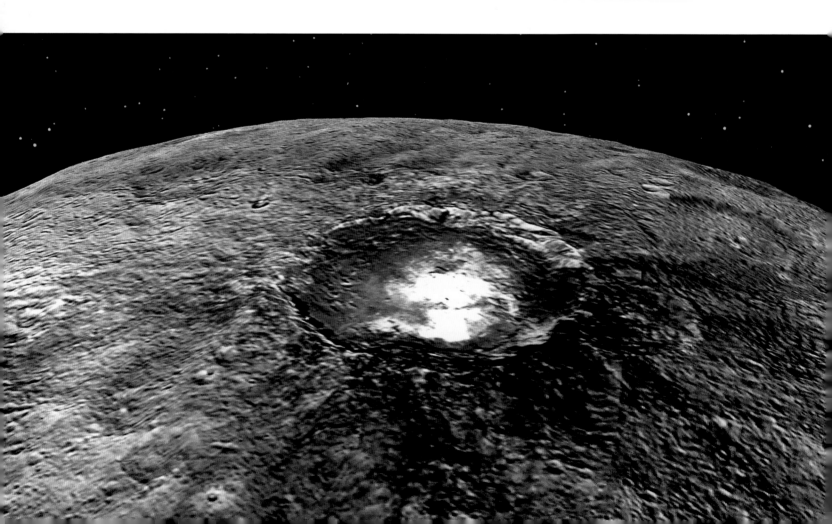

Strange Orbit

Neptune

The discovery of Neptune involves an interesting chain of events. As the orbit of Uranus was observed, troubling discrepancies arose—the planet didn't seem to be moving the way Newtonian science predicted that it should. Two astronomers—John Couch Adams (1819–1892) in England and Urbain Le Verrier (1811–1877) in France—realized that the discrepancies could be explained if there was another planet exerting a gravitational force on Uranus—a planet whose orbit was farther out. Their calculations specified where that planet had to be, and in 1846 astronomers in Berlin found the planet we now call Neptune. □

Above: A portrait of British mathematician and astronomer John Couch Adams, who was one of two scientists to mathematically prove the existence of the planet Neptune by its gravitational force on neighboring Uranus.

Right: A view of Neptune from its largest and closest moon, Triton.

▷ 1930

Planet X

Pluto, the Problematic Planet

The discovery of Pluto in 1930 used to be seen as the final step in the exploration of our solar system. Instead, we now see the planet as the beginning of the vast and largely unexplored outer reaches of that system.

This idea was the farthest thing from the mind of a Kansas farmboy named Clyde Tombaugh (1906–1997) when he made some sketches of Mars using his home-made telescope. He sent them off to the Lowell Observatory in Flagstaff, Arizona, for comments, but instead of a critique he got a job offer. (His comment to the author of this book years later: "Hell, it beat pitchin' hay.")

At Lowell he was assigned the tedious task of looking for what was called Planet X, which was supposed to be outside the orbit of Neptune. The search involved taking

> ⊕ The 2015 flyby of Pluto by the New Horizons spacecraft was one of **the crowning achievements of the American space program.**

pictures of the same region of the sky a couple of weeks apart, then looking for something that moved the right distance to be a planet. In 1930, the search paid off, and Tombaugh became the third person in history to discover a new planet.

But from the start there were problems. Pluto was small and rocky while it should have been a gas giant. Its orbit was tilted with respect to the orbits of other planets, and it spent part of its "year" inside the orbit of Neptune. With the discovery of the Kuiper belt (see page 176), the reason for these discrepancies became clear. Pluto was not the last of the inner planets, it was the first part of the Kuiper belt—our introduction to the next great region of the solar system. In 2009 the International Astronomical Union recognized these facts by designating Pluto as a dwarf planet and naming all planets in the Kuiper belt as "Plutoids." ▫

Left: A close-up of Pluto taken by the New Horizons spacecraft.

▷ 1951

Cosmic Leftovers

The Kuiper Belt

Out beyond Pluto we encounter a flat disk that extends about 50 times farther into space than Earth is from the sun. This is material left over from the formation of the solar system, and it's called the Kuiper belt (rhymes with "viper") after the Dutch American astronomer Gerard Kuiper (1905–1973) who suggested its existence in 1951. Similar in composition to the asteroid belt, though probably more icy, the Kuiper belt is still being explored and understood.

Starting in 1992, astronomers began finding objects in the Kuiper belt that can only be described as planets—objects not much different in size from Pluto but farther out. It is estimated that there may be as many as a dozen or more such objects out there, along with all the smaller debris. These planets are now known as plutoids, and are seen as a third type of planet in our solar system, in addition to their terrestrial and Jovian cousins. □

Above: Artist's conception of one of the larger Kuiper belt objects (nicknamed "Xena" by its discoverers) and its moon.

Right: An artist's conception of the small, rocky Kuiper belt objects. In actuality, these objects would be much farther apart than shown.

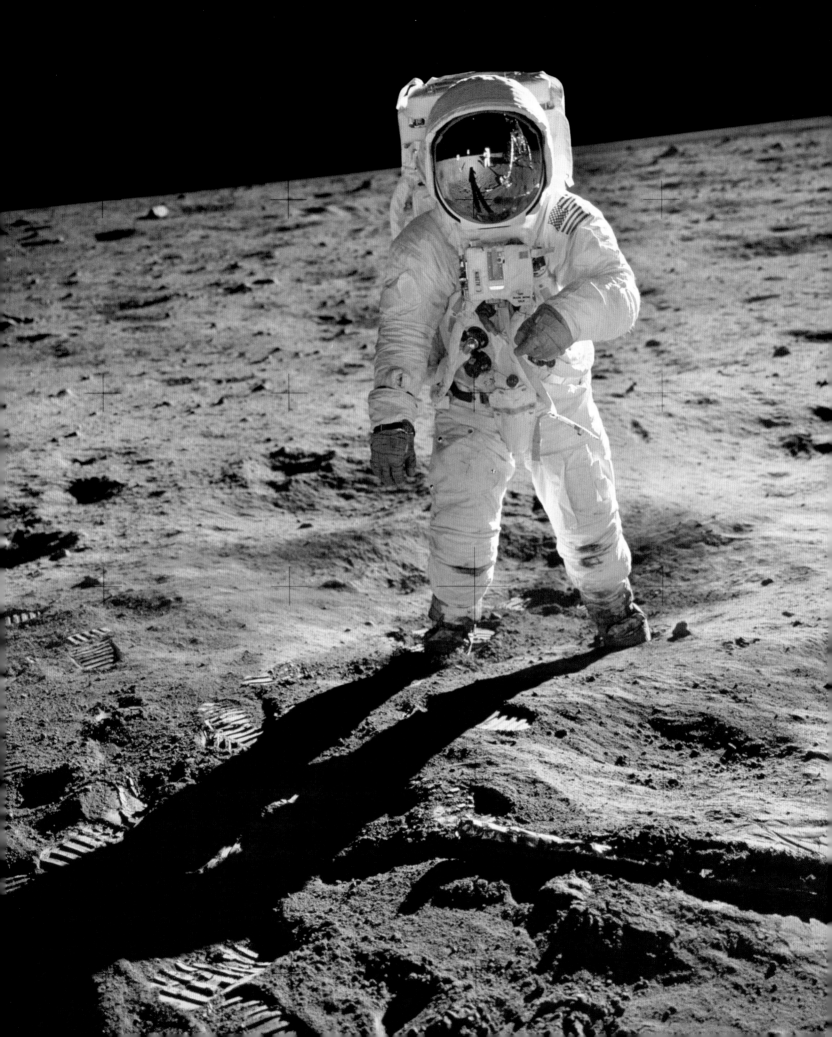

1969

"One Giant Leap for Mankind"

Earth's Moon Up Close and Personal

The moon remains the only celestial body that humans have visited in person, starting with Neil Armstrong's (1930–2012) "giant leap for mankind" in 1969. Since then, a select few astronauts have walked on the moon, including Edwin ("Buzz") Aldrin Jr., shown in the photograph opposite. Subsequent missions brought back geological material from the moon that allowed scientists to learn a great deal about our nearest neighbor. And today, visitors to the Smithsonian National Air and Space Museum in Washington, D.C., line up for a chance to touch a piece of rock from the moon. ☐

Right: A rock brought back from the moon during the Apollo program.

Opposite: American astronaut Edwin ("Buzz") Aldrin Jr. walks on the moon in 1969.

🔍 A simple strategy allowed the Soviet probes to survive the descent to Venus's superhot surface—during the flight out **the probe was opened to the cold of space,** and as it descended it would keep operating until the heat of the surface warmed it up.

1970

A Hostile Planet

Visiting Venus

The first spacecraft to land on the surface of Venus arrived in 1970, launched by what was then the Soviet Union. Scientists found an incredibly hostile planet—temperatures around 800 degrees Fahrenheit with an atmosphere of carbon dioxide laced with clouds of sulfuric acid. Although Venus is only a little smaller than Earth, the fact that it has no oceans means that when volcanoes pump carbon dioxide into the atmosphere there is no way to get rid of it. Consequently, the planet is an example of something called a runaway greenhouse effect. ☐

Left: The surface of Venus as revealed by the Magellan spacecraft.

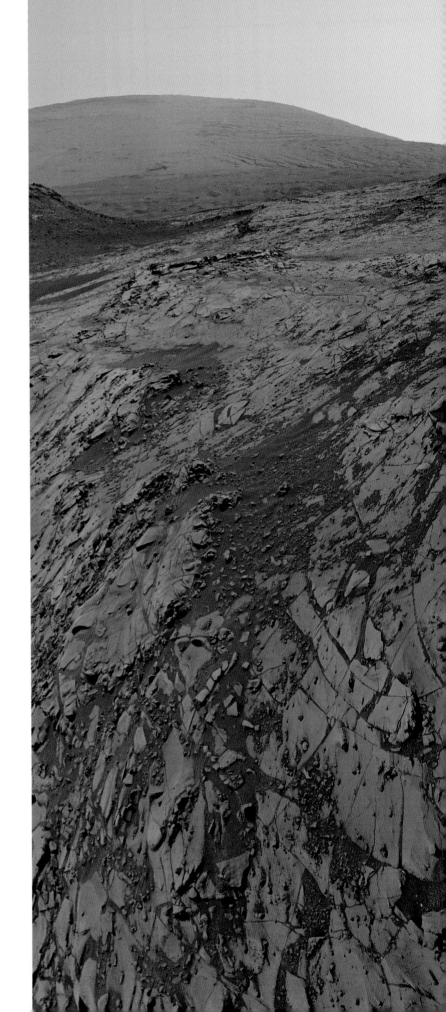

Past, Present, or Future Life?

Mars, Our Closest Neighbor

Our exploration of the solar system has concentrated on Mars—indeed, over the past few decades a veritable flotilla of orbiters and landers from many countries have made the trek out to our nearest planetary neighbor. And starting with the Mariner 9 going into orbit in 1971, these visits have yielded one surprise after another.

First there were the images of geological formations that looked just like river systems on Earth, suggesting that liquid water had flowed on the Martian surface in recent times (geologically speaking). More recently, we have seen salty streaks on the surface that, again, suggest the presence of liquid water on the surface (although it's likely that they are the remains of a briny sludge rather than freely flowing water). We learned that for the first billion years of its existence, before it lost its atmosphere to space, Mars had large oceans and wasn't too different from Earth. The *Curiosity* rover, which is still sending back data from the Martian surface, found clear evidence that liquid water had been involved in the formation of the minerals it was examining.

No one questions the existence of water on Mars—the polar caps are partly water ice, after all. The presence of liquid water, however, would open the possibility of life surviving on the planet—a topic to which we will return in the next section. ☐

Above: Photographs of the Martian surface suggest the presence of running water at some point in the planet's history.

Right: The *Curiosity* rover on the surface of Mars. The instrument has added immeasurably to our knowledge of the Red Planet.

▷ 1995

Liquid Water Discovered on Jupiter's Moon Europa

Galileo Probes Jupiter and Its Moons

The Galileo spacecraft was launched in 1989 and arrived at Jupiter in 1995. It found a planet profoundly different from its terrestrial cousins because Jupiter is the first planet we've encountered that formed outside the frost line (see page 167). At its center is a rocky core, perhaps 20 to 40 times larger than that of Earth, covered by layers of hydrogen and helium. Because of the high pressure inside the planet, much of the outer layers is composed of metallic hydrogen, a material unknown outside of laboratories on Earth. The outer atmosphere, consisting largely of hydrogen, helium, and ammonia, presents a banded structure due to the planet's rapid rotation (the Jovian day is ten hours long).

Although the Galileo spacecraft sent back a lot of information about Jupiter and even dropped a probe into its atmosphere, its most important discoveries concerned the

Above: A cutaway view of Jupiter's structure.

nature of the giant planet's moons. Instead of a bunch of inert rocks, they were seen to be separate worlds in and of themselves, each with its own story to tell us.

The innermost moon, Io, for example, turned out to be dotted with volcanoes—more than 400 at last count. Material brought up in volcanic eruptions gives the moon a pockmarked appearance, making it look something like a pepperoni pizza.

It was what Galileo found on Europa, the sixth-largest moon, however, that sent shock waves through the scientific community. Some background: Europa has a smooth surface made of water ice, and the lack of craters indicates that the surface was formed recently (geologically speaking). This led theorists to suggest that underneath a thick layer of ice was an ocean of liquid water—a subsurface ocean. Measurements by the Galileo spacecraft confirmed this suggestion, so for the first time we had evidence for an ocean of liquid water elsewhere in our solar system.

Europa's oceans are kept heated by a phenomenon known as tidal flexing. As Europa moves around in Jupiter's gravitational field, the changing forces twist it around, heating it in the process. (If you take a strip of metal and bend it back and forth rapidly, it will get warm. This, basically, is what Jupiter does to Europa.)

The existence of a subsurface ocean has made Europa a prime candidate for a home for life in our solar system. Both NASA and the European Space Agency have plans for further missions, perhaps aimed at drilling through the overlying ice to sample the water. In addition, it appears that subsurface oceans like Europa's are quite common—they have been found on other Jovian moons, for example, and most recently on Saturn's moon Enceladus. ☐

🔍 In order to avoid possible contamination of Europa by terrestrial microbes, the **Galileo** spacecraft was **deliberately crashed into Jupiter** in 2003.

On the Horizon

▷ Exploring Europa

The European Space Agency is tentatively planning to launch its Jupiter Icy Moon Explorer (JUICE) spacecraft in 2022. The craft would arrive at Jupiter in 2030 and do an exhaustive analysis of the Jovian moons Ganymede, Callisto, and Europa, all of which have subsurface oceans. Mapping the thickness of the overlying ice is an important first step in probing those oceans for living organisms. ■

Artist's conception of JUICE in orbit around Jupiter

▷ 2004

Cassini Visits the Ringed Planet

Saturn's Spectacular Sights Up Close

The Cassini spacecraft was launched in 1997, arrived at Saturn in 2004, and is still returning data as of this writing. It remains our best source of information about the planet, its moons, and its rings.

Saturn is the farthest planet in the solar system visible to the naked eye, and has been observed since ancient times. Like Jupiter, it has a rocky core surrounded by layers of hydrogen and helium. From our point of view, however, the most interesting things about the Saturn system are its spectacular rings and the moon Titan.

Rings

Arguably the most spectacular sight in the solar system, the rings of Saturn are actually fairly insubstantial structures. Their primary components are chucks of water ice, whose high reflectivity makes them stand out. The rings are actually quite thin—most have a thickness that would fit comfortably in a ten-story building. The rings are marked by divisions, the first of which was discovered by the Italian astronomer Giovanni Cassini (1625–1712) after whom the spacecraft is named.

Titan

The second-largest moon in the solar system (after Jupiter's moon Ganymede), Saturn's moon Titan has

Above: A composite photo of Saturn's moon Titan.

long fascinated scientists. In 2005 the Cassini spacecraft dropped a probe into the moon's atmosphere and gave us our first glimpse of the surface. What was surprising was how familiar that surface looked—one astronomer characterized it as familiar structures made from unfamiliar materials. There are, for example, dunes made of granular organic materials (think coffee grounds) and lakes of liquid

⊕ In 1837, the English clergyman Thomas Dick confidently predicted that we would find exactly **8,141,963,826,080 people living** on the rings of Saturn.

methane. In addition, there are suggestions that, like other moons, Titan has a subsurface ocean of liquid water as well as layers of water ice in its interior.

What interests scientists most about this moon is the fact that chemical reactions producing organic molecules can take place on its surface—albeit slowly because of the temperature. Thus the moon is seen as a kind of laboratory for the process by which life might have originated on Earth. ☐

▷ 2011

MESSENGER

Mercury Revealed

The MESSENGER spacecraft (MErcury Surface, Space ENvironment, GEochemistry and Ranging) was launched in 2004, went into orbit around Mercury in 2011, and was intentionally crashed into the planet in 2015. It found a small planet of surprisingly high density, leading some astronomers to suggest that it had started as a larger planet, underwent differentiation, and then had its outer coating blown off in a collision. The most interesting surface feature is a giant crater 1,000 miles across on one side and, directly opposite, a jumbled region astronomers have called the weird terrain. This chaotic landscape was presumably caused by seismic waves from the collision that produced the crater. ☐

Left: Artist's conception of the MESSENGER spacecraft in orbit around Mercury.

▷ 2015

Pluto and Beyond

Not a Planet Perhaps, but Fascinatingly Complex

In 2015 the New Horizons spacecraft flew by Pluto, giving us our first close-up view of the planet. It was astonishing! Instead of the cold, dead world we had expected, we found a world of enormous complexity. There is evidence for recent (geologically speaking) changes in the surface, possibly because of something analogous to plate tectonics on Earth (see page 195). Mountain ranges of water ice (hard as steel at these temperatures) trade places with glaciers of solid nitrogen and plains that are the remains of vanished lakes that were once filled with some impossible liquid. Scientists will spend years unraveling the mysteries of Pluto. ☐

🔍 It took the New Horizons spacecraft **a year to send back all the data** from its flyby of Pluto.

Above: Artist's conception of New Horizons approaching Pluto and its moon Charon.

Left: New Horizons view of the surface of Pluto.

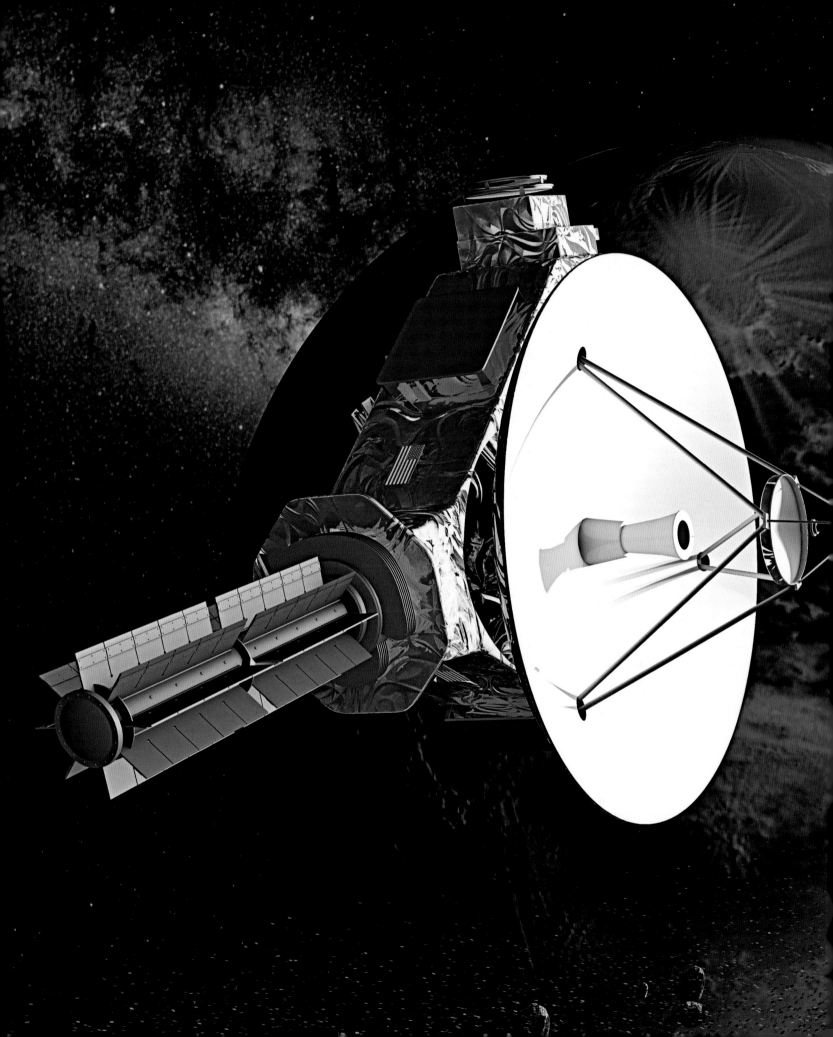

On the Horizon

▷ Exploring the Kuiper Belt

After its flyby of Pluto, the New Horizons spacecraft was directed out into the Kuiper belt, where, a billion miles farther out, it will encounter a smallish object called 2014MU69 in 2019. This will be an important event because it will shed light on the question of whether or not Pluto is typical of the worlds we have yet to find. If it is, we can expect many more surprises as our attention moves to the outer reaches of our solar system. ∎

New Horizons is now on its way into the Kuiper belt.

EARTH—OUR HOME

🔍 About half of the heat coming from Earth's interior is **left over from the Great Bombardment.** The other half comes from **radioactive decay of nuclei.**

PLANET

Earth is the only planet in the solar system whose surface is constantly changing.

▷ 4.5 Billion Years Ago

The Great Separation

The Formation of Earth

Like the other terrestrial planets, Earth was formed when grains of rocky materials coalesced in the collapsing disk that formed our solar system (see page 166). As planetesimals accumulated to form a protoplanet, the nascent Earth moved in orbit, sweeping up the planetary debris in its path. Had you been standing on the protoplanetary surface, you would have seen a constant rain of falling meteorites. This is a period known as the Great Bombardment. Each impact would have heated the planet until it melted all the way through. At this point a process known as differentiation began. The heaviest materials, such as iron and nickel, fell to the center to form Earth's core. (There are actually two layers of the core—an outer liquid layer and, closer to the center, a solid core produced by the great pressures involved.)

Above the core, lighter materials, such as basalt, form a thick layer known as the mantle. Then, at the very top, the lightest materials, such as granite, produce the outermost layer and form the base of continents. As it happens, there is only enough of these lightest materials to cover about a quarter of Earth's surface. This means that you can picture Earth's surface as having two layers: a lower level of basaltic rocks that form the ocean floors, and a higher, lighter level of granite that makes the continents. This sort of process took place on all the terrestrial planets. □

Above and opposite: Cutaway views of Earth, showing the two layers of the core, the mantle, and the outer crust. The structures are not to scale.

The Great Debate

Catastrophism Versus Gradualism

Starting in the 18th century, a major scientific debate erupted over the history of Earth. One group, influenced by the biblical story of Jonah's flood, held that changes in our planet took place suddenly, through catastrophes. They were called Neptunists at the time, but they would be called Catastrophists today. The other group argued that the current state of Earth resulted from the accumulation of gradual change over time. The most prominent of the so-called Gradualists were the Englishmen James Hutton (1726–1797) and Sir Charles Lyell (1797–1875).

Evidence for gradualism came from the study of geological formations. Two examples illustrate this point. In 1785 Hutton found a formation along the banks of the Tilt River in Scotland in which layers of sedimentary rocks, which are created by layers of sediment falling to the bottom of bodies of water, were infiltrated by intrusions of granite. This could only have happened if the granite had flowed into the sedimentary rocks after those rocks had formed. This strengthened Hutton's argument that rocks were constantly being formed—that geological processes acting over time really existed.

The second formation is found in Jedburgh, Scotland. It involves two layers of sedimentary rocks arranged like a *T*, with one horizontal layer capping another vertical layer. Since sedimentary rocks can only form in horizontal layers, the only way to explain this formation is by a series of events: a sedimentary layer had to form, then geological forces had to buckle the layers, then erosion had to remove the curved top of the buckling, and finally a new layer of rocks had to be deposited to form the top of the *T*. The existence of this sort of formation argued for the long-term operation of gradual geological forces on the planet.

Charles Lyell assembled this sort of evidence to buttress a picture of Earth history in which gradual processes—processes still operating today—worked over long periods of time to shape the planet. His mantra— "the present is key to the past"—is now universally adopted by Earth scientists. ☐

Right: Glen Tilt in Scotland, where scientists first uncovered evidence for geological processes that indicated a hugely long history for the Earth. In this photo, sedimentary rocks (the grey sheets) were infiltrated by granite (pink and brown), showing that geological processes over billions of years have changed the Earth.

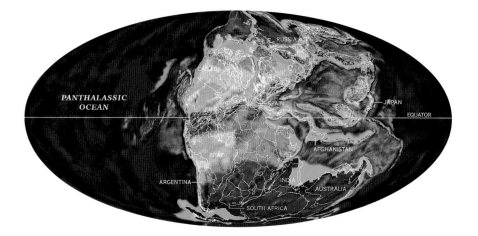

PANTHALASSIC OCEAN

EQUATOR

▷ 1960s

It's Not Your Father's World

Discovery of Plate Tectonics

Look at a map of Earth and imagine sliding Africa to the west—notice how it fits into the coastline of the Americas? In the 1920s the German meteorologist Alfred Wegener (1880–1930) used this as the opening argument for what he called continental drift. Coupled with other data—the existence of geological formations that seemed to continue from South America to Africa, for example—he suggested that about 200 million years ago all the continents were joined in a single land mass he called Pangaea ("All Earth") and have since drifted apart.

This changed in the 1960s. The research vessel *Eltanin*, as part of the general explorations of the oceans at the time, was taking measurements of the magnetism of rocks on the ocean bottom off Puget Sound.

A word of explanation: Seafloor rocks can include grains of iron compounds—think of each grain as a tiny magnet that will line up and point toward the North Pole if it is free to do so. These little magnets, in turn, will produce their own (weak) magnetic field. The ship towed an instrument that could detect this field and thus find out which way the tiny magnets were pointing.

Imagine their surprise when they found a strange pattern in the magnetism. As they moved along, they found that, first, the little magnets pointed north, then south, then north again, and so on. Furthermore, there was a symmetric pattern around a line in the middle of the pattern.

🔍 If you are in North America, multiply your age by two inches. This is roughly how much **farther you are from Paris** than you were the day you were born.

When Wegener, a highly respected member of the scientific community, published his theory, it triggered a major debate. Some scientists criticized his data—American geologists, for example, argued that he had mischaracterized his geological formations. Mainly, however, the theory was rejected because no one could figure out how to move continents around.

Above: The surface of Earth as it existed during the time of Pangaea. Present-day national boundaries are shown in white.

Scientists who saw the data immediately connected it to the fact that Earth's magnetic field reverses itself periodically, so that sometimes the north magnetic pole is in Canada, sometimes in Antarctica (we know of several hundred such reversals in geological history). The *Eltanin* data were then explained this way: Hot magma was coming to the surface as a liquid, so the magnetic grains could align themselves, pointing to wherever the north magnetic pole was at that point in time. As the magma cooled, the grains were locked in, and as new magma rose, its magnets would point in a different direction if the field had reversed.

Above: A converging boundary, in which two plates are pushed together, causing one to slide under the other. The Andes mountains are formed by this process.

Right: A diverging boundary, in which two plates are pushed apart by upwelling magma. The mid-Atlantic ridge is formed by this process.

Bottom: A transform fault boundary, in which two plates slide by each other. The San Andreas Fault in California is formed in this way.

Thus the stripe pattern tells us that the ocean floor is spreading, moving the continents in the process.

So the final picture of how our planet works is this: The interior of the planet is hot, partly because of leftover heat from the Great Bombardment, partly because of radioactive decay. To bring the heat to the surface, the mantle "boils"—hot magma rises in some places, cools, and then sinks in other places. This process takes hundreds of millions of years, but the net effect is that the light material that makes up the continents floats along, moved here and there by forces deep beneath our feet. This is the picture we call plate tectonics, in which Earth's surface is composed of lightweight segments, called plates, that move around in response to the boiling of the mantle. Thus Earth, alone among the planets, has a surface that is constantly changing. □

On the Horizon

▷ Asteroid Impacts

The Catastrophist–Gradualist debate flared briefly in the 1980s, when scientists proposed that the extinction of the dinosaurs was caused by the impact of a large asteroid 65 million years ago—a catastrophic event if there ever was one. The debate triggered an intense search for evidence of impact craters, and eventually the "smoking gun" was found in a crater buried under sediment off the coast of Yucatán. Today new evidence of such impacts continues to accumulate, and the argument has shifted to the question of how deeply the evolution of life on Earth was influenced by these events.

▷ Earthquake Prediction

Imagine bending a pencil with ever-increasing force. We can make two statements: (1) the pencil will eventually break, and (2) it is extremely difficult to predict when this will happen. The same thing happens at transform fault boundaries—rocks on the two sides of the fault stick together as the plates move, releasing suddenly at a time that is very difficult to predict. This is why, in places like California, attention is paid to coping with earthquakes rather than predicting them. Current efforts focus on building codes that require structures to be able to withstand the stresses generated by a major earthquake. Warning systems have recently been built to warn people that an earthquake wave is traveling toward them. This gives officials several minutes to shut down gas and electricity lines and move emergency vehicles out of buildings before the wave hits. ■

The results of a 2011 earthquake in Turkey that killed 604 people and injured thousands.

There are many cycles operating on our planet, and they all fit together in a marvelous machine.

HOW EARTH

▷ **20th Century**

It All Goes in Cycles

Earth Cycles

Earth started out as a hot, airless ball in space. As it cooled, two things happened. The surface magma cooled into solid rock. Geologists call this type of rock igneous (fire formed), and we can see rocks like this in volcanic eruptions today.

The second thing that happened was that the planet acquired an atmosphere, some of which came from volcanoes and some of which was brought in by meteorites and comets. When the atmosphere cooled to 212 degrees Fahrenheit, an extraordinary event happened—the first drop of rain condensed and fell from the sky. As rain washed down into the ocean basins it eroded little chips of rock. These processes created the first oceans and the first beaches.

The Rock Cycle

As grains of eroded rock build up, pressure and various chemical processes change them into a rock—think of it as being something like pouring glue over a mound of sawdust. These are called sedimentary rocks. Tectonic activity can then push the rocks up into mountains, and

Above: Artist's conception of the early Earth and moon, each showing the bright red scars of recent impacts.

WORKS

Right: Kayakers paddle past a glacier, representing a part of the planet's water cycle.

rains can once again erode the grains and carry them to the sea to form new sedimentary rocks. This constant reshuffling is called the rock cycle.

Sometimes tectonic activity can push rocks deep underground, where temperature and pressure rearrange their molecules into a new mineral form. These new rocks are called metamorphic rocks, because they have changed in form. Thus shale, formed from mud in river deltas, becomes slate, and limestone, formed from the skeletons of plankton on the ocean bottom, becomes marble.

The Water Cycle

The sun evaporates water from the oceans and lakes, and the water falls as rain or snow. Flowing back into surface rivers and underground aquifers, the water replenishes the lakes and oceans from which it came. This is the water cycle.

To a reasonable approximation, the amount of water on Earth is fixed. Thus, during Ice Ages, where a lot of water is stored in glaciers, ocean levels drop. During the last Ice Age, for example, the east coast of North America was over 100 miles farther out than it is today, and it was possible for the ancestors of Native Americans to walk from Siberia to Alaska on solid ground.

Atmospheric Cycles, Weather, and Climate

The planet's atmosphere also moves in cycles. We call the short-term aspects of the cycle weather and the long-term aspects climate. The two are different—the weather in Tucson today may be rainy, but the climate in Tucson is hot and dry, for example.

The key factor that drives the atmospheric cycle is simple: There is more energy from the sun falling on the tropics than at the poles. The air moves to redistribute the resultant imbalance of heat. If Earth didn't rotate air would rise at the equator and travel to the poles, where it would cool off, sink, and return to the equator along the surface. The prevailing winds in the Northern Hemisphere would then blow from the north. Because of Earth's rotation, however, the flow of air is more complicated. Near the equator surface winds blow from the east—the so-called trade winds. At midaltitudes it blows from the west— the so-called prevailing westerlies, and around the poles it blows from the east again.

> ⊕ John McPhee referred to the understanding of the rock cycle as **the discovery of "deep time."**

The transfer of heat from the equator is also aided by the great ocean currents. The Gulf Stream, for example, carries heat northward, keeping Europe warmer than it would otherwise be. The water returns to the equator in the Canary Current, which flows along the west coasts of Europe and Africa. ☐

Life Goes On

Ecology and Ecosystems

When we add the effects of living systems to our analysis of the way the planet works, new aspects of Earth become visible. For example, the fact that 20 percent of the atmosphere consists of oxygen is a direct result of the photosynthetic activity of living things.

The key concept in studying the way living systems fit into Earth's operation is that of the ecosystem. An ecosystem is defined to be all the living things that occupy a given area, together with the physical environment that exists there. Thus an ecosystem can be as small as a patch of lawn or as large as a planet.

One crucial feature that scientists measure when they study ecosystems is the diversity—the number of different species of plants and animals found there. If we consider the global ecosystem, this translates into a question that is very difficult to answer: How many species of plants and animals are there on the planet?

The problem is that most of the species on our planet have not been cataloged, so we are forced to make estimates of the total number. There are something over a million species known, and scientists using mathematical models of the rate of discovery estimate that the total number of species, when and if we ever measure it directly, will turn out to be 7 or 8 million. Other estimates run as high as 30 million, but there is little scientific support for that sort of number. ☐

Above: The praying mantis shown here represents one of millions of species of insects. Every species is part of our ecosystem, and their existence keeps everything in balance.

🔍 Insects make up the greatest percentage of living species. The British biologist, J. B. S. Haldane (1892–1964), when asked what his studies of nature had **taught him about God,** replied, **"He has an inordinate fondness for beetles."**

On the Horizon

▷ Climate Change

There is one central fact we have to understand—the climate is always changing. There have been times when the planet was much colder—when the oceans froze over, for example—and times when it was much warmer and there were tropical swamps in the Arctic. Today the subject of climate change arises with regard to the question of whether humans, by burning fossil fuels and putting more carbon dioxide into the atmosphere, are contributing to another warming trend.

▷ Extinctions

The fossil record (see page 84) tells us that 99 percent of the species that ever lived on Earth have gone extinct. Sometimes these extinctions occur suddenly and drastically in what is called a mass extinction. Sixty-five million years ago, for example, an asteroid hit Earth and wiped out two-thirds of all the species that existed at the time, including the dinosaurs. Depending on how you count, there have been anywhere from five to over a dozen such extinctions in Earth's history. Scientists are still trying to discover the causes of most of them. ■

While most of the smoke from this chimney is water vapor, some may contain ingredients that could cause harm.

EXOPLANETS

▷ 1992

To Seek Out New Worlds

The Search for Exoplanets

The ancient Greeks believed that Earth was the center of the universe, so, for them, searching for other Earths was tantamount to searching for other universes—a concept they rejected. In the Middle Ages, theologians argued that to deny the existence of other worlds was to limit the

power of God—a heresy. But it wasn't until 1992 that the first firm evidence for planets around other stars came in.

The early search technique involved something called a radial velocity measurement. The basic idea is this: If a planet is between you and its star, the star will be pulled toward you. Conversely, if the planet is behind the star, then the star will be pulled away from you. This back and forth motion of the star will produce a periodic change in the frequency of the light it emits—a change that can be detected from Earth. The first discovery of an exoplanet in 1992 came in a completely unexpected place, however, since the planet was orbiting a pulsar. Pulsars are the remnants left behind

> ⊕ The most surprising fact about other solar systems is **how few of them are like our own.**

after the explosion of a large star in a supernova—an event that no planet should survive.

However the pulsar planets came to be (they might, for example, have formed after the explosion), astronomers quickly began to find exoplanets around normal stars, where one would expect them to be. Even here, however, we encountered surprises. The planets we found were very large—many times the size of Jupiter—and orbiting closer to their stars than Mercury is to ours. For a while, scientists worried that these so-called hot Jupiters were the only other kind of planet out there. In the end, however, this turned out not to be the case. It was just that, if you use the radial velocity technique, the first planets you'll

Above left: The Kepler spacecraft has detected over 4,000 planets in other solar systems.

There are more planets than stars
in the Milky Way galaxy.

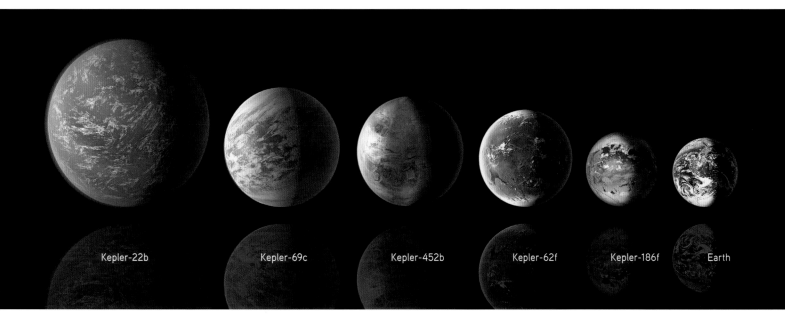

Kepler-22b Kepler-69c Kepler-452b Kepler-62f Kepler-186f Earth

detect will be big ones close to their stars, since they have the biggest gravitational effect on their stars.

The exoplanet search program took a huge step forward with the launching of the Kepler spacecraft in 2009. Kepler is designed to monitor the light from about 145,000 stars, watching for a telltale dip in brightness which indicates that a planet is passing in front of the star. This so-called transit method will see all planets, regardless of their size and distance from the star.

Since the launch of Kepler, scientists have verified the existence of over 4,000 planets circling other stars. The diversity of these objects is almost unbelievable, as seen in the following examples:

- A planet so close to its star that the temperatures on the "day" side are high enough to vaporize the surface minerals, so that when the planet rotates to "night" it rains solid rocks
- Rogue planets wandering around the galaxy on their own, without a star
- "Styrofoam world"—a planet so light that we can't figure out why it doesn't collapse under its own weight

We could go on, but I think the point is clear: our own solar system is just one example in a galaxy full of planetary systems. ☐

▷ 2010

Juuust **Right**
Life and the Planets Like the Earth

The question of whether life exists elsewhere in the galaxy is what is on most people's minds when they think about exoplanets. Since we know of only one type of life—that on our own planet—our analysis of exoplanets focuses on the conditions needed to produce life similar to our own. This means that we have to look for planets that could have liquid water on their surfaces for long periods of time.

If a planet is too close to its star, any oceans that try to form will vaporize. If it's too far away, the surface of the planet will freeze solid. Between the two, in what is called the continuously habitable zone (CHZ), is where surface oceans are possible. In our solar system, only Earth is in the Sun's CHZ.

Thus the search for a home for life tends to concentrate on a planet that is not too hot, not too cold, but *juuust* right—the "Goldilocks Planet." ☐

Above: A sampling of the planets detected by the Kepler spacecraft.

On the Horizon

▷ The Goldilocks Planet

As we confirm the existence of more and more planets, we are starting to find a few that satisfy the conditions for life in the sense of being in their star's "continuously habitable zone" (CHZ). You will see headlines when one of these planets is found to be Earth-like (or at least Earth-sized). One thing to keep in mind, however, is that, if or when we find life out there, it may not be like us at all. In our own solar system, after all, there are many subsurface oceans on the moons of the outer planets (see page 182), and any life that develops there could well be very different from life on Earth.

▷ Future Planet Hunters

There will be many follow-on missions to search for and examine exoplanets. In 2013 the European Space Agency launched the Gaia satellite. Although its primary mission is to obtain accurate positions for a billion stars, it will also search for exoplanets by the transit method. NASA is scheduled to launch TESS (Transiting Exoplanet Survey Satellite) in 2019. This spacecraft will examine thousands of exoplanet candidates in solar systems close to Earth, including an expected 500 Earth-type planets. The goal of TESS will be to gather data to be used by future generations of spacecraft.

▷ Finding Evidence of Life

The ultimate goal of planet hunting spacecraft is to find planets that might support life. Current plans call for future generations of instruments that will examine the atmospheres of candidate exoplanets for the presence of oxygen, a finding that would indicate the presence of living organisms. ■

The Gaia spacecraft mapping the Milky Way galaxy.

COSMOLOGY

▷ 1928

A Galaxy Far, Far Away
The Discovery of the Big Bang

The American astronomer Edwin Hubble (1898–1953) returned from duty as an infantry officer in World War I and was given a position at what was then the world's largest telescope, on Mount Wilson in California. There he set out to solve a riddle that had plagued astronomy for decades. It was called the nebula problem, and it involved the identity of structures that looked like hazy clouds in the pre-1920 telescopes. Were they in fact clouds inside the Milky Way galaxy, or were they, to use the phrase in vogue at the time, other "island universes"?

Hubble could use the new telescope to pick out individual stars in the nebulae, which allowed him to use a technique that had been developed by Harvard astronomer Henrietta Leavitt (1868–1921) to find out how far away they were. He could also determine, by measuring the wavelengths of the light they emitted, that the galaxies are moving away from us. With this information, Hubble was able to state two fundamental facts about our universe: (1) matter is clumped into galaxies (we now know there are billions of them), and (2) the universe is expanding.

With this picture, it is an easy mental operation to imagine "running the film backward" to find a time when the universe began expanding from an infinitely dense single point. Today we know that this point existed a little less than 14 billion years ago. This picture, in which the universe began in a hot, dense state and has been expanding and cooling ever since, is called the big bang picture.

Decisive corroborating evidence for the theory came in 1964, when American astronomers Arno Penzias (b 1933) and Robert Wilson (b 1936) discovered what has come to be called the cosmic microwave background. This is a sea of microwave radiation that pervades the universe and represents the result of the cooling of the universe from its hot beginning to its current average temperature of about 3 degrees above absolute zero. This cooling is analogous to what you can see in embers of a campfire, which cool from white hot to dull red over time. □

Right: An artist's conception of the big bang. Remember that it is not an explosion in space, but an expansion of space itself.

The universe began in a hot, dense state and has been expanding and cooling ever since.

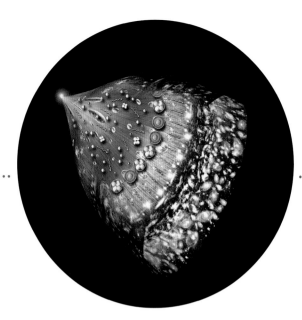

▷ Late 20th Century

In the Beginning

The First Second

As we move backward in time toward the initial event, we find the temperature of the universe to be higher and higher and collisions between its constituent parts to be more and more violent. This, in turn, implies that atoms, nuclei, and even elementary particles will be torn apart as we get closer to the beginning (see page 19). It also implies (see page 20) that, as the energy of the collisions goes up, the fundamental forces of nature will unify. Thus, in what has to be one of the strangest convergences in the history of science, we find that the study of the biggest thing we can imagine—the universe itself—involves the study of the smallest thing we can imagine—the fundamental constituents of matter and the forces between them.

One aspect of the early history of the universe is the rapid increase in size when the universe was about 10^{-35} seconds old. This is called inflation, and it corresponds to having the universe grow from something smaller than a proton to about the size of a grapefruit. This was an expansion of space itself, rather than something moving through space; thus it doesn't violate the prohibition on faster than light travel. Inflation was first discussed by theoretical physicist Alan Guth (b 1947), then at Stanford University, and has been worked out in detail by legions of scientists since. It is an extreme example of what physicists call a phase transition, and you can think of it as being somewhat analogous to the expansion of water when it freezes into ice. ☐

Above: Artist's conception of the history of the universe. The big bang is on the left, followed by the rapid expansion due to inflation and culminating in a universe of galaxies.

The Dark Side of the Universe

Dark Energy and Dark Matter

Our understanding of the universe underwent two major changes in the last half of the 20th century. These changes involved things called dark matter and dark energy—two entities that, despite the similarity in their names, have no connection to each other.

Dark Matter

In the early 1970s, astronomer Vera Rubin (1928—2016), at the Carnegie Institution of Washington, was carrying out measurements of the way stars move within galaxies. She (and other astronomers) expected to find a simple pattern: Close in to the galactic core, they expected the stars to be locked together, rotating like a merry-go-round, with the farthest stars moving the fastest. Then they expected to find a region where all the stars travel at the same speed. Finally, when they were far away from the galaxy, they expected that objects would behave in the same way that planets behave in our own solar system—that is, they expected that the farther out an object was, the slower it would move. This final region they characterized as "Kepler flow," after the man who explained how planets move around the sun.

Well, things didn't turn out that way. No matter how far away from the galaxy they went, they never found the expected slowdown. The only way to explain this was to say that the visible part of the galaxy was embedded in a gigantic sphere of matter—matter that exerted a gravitational force but didn't interact with light or other kinds of electromagnetic radiation. Because it can't be seen, it was called dark matter. Today we understand that about 25 percent of the universe (and 95 percent of the Milky Way) is made of this material.

The next step, of course, is to ask what it is. To answer this question, scientists have built a number of experiments to detect it. The basic idea is that a dark matter wind must be sweeping by Earth (and through your body) all the time. Since dark matter doesn't interact with the electrical force, it will not interact with your atoms very often, so you won't notice it. The idea of the experiments is to have an apparatus sensitive enough to detect those infrequent interactions. So far, even the most sensitive of those experiments—a tank of liquid xenon a mile underground in an old gold mine in the Black Hills of South Dakota—have come up empty.

Dark Energy

The discovery of dark energy came from a completely different (but equally startling) astronomical measurement. In the late 1990s, astronomers established new ways of measuring the distances to galaxies extremely far away. The technique involved something called a type Ia supernova, events that occur in double-star systems where one of the partners is a white dwarf. The white dwarf pulls hydrogen off its partner until the dwarf undergoes a titanic explosion—an explosion that may, for a time, outshine an entire galaxy. It turns out that all type Ia supernovas reach the same maximum brightness, so that you can tell how far away a supernova is by seeing how much light you receive. And, since looking far out into space is equivalent to looking backward in time, this

technique becomes an ideal tool to investigate the history of the expansion of the universe.

The expectation was that, because of the attractive force of gravity, the expansion rate should be slowing down as gravitational attraction "put the brakes" on the expansion. As with dark matter, however, the results of the measurements were completely unexpected. It turns out that, for this first five billion years of its history, the brakes were indeed on and the expansion slowed down. But then, something "stepped on the gas pedal," and the expansion started to speed up. Something had to be acting as a kind of antigravity, pushing the galaxies apart. The entity behind this expansion was called dark energy, and it is now thought to be responsible for about 70 percent of the mass of the universe. We don't know what it is, although there are theoretical suggestions. Finding out what dark energy is remains a central problem (some would say *the* central problem) in cosmology. □

Above: Astronomer Vera Rubin points to the Andromeda galaxy. One of the galaxy's rotation curves led her to the discovery of dark matter.

On the Horizon

▷ Dark Matter Searches

As we have seen, dark matter searches involve detecting particles in the dark matter wind that must be sweeping through Earth. Although these searches have yielded negative results so far, it doesn't mean that they will always be so. The general consensus is that dark matter must be made up of some kind of elementary particle that has not yet been detected. It is possible, therefore, that dark matter particles may be created in collisions at the Large Hadron Collider before they are seen in conventional search experiments.

▷ The Fate of the Universe

Research into the nature of dark energy will shed light on the ultimate fate of the universe. Cosmologists have identified three possible futures. If the amount of dark energy in the universe keeps increasing, as some theorists suggest, then eventually the repulsive force it generates will push not only galaxies apart but also the parts of every atom. This future has been labeled the Big Rip.

On the other hand, it could be that the amount of dark energy is fixed, so that gravity will take over again sometime in the future. This could result in a collapse of the universe (the "big crunch") or a continued but ever slowing expansion, with everything eventually running out of energy (the "big nothing").

▷ The Multiverse

The most striking cosmological suggestion comes from string theory (see page 22). In some versions of the theory, there is not one universe, but an almost infinite number of them—10^{500} in fact. (That's a "1" followed by 500 zeroes). This collection is called a multiverse. The universes are like separate bubbles and can't communicate with each other.

In a sense, the multiverse represents the final triumph of the Copernican principle. Earth is not the only planet in the solar system, the sun is not the only star in the Milky Way galaxy, the Milky Way is just one of billions of galaxies in the universe, and our universe is just one among many in the multiverse.

Quite a change from the old Greek idea, isn't it? ∎

Artist's conception of the multiverse.

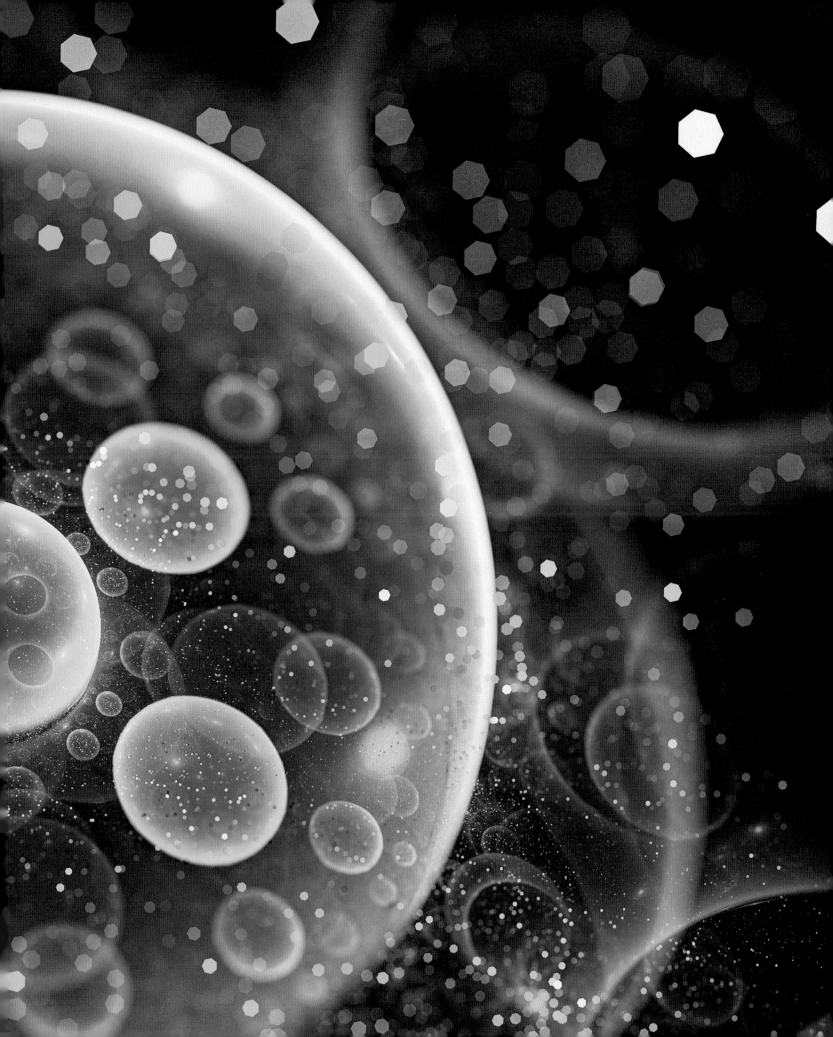

Chapter 5

TECHNOLOGY

Trains and automobiles replace
tired feet and horses making travel
fast, flexible, and accessible to all.

GROUND

▷ 1774

Under Pressure
Steam Engine

The first steam device we know about was built by Hero
of Alexandria (A.D. 10–70). It was little more than a toy,
spinning a metal globe on an axis. The first commercial
steam engine came centuries later, when the Englishman
Thomas Newcomen (1664–1729) built a device powered
by burning coal. Steam pushed a piston up in a cylinder,
and then a spray of cold water condensed the steam so
that air pressure pushed the piston back down. The
device was very inefficient—a room-sized engine probably
developed less power than a modern lawn mower. It was
James Watt (1736–1819) who introduced the modern
steam engine in 1774, ushering in the Industrial Revolution.
For the first time, humanity had a portable, powerful
energy source, and the results were spectacular. ☐

Above: Steam engines like this one in Ohio are still operated for
tourists and railroad buffs. In their day, steam engines ushered in
the Industrial Revolution and had a spectacular effect on the world.

TRANSPORTATION

▷ 1869

East Meets West
Transcontinental Railroad

It is an amazing fact that Julius Caesar and Napoleon Bonaparte had exactly the same means for moving troops and supplies—muscle power. Watt's development of the steam engine changed that with the adaptation of the engine to serve as the driving force for the advent of railroads. The first railroad in the United States was introduced by John Stevens (1749–1838), who ran a demonstration system around his estate in Hoboken, New Jersey. Events followed swiftly. The Baltimore and Ohio railroad opened for business in 1830, and a massive building boom soon saw rail networks connecting much of the eastern half of the country. In 1853 the first "union station"—a central railroad station used by several different railroad companies—opened in Indianapolis. In 1864, George Pullman (1831–1897) introduced the first sleeping car, making multiday trips comfortable for affluent travelers.

In 1869 the world's largest railroad project was completed when men laying track east from Sacramento met men laying track west from St. Louis at Promontory Point, Utah, and the world's first transcontinental rail line was completed. Although the trip from New York to California took five days, which seems long to us, it was a huge improvement over the weeks or months it took to go by boat.

Above right: Signs like this were put up to warn people that trains might be approaching. The smoke-spewing locomotives were slow to stop, and accidents did happen.

Throughout the early 20th century, railroads provided the main means of moving passengers and freight in the United States. By the 1920s, coal-driven steam locomotives started to be replaced be diesel engines, which are easier to operate and maintain, and which remain the main source of power for American railroads. ☐

⊕ Sleeping compartments on trains were called Pullman cars after George Pullman, the designer and manufacturer of the sleeping car, **who donated one of his cars to carry Abraham Lincoln's body** to Illinois after he was assassinated.

Explosive Technology
Internal Combustion Engine

It's hard to think of a technological advance that has had a greater effect on transportation than the internal combustion engine (ICE). Basically, an ICE is a device in which an explosive mixture is detonated in a cylinder and the resulting pressure is used to drive a piston. Devices like this have a long history, but the real impact of the ICE followed the development of the petroleum industry in the 19th century.

The first modern ICE was built in 1876 by the German engineer Nikolaus Otto (1832–1891). It was a four-stroke engine, like those found in most cars and trucks today. The engine works like this: A mixture of gasoline and air is ignited by a spark, driving the piston down. A valve is then opened and the piston is pushed up, removing the exhaust products from the cylinder. The piston then goes back down, drawing in a new gasoline–air mixture. On the final stroke, the piston moves up, compressing and heating the mixture, at which point a spark ignites the mixture and the cycle repeats. Otto's original engine ran on coal gas, but the four-cycle engine was quickly adapted to run on gasoline.

From there on the list of men who built improved versions of the ICE reads like a Hall of Fame of automobile manufacturers. Rudolf Diesel (1858–1913), Karl Benz (1844–1929), Gottlieb Daimler (1834–1900), and many others contributed to bringing the ICE to its present state. □

Right: A cross section of a diesel engine showing the internal engine parts.

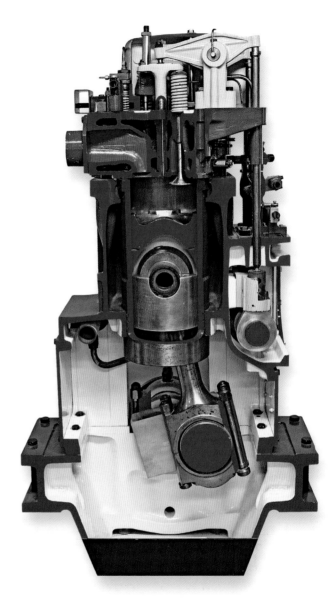

🔍 The Locomotive Act, passed by the British Parliament in 1865, required that anyone operating a horseless carriage on a public road had to be preceded by **a man waving a red flag and blowing a horn.**

Horse Power Without the Horse

Internal Combustion Automobile

In the late 19th century, there were many competing designs for automobiles. Steam-powered cars were some of the first on the road, and for a long time electric cars were popular as well. But the modern automobile era began in 1886, when Karl Benz invented the first car powered by an ICE burning gasoline.

Bertha Benz, Karl's wife, is generally credited with bringing automobiles to public attention. In 1886, dissatisfied with the way her husband's car was being marketed, she loaded her two teenage sons into a car and drove off to visit her mother, some 60 miles away, without telling anyone where she was going. The publicity she got for making the first long auto journey convinced people that cars could play a role in family life.

It was in America, however, that automobile production flourished. Henry Ford (1863–1947) is generally seen as the most important figure in this development. He founded the Ford Motor Company in 1903 and perfected the assembly line method of production, in which the car is carried past the workers on a conveyor belt and each worker performs a specific task. At its peak, Ford's assembly line was capable of producing a Model T automobile in 93 minutes, and over the years more than 15 million of the cars were produced and sold.

The impact of the automobile on American culture has been profound. The growth of suburbs and the development of sprawling metropolitan regions all came about because of the availability of cars to the average citizen. Today a new automotive revolution is under way as engineers look for an alternative to the gasoline-powered ICE. Hybrid cars, using a mix of electric and gasoline power, and all-electric cars are already on the market. □

Below: The Ford Model T was the last word in automotive elegance in 1927. Henry Ford did not invent the automobile, but he made it affordable to the masses, ushering in the automotive era.

▷ 1956

Traffic Arteries

Interstate Highway System

It's hard to imagine transportation in the modern United States without the Interstate Highway System. Well-maintained, limited-access highways form a web across the country, easing the stress of travel for private individuals and commercial truckers alike.

The idea of such a system was first sketched in a report to Congress in 1939, but it really began when President Eisenhower threw his support behind the Federal-Aid Highways Act of 1956. It was not, as has often been stated, a system designed to improve the national defense, nor was it authorized, as is often stated, by the Interstate Defense Highway Act of 1956—an act which, as far as I can determine, never existed. Instead, it was intended to improve the national transportation system and boost the economy—a goal that it has manifestly met.

Depending on how you count, the first segment of the Interstate system was started outside of St. Louis, Missouri, in 1956 (the first segment started after the Act went into effect) or outside of Topeka, Kansas (where a project already started was completed with funds from the Act). In any case, today there are 46,876 miles of highway in the system. The system was largely completed in the 1990s, although there are still a few pieces missing, as anyone who has struggled through the horrific interchange of I-70 and the Pennsylvania Turnpike in Breezewood, Pennsylvania, can attest. ☐

Left: Complex interchanges like this one in Arizona are a necessity when two interstate highways meet.

▷ 1964

Bullet Trains

High-Speed Trains

Perhaps the most interesting development in passenger service has been the introduction of high-speed train lines in countries around the world. The trend began in 1964, with the high-speed *Shinkasen* trains in Japan. Routinely traveling at 150–200 miles per hour, with maximum test speeds of 275 miles per hour, they link all the major cities in Japan with over 1600 miles of track. Emboldened by Japanese success, the French TGV (Train à Grande Vitesse) debuted in 1977, followed by the German ICE (Inter City Express) in 1991. Today, most of the cities in Europe are connected by high-speed train lines. ☐

On the Horizon

▷ Maglev Trains

The maximum speed of trains like those discussed in this section is set by friction between the wheels and the track. You can, in fact, think of a high-speed train as a device designed to convert the energy of burning fuel to heat in the wheels and track. The so-called maglev (short for magnetically levitated) train is a response to this fact.

Here's how it works: Inside the train are a set of superconducting magnets (see page 59). As the train moves, these devices create a changing magnetic field in the metal guide track under the train. This, in turn, will generate electrical currents in the guide track, and these currents will produce their own magnetic field, distinct from that of the superconducting magnets. The easiest way to picture the outcome is to imagine the superconducting magnets creating a kind of mirror image magnet in the guide track. If the superconducting magnet has its north pole down, then the mirror image magnet will have its north pole up, and the repulsion between the two magnets will lift (levitate) the train so that it actually floats a few inches above the guide bar, thereby eliminating wheel friction. It has been estimated, for example, that a maglev train could travel from Washington to New York in an hour— a time that would fundamentally change the way we view interurban transportation.

Although there have been successful prototypes of maglev trains operating in Germany and Japan for many years, commercial acceptance of the technology has been slow, primarily because of the cost of building new track. Today, the only commercial maglev train in operation connects Shanghai airport to downtown Shanghai.

▷ Driverless Cars

It used to be that, when you got into your car, you had to turn on the headlights and windshield wipers yourself. These functions are now automatic, governed by onboard computers. You can think of this development as the first baby step toward the driverless car. Driverless cars used to be strange looking, with cameras mounted in all sorts of strange places. That look is gone, and modern driverless cars have all of their sensing equipment hidden in what looks like a normal design.

The basic idea behind the driverless car is that the passenger gets in and picks a destination. The car, using standard GPS technology, picks a route (perhaps aided by current information on traffic congestion), and starts to drive. Its sensing equipment picks up the twists and turns of the road as well as the presence of other vehicles and gets the passenger to the requested destination. (We should note that there is a technical distinction between autonomous cars, which take over driving only under certain well-defined circumstances, and self-driving cars, which need no human input.)

Today, several states and the District of Columbia have passed laws allowing the testing of driverless cars on public roads. If this technology becomes commonplace, the daily commute will become very different for many people. Your car will take you to your office while you work or catch up with your reading, then go off and park itself at some distant lot until you summon it to take you home. Quite a change!

▷ Smart Highways

It used to be that roads were just stretches of pavement to be driven over. The "smart highway" movement aims to change that. Part of what an eventual smart highway system might look like is already familiar to us—think of the signs on city expressways alerting drivers to accidents and road blockage. Eventually, we can expect that this function will migrate to wireless systems that communicate directly with our cars' computers.

But ideas about smart highways go well beyond information sharing. In the Netherlands, South Korea, and the United States engineers are looking into the possibility of using road surfaces to generate electricity with embedded photovoltaic cells. Various schemes call for using this energy to light the roads at night, melt snow and frost, or even charge passing electric cars. You can understand the potential of this sort of procedure by noting that every hundred miles of interstate highway corresponds to the equivalent of a square mile of paved surface. Using that surface to generate solar energy would convert the Interstate system to the world's largest solar collector. ■

The Shanghai Transrapid is a maglev train that connects the city to its airport.

Few ideas have captured the human imagination so strongly as the wish to be able to fly like a bird.

▷ 1783

A Sheep, a Duck, and a Rooster

Balloons

Humans could not fly like birds, but that didn't mean we couldn't fly—it just meant that we'd have to find a different way to do it. The earliest of these alternate techniques—one still in recreational use today—was the hot air balloon, which depends on the fact that hot air is less dense than ambient air. Like a cork released at the bottom of a pond, the hot air balloon rises of its own accord. In the third century, Chinese armies used small hot air balloons for signaling, and in 1783 the Montgolfier brothers (Joseph-Michel, 1740–1810, and Jacques-Étienne, 1745–1799) demonstrated the first modern hot air balloon at Versailles, near Paris. ☐

🔍 Rather than risk sending people up on the first flight, the Montgolfier brothers **sent a sheep, a duck, and a rooster, all of which survived.**

Left: Modern hot air balloons like the one pictured here are the descendants of the first successful human flight.

▷ 1852

A Bright Future Combusted

Dirigibles

The problem with hot air balloons is that you have to keep heating the air to keep them afloat. A more efficient scheme would be to fill them with a gas that is lighter than air, and English scientist Henry Cavendish's (1731–1810) discovery of hydrogen in 1766 seemed to fit the bill perfectly. The first hydrogen balloon was demonstrated in Paris in 1783, the same year as the Montgolfier flight. It was followed by a rapid development of hydrogen balloon technology, and, although it seems strange to say this today, in the 1920s and 1930s many saw dirigibles as the future of air travel.

The German dirigible *Hindenburg* was the flagship of the world dirigible fleet, inaugurating its regular transatlantic service in 1936. It was almost three football fields in length and took only two and a half days to make the crossing—half the time of the fastest ocean liner. For the passengers it was luxury personified, with an elegant dining room, a dance band, and a lounge.

Unfortunately, when it was coming in for a landing at Lakehurst, New Jersey, on May 6, 1937, the *Hindenburg*'s hydrogen ignited, destroying the vessel and killing 35 of 97 people on board and one person on the ground, thereby effectively ending commercial dirigible travel. Today's blimps are filled with nonflammable helium—heavier than hydrogen, but safer. ☐

Below: The 1937 Hindenburg disaster ended commercial dirigible travel.

Up in the Air and Under Control

The Wright Brothers

The problem people faced in producing heavier than air flight wasn't power—by 1900 there were many gasoline-powered engines capable of propelling an aircraft. The problem was controlling the craft in the air—a complex three-dimensional process that had never been addressed by engineers accustomed to craft that stayed on the two-dimensional ground or water surface. The brothers Orville (1871–1948) and Wilbur (1867–1912) Wright, operating out of their bicycle shop in Dayton, Ohio, devised a method of control that involved changing the shape of the wings on their craft—a technique borrowed from the flight strategy of birds. During repeated trips to the Outer Banks of North Carolina, they built

gliders to perfect their control system. Finally, in 1903, they added a light gasoline-powered engine and on December 17, 1903, achieved the first powered flight.

Much of their life after that was involved in developing their aircraft and in legal battles over their patent (#821,393). In one notable event, in 1944, aircraft tycoon Howard Hughes (1905–1976) stopped off in Dayton to give Orville a ride on the new Lockheed Constellation. Orville's comment: The wingspan of the Constellation was longer than the distance of their historic flight at Kitty Hawk. □

The first powered flight by a heavier than air machine—Kitty Hawk, North Carolina, 1903.

She's Got a Ticket to Fly
Commercial Air Travel

Believe it or not, the first regularly scheduled air service was started between St. Petersburg and Tampa, Florida, in 1914. The seaplanes involved took 23 minutes to make the trip, flying about five feet above the water. A one-way ticket for the single passenger cost $5 (about $120 in 2015 dollars). The airline folded after three months of operation.

Despite this inauspicious start, commercial airlines flourished quickly. By 1918 the first regularly scheduled airmail service was started in the United States. The service began when Congress authorized a service between Washington, D.C., and New York, but it spread from there. Henry Ford even got into the act by diverting some company planes that had been used to deliver auto parts to carrying mail.

By 1929 a strange hybrid system of transcontinental travel had developed. Travelers took a train from New York to Columbus, Ohio, then flew to Oklahoma, took another train to Clovis, New Mexico, and finally got on a plane to California! The trips by train being necessitated by the fact that it was considered dangerous to fly at night.

One of the most important propeller-driven aircraft in the postwar period was the Lockheed Constellation. Powered by four engines, it was capable of crossing the United States in less than eight hours. It was originally built as a military transport in World War II but was quickly converted to civilian use after 1945. To travel across the Atlantic on the Constellation, passengers would stop at Gander, Newfoundland, and Shannon, Ireland, for refueling.

The jet age was ushered in with the British-built de Havilland Comet in 1952. Unfortunately, the aircraft suffered from metal fatigue, a poorly understood phenomenon at the time. It was quickly followed, however, by the Boeing 707 in 1959, an aircraft capable of carrying 181 passengers and flying at speeds of 500 miles per hour. With this airplane, the modern world of air travel can be said to have begun. ☐

Below: There may be a hundred or more aircraft at a modern airport at a given time.

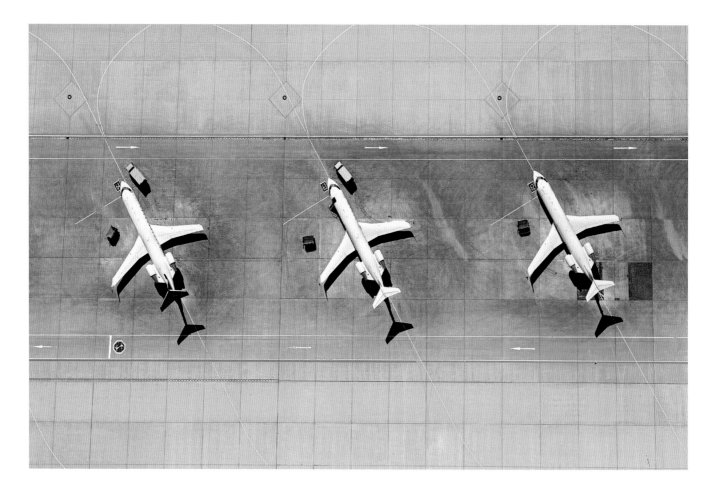

▷ 1944

Propulsion Compulsion

The Jet Engine

By the 1930s, engineers realized that they were nearing the limits of what could be achieved with propeller-driven aircraft—basically, as the speed of the tip of the propeller approached the speed of sound the system began to lose efficiency. This led a number of engineers in Germany and England to start thinking about a totally new propulsion system, the jet engine.

The basic principle of the jet engine goes back to Sir Isaac Newton (1642–1727) in the 17th century, and to his Third Law of Motion, which says that for every action there is an equal and opposite reaction. Blow up a balloon, let it go, and it flies off. Why? The pressure in the balloon exerts a force on the air that it pushes out of the nozzle, and Newton tells us that an equal and opposite force will be exerted on the balloon, making it fly off. This, in essence, is how a jet engine works.

In a jet engine, air is brought into the front of an engine and fed through a series of rotating fans that compress it. The compressed air is then mixed with fuel in a combustion chamber and the mixture is ignited. Like the air in the balloon, the resulting hot gases blow out of the back of the engine, and the airplane is thrust forward, while some of the energy of the exiting gas is used to turn the compressors that started the whole process.

In the engines used in most modern aircraft, an extra fan at the front of the engine diverts some of the air around the combustion chamber and adds it to the exhaust. This increases the efficiency of the engine and, additionally, makes the engine operation quieter. ☐

Above: The jet engine made the modern commercial air system possible. The basic principle goes back to Sir Isaac Newton.

⊕ Although many countries experimented with jet engines for **fighter aircraft during World War II,** the first to become operational and enter mass production was the **Messerschmitt 262 late in 1944**.

▷ 1982

Now You See It, Now You Don't

Stealth Technology

Perhaps the most striking feature of modern military aircraft is their odd angular shape and matte black color. This departure has to do with making the plane invisible (or nearly so) to radar. Radar works this way: A radio beam is sent out and encounters a metal object like an airplane. The beam is absorbed and reemitted, and the reemitted beam is detected by the radar operator. There are two ways to lessen the chances of detection: divert the reemitted beam so it doesn't go back to the detector, or try to diminish the intensity of the reemitted beam. The angular shape of stealth is designed to achieve the first of these objectives, and special materials in the plane's surface achieve the second. □

Left: A stealth aircraft.

Above: A fighter plane.

🔍 Stealth technology was tested at Area 51, **the government's once-secret facility** at Nellis Air Force Base in Nevada.

On the Horizon

▷ Drones

Drones, or unmanned aerial vehicles, as the Department of Defense prefers to call them, are in the news constantly these days because of their use in military conflicts. There is a long history of such use, dating back to the 19th century when Austrian armies tied bombs to balloons and launched them against Venice. The United States first used military drones in 1964, and by 2012 the U.S. Air Force had almost 8,000 of the craft available.

There are basically two types of drones: those that are piloted by a remote human operator and those that are guided by onboard computers. It is the former type that will have the greatest impact for most people. This is especially true for drones that are equipped with cameras.

The great advantage of a camera-equipped drone is that it can provide a way of seeing areas from the air—a bird's eye view that is hard to obtain without expensive equipment like helicopters. Thus farmers and ranchers don't have to visit every parcel of their far-flung operation to know what is going on—a drone flight will provide that information quickly and cheaply. Similarly, remote power lines and pipelines can be monitored without sending out expensive technicians. Drones have been used to produce images of remote areas to aid in search and rescue missions, and filmmakers have used them to produce aerial views for their films as well. Any situation in which a bird's eye view can be useful—and there are many of them—is one in which drones can be used. Some companies, such as Amazon, are even looking into the possibility of using drones to make home deliveries.

There are issues with drones, of course, as there are with any new technology. One problem is finding a way of keeping drones away from regular commercial aircraft and from sensitive areas. In Washington, D.C. for example, there have already been incidents of recreational drones entering forbidden air space. And then there are privacy issues—does your neighbor have the right to fly a drone over your backyard to see what you're doing? It will be interesting to see how these issues play out.

▷ Ballistic Aircraft

We're used to aircraft staying reasonably close to Earth's surface as we travel from one place to another—30,000 feet seems to be a reasonable altitude to most of us. But if some designs on the drawing boards are actually realized, that may change. Instead of sedate journeys following great circles on Earth's surface, aircraft might be launched into ballistic orbits—their paths might look more like missile launches than conventional aircraft. By spending most of their time above the atmosphere, astonishing flight times could be achieved. One design, for example, is predicted to reduce the flight time from London to Sydney to a few hours.

▷ Shape-Changing Aircraft

If you watch the back edge of the wings on your plane the next time you fly, you'll notice that there is a mechanical device, called an aileron, that is manipulated during takeoff and landing. These flaps are controlled by hydraulic systems that are heavy and awkward. In the future, airplane wings may be made from flexible composite materials whose shape can be changed by lightweight internal actuators. The shape of a flexible wing could then be continuously adjusted in flight to maximize the efficiency of operation and reduce noise.

▷ Airports of the Future

Every commercial flight begins and ends at an airport, so the airport itself is an important part of the flight experience. Airports have had an impressive evolution, starting out as functional but unaesthetic places whose only function was to get passengers onto planes and winding up as today's glitzy mix of transportation, entertainment, and shopping. The trend is to try to make airports places where a traveler might actually want to go, rather than just a place to be endured.

Changi Airport in Singapore is routinely voted the world's top airport, and it illustrates this trend perfectly. It already has movie theaters, a rooftop swimming pool, and a butterfly garden. If you have a long layover, you can even get a free bus tour of Singapore.

The new addition to Changi Airport in Singapore, slated to open in 2018, will feature a five-story garden around a structure billed as the "world's tallest indoor waterfall." Other airports are not far behind. At Munich International Airport passengers can ice skate in the winter and sample beer from the only microbrewery located inside an airport.

Airports are also starting to use communication technology to make the actual mechanics of moving through an airport easier. At Copenhagen, airlines use smart phones to let passengers know where the shortest security lines are located, for example. At Hamad International Airport in Qatar, passengers can print their own luggage tags and just drop their bags off, eliminating long wait times. It is estimated that in 2015 airlines spent $7 billion to implement these sorts of high-tech advances.

So in the future it may be so much fun being at an airport that you won't want to leave! ■

A military drone known as the Reaper prepares for takeoff.

Our ability to cross oceans depended on the wind for most of recorded history.

WATER

🔍 An Egyptian ship with **its sails up could be moving south,** using the wind to overcome the northward push of the Nile's current.

▷ 3400 B.C.

Blowing in the Wind
Sailing Ships

Humans have used rivers and coastlines as major transportation arteries throughout history. The Pacific Ocean and Australia, for example, were settled by people who had little more in the way of oceangoing craft than outrigger canoes. We know that the first Europeans to visit North America were Vikings in their open longboats. The addition of sails to use the energy in the wind made long voyages less perilous for many people.

The operation of sailing boats depends critically on the direction in which the wind blows. The ancient Egyptians, for example, used the fact that winds in their region generally blow from the north. Thus, if they wanted to go south

(against the northward flow of the Nile) they hoisted their sails; if they wanted to go north, they furled the sails and let the current carry them.

In a similar way, after the settling of the New World by Europeans, the large-scale wind patterns in the Atlantic were used to facilitate ocean travel. Ships would drop down to the Canary Islands to pick up the winds blowing from the east to cross to the Americas (that's why they are called trade winds), then go north to pick up the prevailing westerlies for the return trip.

The fastest commercial sailing vessels ever built were the so-called clipper ships of the mid-19th century. They were narrow ships with huge sails, primarily designed for the tea trade with China. There are examples of these ships traveling as much as 800 km (over 500 miles) in a single day. Their use declined as steam-powered ships were developed (see page 235). Early steamships weren't as fast as clippers, but, because they didn't depend on the wind, they were more reliable. Clipper use declined rapidly after the opening of the Suez Canal in 1869. ☐

▷ Mid-1400s

In Fourteen Hundred and Ninety-two Columbus Sailed the Ocean Blue
Voyages of Discovery

Humans have sailed the oceans from the beginnings of civilization. The records of the earliest voyages are known to us only through historical analysis. We know about the

---

Above: The Vikings used ships like the model shown above to discover and settle Greenland and Newfoundland.

TRANSPORTATION

trans-Atlantic voyages of the Vikings, for example, because of the discovery of their settlement at L'Anse aux Meadows in Newfoundland. It wasn't, however, until the so-called Age of Discovery, from the 15th to the 18th centuries, that European explorers began mapping the oceans and opening trade routes all over the world.

In the mid-1400s the development of a ship known as a caravel allowed sailors to travel over the open ocean—before this, European sailors (the Vikings excepted) had traveled close to shore in clumsy, bargelike craft. Prince Henry the Navigator (1394–1460) established a center for exploration in Portugal, and throughout the latter half of the 15th century, Portuguese sailors explored the west coast of Africa. In 1497–1499, Vasco da Gama (ca 1460–1524) sailed around the Cape of Good Hope, proving that it was possible to reach India and what is now Indonesia by sea, thus opening up the lucrative spice trade to the

Portuguese. This tradition of exploration reached a climax from 1519 to 1522, when an expedition started by Ferdinand Magellan (ca 1480–1521) circumnavigated the globe.

At the same time explorers sent out by the Spanish crown were trying to find ways to India by traveling west across the Atlantic. The celebrated expedition led by Christopher Columbus (1451–1506) was just one of these. Eventually it dawned on people that there was a continent-sized barrier—the Americas—blocking their way, and the emphasis shifted to exploring the new world. In subsequent centuries, sailing ships sailed all the oceans of Earth, mapping out our planet in detail.

Before we leave the era of sailing ships, we should mention what was perhaps the most impressive sailing fleet ever assembled. It was led by the Chinese admiral Zheng He (1371–1433). It traveled along well-known trade routes in the Indian Ocean and had a fleet of 317 ships and carried 28,000 men. The largest boats were over 400 feet long—several times the size of European caravels. After several voyages, the fleet was disbanded due to political changes in China. ☐

Below: Artist's conception of Magellan's ships starting their historic voyage around the world.

▷ 1787

Steamed Up

The Arrival of Steam

The invention of the modern steam engine (see page 214) changed a lot of things. It made energy stored in coal available for human use. It powered the factories and railroads that drove the Industrial Revolution, and, in the process, destroyed a lot of old technologies. These included the extensive canal systems that had been built by the early 19th century and the use of wind to drive commercial ocean traffic.

The first steam-powered ship took to the water in 1787 in Philadelphia. Designed by the American inventor John Fitch (1743–1798), its maiden voyage was observed by the men who had come to the city for the Constitutional Convention. The move to steam-powered oceangoing craft was a complicated one. The first oceangoing steamships were strange hybrids—they had steam engines running a paddle wheel but had sails as well. In 1819, the American ship S.S. *Savannah* was the first such ship to cross the Atlantic. The first fully steam-powered crossing took place in 1827, and the first regularly scheduled commercial steamship service began in 1839.

The most important technological advance in this early period was the development of the screw propeller to replace the paddle wheel. The first such ship, the S.S. *Archimedes* was built in Britain in 1839. From there on, ship design and efficiency improved steadily throughout the rest of the 19th century as steamships took over commercial ocean traffic.

There was one interesting sidelight, however. In order to operate, steamers needed to carry a great deal of coal to run the engines—the longer the voyage, the more coal was needed. This cut into the space available to carry cargo, a fact that made it difficult to compete with clipper ships (see page 232) on runs to China. In the 20th century, the mode of power for ships shifted from steam engines to diesel internal combustion engines, which now power nearly all commercial and military craft, with some military submarines powered by onboard nuclear reactors.

The main modern advance in commercial water transportation was the development of the container ship. Invented in 1956, the container is a standard-sized steel box that, once loaded, can be stacked on a ship by overhead cranes and, at its destination, loaded on a railcar or truck without ever being opened. This kind of seamless operation has made ocean commerce highly efficient. Today, much bulk cargo on the oceans is carried on container ships. ☐

Left: The steamship *Earnshaw*, which still sails in Lake Wakatipu in New Zealand.

On the Horizon

▷ The Crewless Ship

Just as companies like Google are developing the driverless car, engineers are working on the design of container ships that will be run by computers, without the need of a human crew. The British firm Rolls-Royce is developing what they call drone ships, a system in which a few operators at a remote location will be able to operate hundreds of ships on the high seas. Such a system would represent the ultimate in efficient (and safe) water transportation. ■

Artist's conception of what a crewless ship might look like. All space on the ship is devoted to cargo, and it would be guided by remote operators communicating with the ship electronically.

BUILDINGS

How high a building can be built depends on the kinds of materials available.

▷ From Prehistoric Times
What's It Made Of?
The Evolution of Building Materials

People have always needed buildings—for shelter, for community activities, for commerce, for storage, and all sorts of other reasons. The kinds of buildings they constructed depended on the kinds of materials they had available. We can identify three distinct phases: wood, stone and concrete, and steel.

Wood

The earliest building materials were plant products—branches and leaves in the earliest structures, wood later on. Wood is actually a splendid building material. It is easy to shape, nails can be driven through it, and it's readily available. Go to any suburban construction site today and you will see wood framing being put up to support apartments and shops.

There are, however, limits to what we can do with wood. The easiest way to picture the structure of wood is to imagine a handful of straws. The straws represent the

> 🔍 The observation deck of the Empire State Building **can sway as much as two feet from the vertical** during a storm.

grain of the wood. If you put a weight on top of a handful of straws, they can support it if the weight isn't too heavy. If the weight becomes too great, however, one of the straws will start to buckle, pushing against its neighbors and causing them to do the same. This means that there is a limit to how tall a wooden building can be. Typically, wood structures are less than three stories tall.

Right: A cross section of wood showing the ends of the vascular channels that produce the characteristic grain.

Stone and Concrete

To go higher, ancient architects used stone. Buildings like the pyramids of Egypt are basically piles of stone hundreds of feet high, with very little usable space inside. They are not, however, tall enough to tax the ability of stone to support their considerable weight.

The great cathedrals of Europe, with their spires reaching hundreds of feet into the air, are examples of stone buildings with usable space inside. Because of its internal atomic structure, stone is a material that is very good at supporting weight—Mount Everest, after all, can be thought of as a pile of stone five miles high. Stone is not, however, very good at resisting lateral force. You may be able to stack stones or bricks a mile high, but push sideways on the stack and it will topple. The inability of stone to withstand this sort of sideways force (what engineers call shear) limits the height you can achieve with stone buildings to several hundred feet.

Brick and concrete can be thought of as examples of "artificial" stone. Brick is made from clay that has been fire hardened. Concrete is a bit more complex. It is a mixture of sand and gravel held together by cement, which is itself a mixture of ground limestone and clay that has been baked to drive off water. When water is added to the concrete

mixture, minerals formed from calcium in the limestone form long, interlocking grains and, as the water evaporates, hardens into a substance very much like stone.

The Romans developed concrete as a building material, mixing in volcanic ash to make it water resistant. The Pantheon in Rome is one of the oldest concrete structures in the world. Today concrete is probably the most widely used building materials in our cities. If steel reinforcing rods are embedded in concrete, the problem of shear can be overcome. In effect, in this situation, the concrete carries the load and the steel resists the shear.

Modern concretes have been engineered to be much stronger than in the past, and some tall buildings—Water Tower Place in Chicago, for example, at 859 feet—are built entirely of reinforced high-strength concrete.

Steel

We have discussed the Bessemer process and the widespread availability of steel elsewhere (see page 43). This new technology changed forever the shape of modern buildings and modern cities. The basic point is that steel is strong against both compression and shear, and so

combines the strengths of the other building materials without their weaknesses. This ability is used in modern buildings in a way that represents a new kind of construction technique.

In stone and brick buildings the walls perform two functions: They support their own weight and that of the roof, and they act as a barrier between the inside of the building and the outside. In a modern steel-frame building these functions are divided. The steel-frame acts as a kind of skeleton that supports the weight of the structure, and the walls serve as the barrier against the outside environment. This is why you often see modern buildings, particularly the skyscrapers we discuss in the next section, with walls made completely of glass. The glass obviously can't support any weight, but it doesn't have to—that is taken care of by the steel frame. ☐

Above: The pyramids in Giza, Egypt, are arguably the most famous stone structures in the world. A remarkable feat of engineering, they were one of the Seven Wonders of the Ancient World and the only one that survives to this day.

▷ 1889

How High?

The Skyscraper

The modern skyscraper was born in Chicago. Architectural historians generally regard the Home Insurance Building in that city—a mere 10 stories tall—as the first modern skyscraper, whereas the Rand McNally Building (also in Chicago), built in 1889, was the first steel-framed sky-scraper. The surge in tall buildings that followed—New York's Woolworth Building (55 stories, 702 feet) in 1913 and the Chrysler Building (77 stories, 1046 feet) in 1927—forever changed the look of modern cities.

But the construction of the Empire State Building (102 stories, 1250 feet) in 1931 cemented the skyscraper in modern folklore. Who can forget Deborah Kerr and Cary Grant agreeing to meet there in *An Affair to Remember*, or King Kong meeting his sorrowful end on its highest tower? (Full disclosure: the author proposed to his wife on the observation platform of the Empire State Building and, miraculously, was accepted.)

The Empire State Building was put up in a mere 410 days by an improbable crew made up mostly of European immigrants and Mohawk Indians. It was officially opened when President Herbert Hoover pressed a button in the White House and turned on its lights.

The Empire State Building reigned as the world's tallest building for 40 years. For a while, what was then called the Sears Tower in Chicago (110 stories, 1454 feet) held the title, which was then claimed by skyscrapers in Asia and the Middle East. Since 2010 the world's tallest building title has been held by the Burj Khalifa in Dubai (163 stories, 2722 feet).

Before buildings this tall could be built, a large number of technical obstacles had to be overcome. We will look at just three of them: wind, vertical transport, and air-conditioning.

Wind

As strange as it may seem, given their massive size, it is not the force of gravity that is the major concern of the engineers who design skyscrapers. Instead, it is the wind. There are several reasons why this is so. A skyscraper is like a huge sail set in the ground, so a large force will be exerted on it. Furthermore, as we go up in height the wind gets stronger.

Right: These skyscrapers in Manhattan illustrate two important points about the use of steel as a building material: (a) it allows us to make the buildings very tall, and (b) it allows us to cover the outside of the building with materials like glass, which do not add to the building's strength.

One way to think about the effect of wind is to imagine a skyscraper as being like a bridge that has been tilted to a horizontal position. Instead of the weight of traffic pressing down on a bridge, we have the force of the wind pushing horizontally on a building. This force can become quite large—if you laid a 200-story building down next to the Golden Gate Bridge, the force exerted by a 100 mile per hour wind would be the equivalent of parking several hundred fully loaded dump trucks along its length.

Steel is a remarkably flexible material, so tall buildings can sway in the wind like a tree. The design limitations associated with the need for tall buildings to sway are not dictated by materials, but by how much movement the human occupants of the building can tolerate.

Vertical Transport

It would not have been possible to build tall structures if we didn't have a way of moving people up and down rapidly—no one wants to climb 40 flights of stairs to his or her office. The invention of the safety elevator in 1852 opened the way for buildings to go higher, just in time to anticipate the skyscraper boom. Elisha Otis (1811–1861) devised a simple system that would lock an elevator in place if the supporting cable broke. At the 1854 World's Fair in New York, he amazed crowds by standing on a platform equipped with his elevator brake suspended several feet in the air, then having a colleague cut the rope holding up the platform. He would doff his hat to the crowd when the platform didn't fall.

In modern high-rise buildings, elevators are so common that we hardly notice them. It is not unusual to place more than one elevator in a shaft, with some servicing the upper floors and others the lower floors. In the Willis Tower (formerly the Sears Tower) in Chicago, for example, there are 87 elevators operating in only 40 shafts.

Air-Conditioning

It would be impossible to sustain businesses functioning in skyscrapers without the availability of air-conditioners. The introduction of modern air-conditioning systems is generally attributed to the American engineer and inventor Willis Carrier (1876–1950). Working for a client in New York City, he designed the first system in 1902. Oddly enough, that first system was more concerned with controlling humidity rather than temperature, and more concerned with maintaining the temperatures needed for the manufacturing process of his client rather than making people comfortable.

The acceptance of air-conditioning in America was aided by the operators of movie theaters. Starting in the 1920s, advertising cool interiors during sweltering urban summers brought crowds in. Today, workers (and computers) in even the hottest regions of the country can maintain productivity year round because their workplaces are air-conditioned. ☐

On the Horizon

▷ Jeddah Tower

In 2020, a new tallest building is scheduled to be completed in Jeddah, Saudi Arabia. Although, as is customary, the design details are being kept secret during construction, it is expected to be 3281 feet tall (about one kilometer!) and have 252 stories. ■

Artist's conception of what the Jeddah Tower will look like when completed.

COMPUTERS

The ability to manipulate information in digital form has already changed the world and will continue to do so.

▷ 1837

The Birth of the Computer

Analog Computing Ahead of Its Time

Ever since the invention of numbers, people have needed devices to help with calculations. The abacus and the slide rule, for example, were both widely used in the 20th century. The birth of the modern computer, however, is generally credited to the English mathematician Charles Babbage (1791–1871) who, in 1837, designed what he called an analytical engine. It was a large, complex piece of machinery, full of gears and levers, but designed along the lines of modern digital computers.

Unfortunately, Babbage's "engine" was never actually built—the British government cut off funding before it was finished. Over a century would pass before another

---

Above: A model of Babbage's analytical engine. It was never built during his lifetime due to lack of funding. But it would have been the world's first analog computer.

machine, operating with very different components,
would carry the development of the computer forward.

Had Babbage's machine actually been built, it would
have been what we call today an analog computer. By
this we mean that a particular output—the position of a
dial or the strength of an electrical current—would indicate
the numerical answer to the problem being posed. This
is in contrast to the modern digital computer in which the
numerical answer comes out directly. During the 19th
century a number of analog computers were built for
specialized use, including, in 1872, a device for calculating
the tides. □

▷ 1936

The Turing Machine
Computer Science Is Born

The concept of the modern programmable digital computer
was introduced by British mathematician Alan Turing
(1912–1954) in what is now called a Turing machine. In
its simplest form, a Turing machine can be thought of as
a tape with symbols on it, a device for reading the tape,
and a set of instructions about what to do for each symbol.
The tape might, for example, be divided into segments,
each of which has a letter of the alphabet. An instruction
might be "If there is a letter A in this segment, change it
to a letter B." As the tape is fed through the machine, the
instructions are applied one segment at a time.

The point about Turing's paper is that he showed that
any program running on a computer could, ultimately, be
thought of (and analyzed) as a Turing machine. This work
is seen as the beginning of modern computer science. □

Above: A model of what a Turing machine might look
like—the rectangular box in the center is where the tape
is read and changed. The tape-fed instructions made
it a programmable computer.

▷ 1944

ENIAC

The First Modern Computer

What distinguishes modern digital computers from analog machines, such as Babbage's analytical engine (see page 244) is the fact it represents numbers in binary form, rather than as the position of a gear or the strength of an electrical current. Binary numbers can be represented as a string of 0s and 1s. The following gives the binary representation of a few familiar numbers:

1	1
2	10
3	101
4	110
5	111

Representing numbers in this way requires a device that can have two values. For example, three lightbulbs arranged on–off–on would represent the number 5. The most common devices used to represent binary numbers are electronic devices that can be on or off and magnetic materials that can have the north pole pointing up or down. As with the Turing machine, the modern computer has a complex set of instructions, called a program, that tell it what to do when it encounters a 1 or a 0.

During the 1930s, the navy experimented with systems where the "on or off" device was an electrical relay that could be open or closed. It wasn't until 1944 that scientists at the University of Pennsylvania built the first modern electronic computer using a device called a vacuum tube. This was a glass bulb in which electrons were boiled off a wire on one side and pulled to the other side by a strong voltage. Between these two sides was a grid. Electrons could be pushed onto the grid or pulled away from it. The idea was that if you ran electrons onto the grid you could shut off the current through the tube, so the device could be either on or off.

Each vacuum tube was about the size of a tube of lipstick. The tubes would be wired together in racks to make the computer. The Pennsylvania machine was called the Electronic Numerical Integrator and Computer (ENIAC) and was primarily designed for military use. It was the first machine that could be reprogrammed without being rewired. ☐

Above: ENIAC was a huge machine with very little computing power by modern standards. The machine filled a large room and required a large crew to keep it running.

Better and Better

The Transistor and Integrated Circuits

The invention of the transistor (see page 60) changed the computer forever. As we pointed out, you can think of the transistor as a "sandwich" made of doped semiconductors. By running electrons onto the transistor base (the "meat" of the sandwich), you can keep a current from flowing through it. Thus the transistor can function as an on or off device like the vacuum tube already described. Unlike the vacuum tube, however, it can be very small and doesn't wear out. Thus it is an ideal device for processing information in binary form.

The real technological breakthrough came from the ability to put transistors together in what is called an integrated circuit. By modern standards, the first transistors were huge—the size of golf balls. The size quickly diminished, however, and in 1958 the American electrical engineer Jack Kilby (1923–2005) built the first integrated circuit. This is a system in which the circuit elements—transistors and other devices—are built in one process. We'll describe the details in a moment, but here let us point out that, compared to the traditional technique of building the circuit components separately and then assembling them, this represents an enormous step forward. Kilby received the Nobel Prize in 2000.

> 🔍 The first portable computer, the Osborne 1, came out in 1981. **It weighed more than 20 pounds!**

A typical integrated circuit might be built this way: A mask is laid down over a slab of silicon. The mask will have holes in places where we want a particular piece of the circuit—a layer of doped semiconductor, for example (see page 57). Then a vapor of silicon and the doping atom are introduced and allowed to plate out on the open parts of the mask. Then a new mask is laid on, a new vapor introduced, and so on. In this way the three layers of a transistor would be assembled and, using different masks, the other circuit elements and connecting wires would be assembled. The result: a complete circuit on the original base of silicon. From a few transistors on the original integrated circuit, we have now reached the point where we can put billions of transistors on a piece of silicon the size of a postage stamp. Such a system, often referred to as a microchip, is an example of Moore's law in action (see page 62). ☐

Below: Integrated circuits are compact, despite the fact that they can contain many transistors.

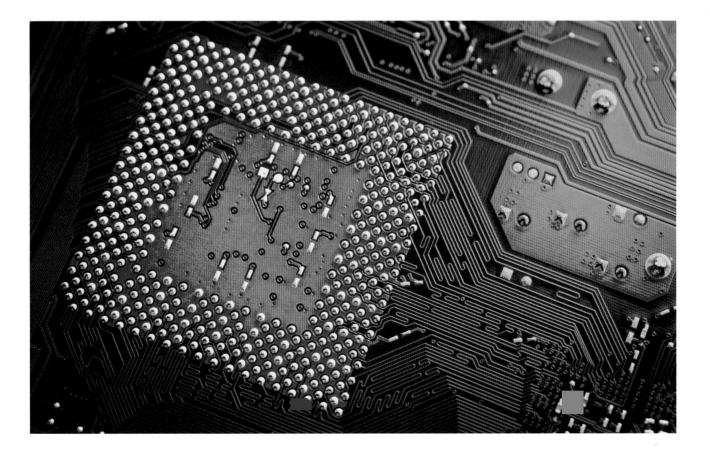

Sir Tim Berners-Lee, the man who invented the World Wide Web and revolutionized human communication.

▷ Late 1970s, early 1980s

The Computerized World

Personal Computers

Thomas J. Watson (1874–1956), chairman of IBM, is often quoted as saying, "I think there may be a world market for maybe five computers" in 1943. And, although scholars doubt that Watson ever actually said this, there were many other prominent scientists and businessmen who made similar statements in the 1940s and 1950s. How hard it would have been to imagine anything like our computer-driven world in those postwar years.

> **⊕ The world's most powerful computer is the Sunway TaihuLight in China.**

The earliest computers, like ENIAC, were huge main-frame devices. They were often housed in dedicated buildings and required multiperson crews to operate them. Users communicated with the machine, usually with punched cards, through interactions with members of that crew.

The idea of a personal computer, one with which the user could interact directly, grew in the 1970s. Throughout the decade there were many attempts to market such a machine, primarily to enthusiasts, but it wasn't until the late 1970s and early 1980s that machines we would recognize—the Apple II and IBM PC—became available. The shrinking size was the result of the development of integrated circuits and microchips, as already discussed.

The modern smart phone represents the ultimate in computer downsizing. In a machine that can fit in your pocket, you can now have more computing power than was available in those early mainframes. In fact, some engineers claim that the ultimate limit in computer size is not set by the circuitry but by the size of the human finger needed to type in the data. □

Opposite: The original Apple Macintosh computer from 1984. This computer was one of this first desktops available to the public.

▷ 1969

Connecting the World

The Internet

The Internet has become so much a part of our lives that it's sometimes hard to remember how recently it was developed. It all began in 1969, when the Advanced Research Project Agency (ARPA, part of the Department of Defense) funded a system called ARPANET to allow selected computers in different locations to share data with each other. The original system linked only four computers. As the networks grew, several important changes occurred. The first private service providers were created in 1989 to give users access to the networks, and in 1992 Congress expressly allowed commercial activity on networks developed by the government. In 1989, British computer scientist Sir Timothy John (Tim) Berners-Lee (b 1955), working at the European Organization for Nuclear Research (CERN) introduced what has come to be known as the World Wide Web (that's where the "www." comes from), working from systems that had been developed to link CERN computers. From there a dizzying succession of technical advances led to our present system, where anyone with a computer can have access to what is, in essence, the accumulated knowledge of the human race. □

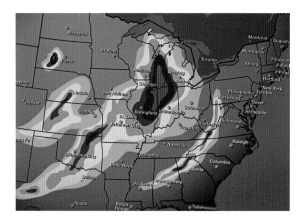

▷ 21st Century

Big Data

Bigger Is Better

There has been a quiet revolution going on in science, a revolution that has attracted little attention. It is based on the ability of computers to store and manipulate large amounts of data. Before the availability of computers, scientists could analyze only relatively simple systems, and this, in turn, limited their ability to deal with the complexity of the real world. Today, on the other hand, realistic simulations of nature are becoming common. This trend affects everything from weather forecasting to the analysis of census data and sometimes goes under the name of Big Data.

It has also affected the skills young scientists need to acquire. Being able to manipulate and "mine" huge data sets is now as important as being able to solve differential equations was a century ago. □

Above: Fast computers allow us to analyze complex weather systems and issue timely warnings.

▷ 21st Century

Smart Materials

Programming Matter

The availability of miniaturized microprocessors is leading to the development of what are called smart materials—materials in which computers are actually embedded as part of the structure. Imagine, for example, a bridge that had miniaturized sensors built into its concrete and steel, and imagine further that those sensors communicated with an embedded computer. Such a bridge could actually tell engineers when problems were starting to develop. Or imagine the operating system for a cell phone built into clothing, with the energy of normal body movements continually recharging the phone's battery. There is almost no limit to what might result from this sort of technology. □

Cloud Computing

Making the Most of the Internet

Cloud computing came into its own in the 21st century. Essentially, it is a system that allows data and programs to be stored in remote locations and accessed locally. The "cloud" can be thought of as the array of computers that make up the Internet. In commercial interactions, cloud computing allows companies to avoid the cost of providing expensive infrastructure to store information. For individual users, it makes systems less vulnerable to the crash of individual computers. ☐

> ⊕ Much of the current debate about **climate change** involves the **use of complex computer codes** known as global circulation models.

Above: The symbol that represents cloud computing. The term "cloud" is simply a metaphor for the system of computers in which information can be stored.

Left: In the future, smart materials will control the environment in buildings. Buildings like this will have sensors that automatically adjust things like window opacity and temperature.

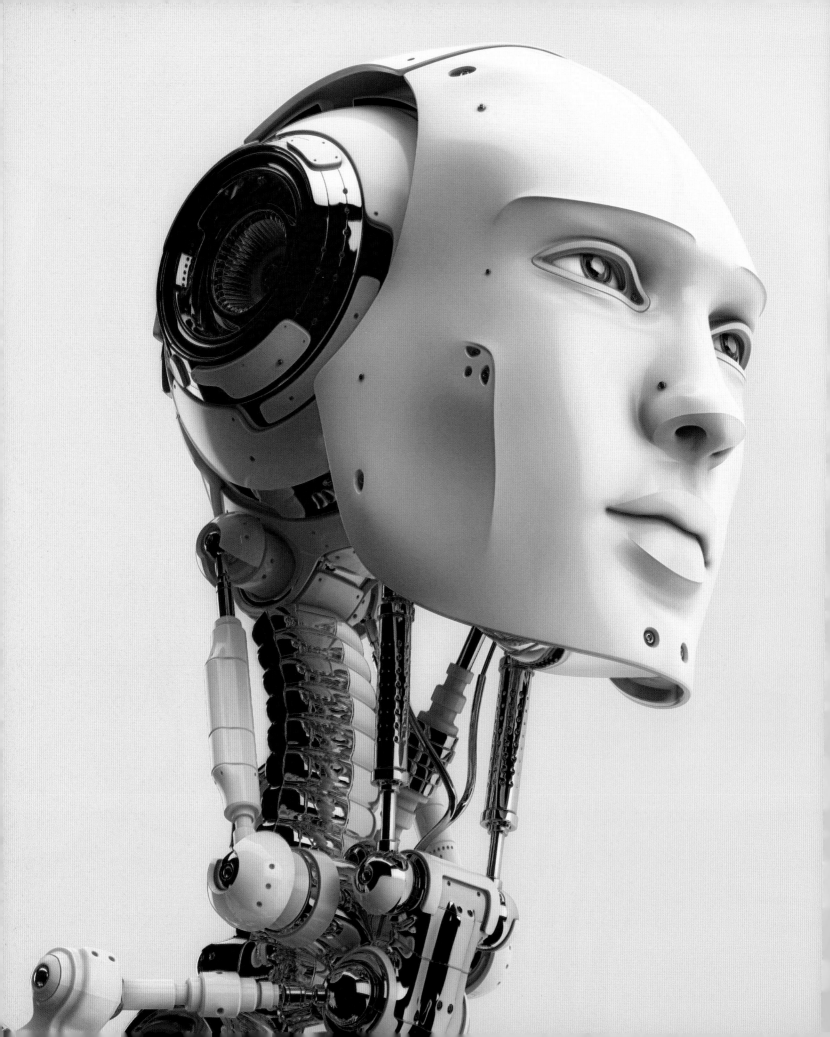

On the Horizon

▷ Quantum Computing

As we have pointed out, modern computers depend on transistors that are either on or off—a situation we have characterized as being either 1 or 0. In quantum mechanics (see page 72) systems can be characterized by the probabilities that they are 1 or 0—in effect, they can be thought of as being in an intermediate state between the two. It has been known for a long time that this introduces the possibility of developing computers that would operate much faster than transistor-based machines. At the moment, technical difficulties are slowing the development of quantum computers, but if they ever become a reality, they would be able to crack the modern encryption systems that underlie financial and government communications.

▷ The Turing Test

In 1950 Alan Turing proposed a method for testing the ability of a computer to "think." The test was this: A panel of (human) judges interact with an entity through a screen and keyboard, then try to guess whether that entity is a machine or a human being. If the entity is a computer and the judges think it is human, the machine will be said to have passed the Turing test. Since 1991 a competition known as the Loebner Prize has been held to see how well machines do in this situation. To date, no machine has passed, but there will surely be headlines when one does.

▷ Artificial Intelligence

The idea that we might be able to build computers that mimic human thought processes has been around for a long time. Many advances in this field depend on a process called machine learning, in which a computer examines data samples (voices on a telephone, for example) and, by a process of trial and error, learns to interpret them. You encounter the results of this process whenever you deal with recorded messages when interacting with a business on the telephone. As computers acquire more capability, there will be a steady stream of new applications like this. The next step will probably be artificial intelligence systems that will help you drive your car—they might warn you about dangerous situations, for example. ■

Will research on artificial intelligence produce humanoid robots? Many scientists are working on it.

NEW MATERIALS

Above: A Chinese gilded mask made mostly of bronze, an alloy of copper and tin. The discovery of bronze was a major innovation.

▷ 2 Million B.C.

Everything Is Made from Something

The Use of Materials from Ancient Times

Ever since the first *Homo habilis* chipped the edge off of a stone to make a crude tool two million years ago, humans have used different sorts of materials to deal with the world. At first, like *Homo habilis*, we used the materials that nature supplied. Our buildings were made of wood and stone (see page 238), our clothing from natural products like wool and cotton. As time went by, however, we began to make our own materials, materials better suited to our needs than those supplied freely by nature. The Romans found that they could use concrete to make "stones" in any shape they needed (see page 239), and metal workers found that they could produce alloys that had better properties than pure metals. Bronze (a mixture of copper and tin) replaced pure copper and, in the 19th century, mass-produced steel (see page 43) changed the very fabric of our cities. Plastics (see page 33) began to be used for all sorts of functions previously reserved for natural materials. We even began to refer to historical periods by the materials people living in those periods used—Stone Age, Bronze Age, Iron Age, and so on.

Today scientists and engineers produce new materials at a dizzying rate. The reason for this is that we now understand the atomic structure of matter and can use that knowledge in the laboratory. In what follows, we survey a small sample of the kinds of new materials that have become available in modern times. ☐

🔍 The earliest objects **made from glass are Egyptian beads** dating to about 3500 BC.

Our ability to produce new materials has been a constant source of improvement for the human race.

▷ 1500s B.C.

In Unity There Is Strength

Composite Materials

The essential point of a composite material is that it has two or more components, with the strength of each component compensating for the weakness of the other. Typically, the composite has one substance, called a matrix, that holds everything together and one or more other substances embedded in the matrix.

In the Old Testament, for example, the Hebrews were told to make bricks without straw—one of the events that led up to the Exodus. Bricks made with straw are a good example of a composite material. The clay in the brick supplies strength against compression but is weak against a sideways force (what engineers call shear). The straw,

> 🔍 The Boy Scouts have a **Composite Material** merit badge.

on the other hand, is strong against shear but weak against compression. The two materials together, then, are stronger than each individually. The same principle applies to modern reinforced concrete (see page 239), where steel-reinforcing rods take the place of straw, and the matrix is the cement that holds everything together. Plywood is another everyday composite material, with layers of wood arranged so that the grain of each layer is perpendicular to the layers above and below it.

Modern composite materials tend to be more sophisticated and are found in everything from golf clubs to spacecraft. The matrix in modern materials is typically a polymer—a long molecule, probably containing carbon and being similar to the molecules found in plastics. The strengthening material is often a fiber (carbon fibers are commonly used). This yields a composite material that is both light and strong, which explains its extensive use in aircraft construction. ☐

Above right: Plywood's strength comes from layering wood so that the grain of each layer is perpendicular to the contiguous layers.

▷ 1888

What Time Is It?

Liquid Crystals

Chances are you've looked at dozens of liquid crystal displays in the last 24 hours. They're used in digital wristwatches, control panel displays in cars or on ovens, and on ordinary alarm clocks, to name just a few of their many uses. They were first discovered accidentally by Austrian

> 🔍 **Liquid crystals** are an example of a scientific discovery that **seemed to be useless** for decades, until the advent of the LCD.

chemist Friedrich Reinitzer (1857–1927) in 1888. He noticed that a particular molecule related to cholesterol had a strange property—it seemed to have two melting points. The solid phase would melt at one temperature, producing a cloudy liquid, but at a higher temperature there would be another "melting" and the liquid would become clear. When examined under a microscope, the intermediate phase showed a clear, crystal-like structure, a quality that led to the name "liquid crystal."

Above: Modern iPhones are made of many composite materials, and the display often makes use of liquid crystals

Liquid crystals remained something of a scientific oddity for almost 80 years, although a few researchers did investigate their properties. It wasn't until 1962 that the first practical liquid crystal display (LCD) was built. This is its basic operating principle: The molecules in a liquid crystal are long—think of them as spaghetti straws. Normally the molecules are oriented randomly—think of a pile of straws just thrown on the ground. Apply an electric field to the system, however, and the molecules line up, a fact that means that they will transmit light only if it is polarized in the same direction as their alignment. An LCD is just a liquid crystal sandwiched between two polarizing sheets. If an electric field is applied so that the molecules line up with the polarization of the incoming light, that light will be transmitted, pass through the second polarizer, and produce a visible glow. Thus, by controlling the orientations of the molecules in different parts of a screen, we can create a visible pattern. Look at the next LCD you see—the segments in the display correspond to different areas of the liquid crystal material. ☐

▷ 1962

Let There Be Light
The Light-Emitting Diode

A light-emitting diode (LED) is a device made from two doped semiconductors (see page 57). When free electrons from one semiconductor wander into the other, they can fall into empty spaces in the atoms there, emitting radiation in the process. The first devices like this emitted only infrared radiation, but in 1962 the American electrical engineer Nick Holonyak (b 1928) built the first LED that emitted visible light (it was red).

In the years that followed, scientists in America and Japan experimented with different materials to produce different colors. By 1971 LEDs that gave off yellow, orange, and green light had been constructed, followed in 1993 by blue. LEDs were first introduced into the commercial market in 1995 and are now used in a wide variety of everyday situations. The next time you are at a stoplight, look at the signal closely. You will notice that the light comes from discrete segments rather than from a continuous luminosity. That's because the light is coming from a bank of LEDs. You'll see the same thing in the taillights of the car in front of you. ☐

Left: Close-up of an LED display. Light-emitting diodes are used in a wide variety of everyday applications.

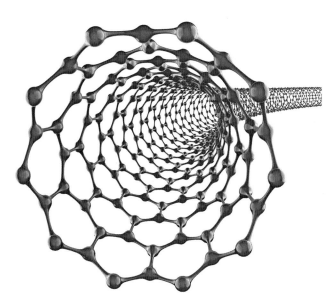

▷ **1985**

Carbon Can Be Weird
Buckyballs and Carbon Nanotubes

We are familiar with pure carbon in two forms—graphite (the "lead" in pencils) and diamond, with the differences between them having to do with the types of chemical bonds (see page 45) in the two materials. In 1985, three scientists at Rice University in Texas—Richard Smalley (1943–2005), Harold Kroto (b 1939), and Robert Curl (b 1933)—produced a third form of pure carbon composed of 60 carbon atoms arranged around the surface of a sphere. It looked something like a soccer ball and reminded the discoverers of a geodesic dome. The dome was invented by American inventor Buckminster Fuller (1895–1983), a fact that led to the new molecule being named buckminsterfullerene, or buckyball for short. The three received the Nobel Prize in 1996 (see page 45).

New versions of pure carbon structures were discovered quickly. Carbon nanotubes, for example, are cylinders whose walls are networks of carbon atoms. These nanotubes are very strong and can be made into strings several inches long. They are being developed as inserts in composite materials to make strong but lightweight parts for airplanes and spacecraft. The nanotube can also be used as a kind of capsule—think of a cylinder with half a buckyball capping each end. Such capsules are being developed as microscopic delivery systems for drugs in the human body. □

Above: Artist's conception of a carbon nanotube.

On the Horizon

▷ Organic Light-Emitting Diode

The latest advance in LED technology is the organic light-emitting diode (OLED), or organic LED. This is a device in which thin layers of organic material produce light rather than layers of semiconductor. Because of the properties of the organic material, display screens made from OLEDs can be incredibly thin—engineers talk of TV screens a quarter of an inch thick, for example. Because organic materials can be flexible, engineers also talk about TVs that can be rolled up when not in use, and even foldable cell phones.

▷ Nanotechnology

In traditional manufacturing, a product is made by starting with a block of material and removing the pieces you don't want. This is called subtractive manufacturing. There is an alternative process, however, in which you add only the atoms you want. This is called additive manufacturing and is an important part of the new field of nanotechnology.

One of the leading examples of this new sort of technology—one that is bursting onto the scene as you read this—is three-dimensional (3-D) printing. In this process, data are fed into a computer telling it where materials are supposed to be deposited, and then the computer controls a small injector that actually lays the atoms down. Shoes, cars, houses, and even human body parts have been made using this technique, and we can expect it to become more ubiquitous as the process is made faster, cheaper, and more efficient.■

OLED displays, such as these monitors at a consumer electronics show, hold the promise of incredibly thin flexible screens that could be rolled up or folded.

ENERGY

The kind of energy humans have used has changed as our technologies improved.

▷ **Prehistory–Present**

Energy to Burn
Historical Overview of Energy Use

The first sources of energy available to our ancestors were muscle power (either human or animal) and biomass (mainly wood) for heat. When Europeans settled North America, they found themselves at the edge of a huge forest, and so they used the most easily accessible fuel—wood—to heat their homes. When railroads were first built in North America, in fact, they ran their steam engines on wood.

As the supply of wood near cities began to be exhausted, people adopted two strategies that will sound familiar to modern consumers of energy. First, they developed new sources. For a while, for example, there was a thriving business in shipping boatloads of firewood from Maine to New York. Second, they found ways to use their energy source more efficiently. The invention of the Franklin stove, for example, allowed consumers to get much more useful heat from their increasingly expensive wood supply than they could from its predecessor, the open fireplace.

But it was the 1776 development of the modern steam engine by the Scottish engineer James Watt that really changed the world's use of energy, for it made available the solar energy that fell on Earth millions of years ago and was stored in coal. Over several decades in the early 19th century, the use of wood declined and the use of coal grew until coal was the primary source of America's energy. A similar process occurred in the early 20th century when petroleum began to replace coal for many uses.

There are several lessons we can take from this history. First, people will always use the cheapest and most accessible energy source available to them, and, second, to change from one energy source to another takes a long time—30 years is a good estimate. □

Above left: Coal remains a major energy source in many countries.

🔍 The use of wood in the early railroads gave rise to an unusual way of designating the amount of wood being sold to run the engines. **The "cord" was a stack of wood measuring 4 feet by 4 feet by 8 feet,** a unit still used.

Simply Shocking

Electric Energy

The problem with the steam engine is that if you want to use the power it generates you have to have the engine right there—in the basement of your factory or on your train. The invention of the electric generator by British scientist Michael Faraday (1791–1867) changed all that. It made it possible to generate heat—by burning coal, for example—in one place, convert that heat into electrical energy, and transmit the energy over a grid to be used in a distant place. You can scarcely imagine modern society without this device.

The basic operating principle of the electrical generator is this: If a magnetic field in the region of an electrical conductor is changed, a current will flow in the conductor. There is a source of energy—falling water, steam from a coal fire or nuclear reactor—that spins a wire loop between the poles of a magnet. From the point of view of someone standing on the loop the magnetic field is always changing, which means that current will always flow in the loop. Thus the original type of energy is converted into electric current. ▢

Above: An engraving of British scientist Michael Faraday, who invented the electric generator.

Below: A diagram of a battery-powered electric motor. In this motor, the magnet (shown in red) exerts a force on the loop of wire (shown in yellow), causing it to rotate.

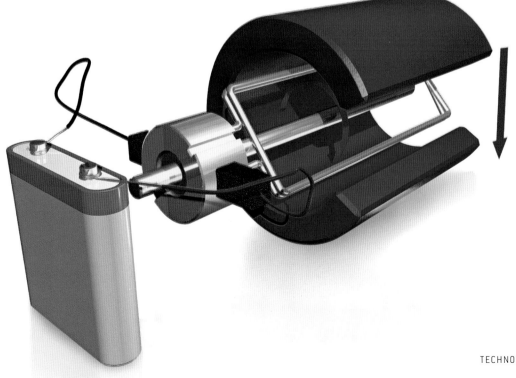

Turning on the Lights

The Electrification of America

Converting something like an electrical generator from a laboratory curiosity to a commercial reality is a long process. The first commercial electrical generating plant was located on Pearl Street in Manhattan and went into operation in 1882. It was built by a company headed by the renowned American inventor Thomas Edison (1847–1931) and used direct current (DC)—that is, electrical current that flowed in the same direction all the time.

An alternative system that used current whose direction switched back and forth—it's called alternating current (AC)—was championed by the Croatian-born American engineer and inventor Nikola Tesla (1856–1943), an eccentric genius who invented a wide range of electrical devices. The competition between AC and DC systems led to one of the most bizarre episodes in the

> 🔍 One public relations ploy used by **advocates of DC** was to point out that **the electric chair ran on AC.**

history of technology, often referred to as the War of the Currents. The basic fact behind the "war" was this: it is easy to step alternating current up to high voltages, which means that it is easier to transmit AC power over long distances. Thus AC was a natural fit for a system with large, centralized generators distributing power over an extensive grid. When Tesla teamed up with American inventor and entrepreneur George Westinghouse (1846–1914), AC systems quickly took over the market.

DC proponents fought back by arguing that the high voltages in AC systems constituted a major health hazard to the public. They publicized cases in which people were killed by falling power lines, for example. By the start of the 20th century, however, the war was over, and AC had won. The Rural Electrification Act of 1936 completed the process of bringing electricity to all regions of the United States. □

Left: A display of electric lights at a show in Chicago in 1911. This was one of the first demonstrations of electric lighting in the United States.

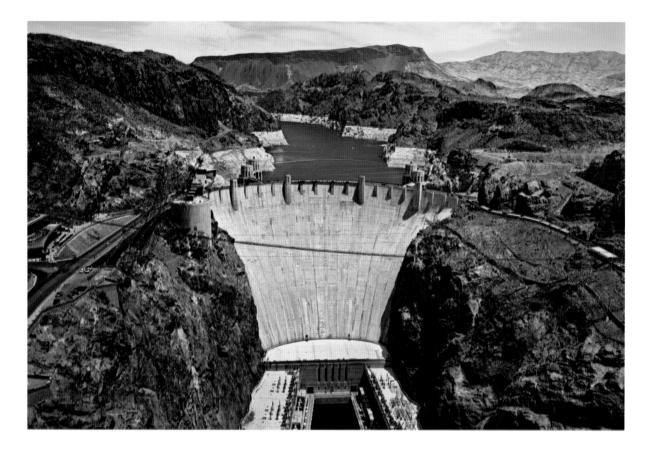

▷ 2016

Where Does It Come From, Where Does It Go?

The American Energy Budget

There are two fundamental questions we can ask about energy usage in the United States: (1) Where does our energy come from, and (2) How is it used?

As the pie chart shows, by far the greatest portion of our energy—over 88 percent—comes from what are called fossil fuels—coal, oil, and natural gas. On any timescale meaningful to human beings, these fuels are not renewable. Once they are used, in other words, they are gone. In addition, when they are burned they produce carbon dioxide as a waste product, a gas whose abundance in the atmosphere we are trying to control. Nevertheless, there are enough reserves of fossil fuels in the world to run modern industrial societies for many centuries.

Nuclear energy is used to produce electricity and has supplied roughly 20 percent of the nation's electricity for decades. It does not produce carbon dioxide, but it does produce radioactive waste that must be stored in such a way that it will not leak into the environment.

The main contribution to the "other" category of energy sources is hydroelectric power, in which the energy of falling water is used to run an electrical generator. The poster child for this kind of power is Boulder Dam (officially named Hoover Dam) on the Colorado River between Nevada and Arizona. Finished in 1936, it generates as much electricity as two large nuclear reactors or coal-fired plants. Hydroelectric power is clean, renewable, and cheap, but by now all the places in the country that could accommodate a dam have been exploited, so this source of energy cannot be expanded easily.

Biofuels and wood make up most of the rest of the "other" energy sources. They are renewable and do not make a net contribution of carbon dioxide to the atmosphere. Although burning them does produce the gas, while the plants and trees are growing they pull carbon dioxide from the atmosphere.

As far as the second question is concerned, we use our energy in roughly equal proportions for residential buildings, commercial buildings, transportation, and manufacturing. ☐

Above: Hoover Dam continues to supply electricity in the southwest, though chronic drought has diminished its hydroelectric capacity.

21st Century

The New Players
Wind and Solar Energy

As we have seen, the history of energy use in the United States is one that involves constant changes in energy sources—wood to coal, coal to oil. We are now at the beginning phase of yet another transition, this time to renewable sources of energy that do not add carbon dioxide to the atmosphere. The most prominent of these new sources are wind and solar energy.

The United States actually has huge potential supplies of both of these resources. The desert regions of the American Southwest are ideal locations for large arrays of solar collectors, and the high plains regions possess steady winds. In addition, there are offshore areas—Cape Cod and the eastern portion of Lake Erie are examples—that are being evaluated as sources of wind energy. Calculations indicate that, in principle, either of these potential resource bases could supply all of the nation's energy.

There are several obstacles to the transition to wind and solar, some technical and some economic. The most important of these is the sporadic nature of both resources—the sun doesn't always shine and the wind doesn't always blow. So long as neither kind of energy constitutes a significant part of the nation's supply, this isn't a problem. The output from wind turbines and solar collectors can just be fed into the power grid without disruption, and on cloudy or windless days their absence can be dealt with by generating more power by other means. When we get farther into the transition, however, we will have to find ways to store the energy we get from wind and solar so that it is available when it is needed. This will, of course, add to the cost.

All new sources of energy will be expensive when they are introduced, but the price drops as the technology improves. Right now, for example, the cost of generating energy from land-based wind turbines is comparable to the cost of energy generated by other means. The extra cost of building offshore facilities still makes energy from those sources more expensive.

Solar energy has always been expensive, but its cost is dropping rapidly—from ten times the cost of conventional power a few decades ago to less than twice that cost now. Engineers confidently predict that the cost will continue to drop in the future.

Finally, we note, as already pointed out, that when wind and solar power begin to supply a significant portion of the nation's energy, the cost of storage will have to be factored in to these economic considerations. □

Below: Arrays of solar panels like this one are becoming a common sight in America.

On the Horizon

▷ Energy Storage

One of the greatest technological hurdles to be over-come in the transition to renewable energy is the prob-lem of how to store energy. One method, already being exploited, is to pump water to a reservoir on top of a hill when the sun is shining, then let it run back down to produce electricity at night. Another technique is to pump air into a cave during the day, then use the compressed air to run generators at night. The most likely storage device, still being developed, is called a capacitor. Small versions of this device are routinely used in electrical circuits, but to use them in our energy system would require that we develop much larger versions. Capacitors store electrical charge, then deliver electrical current directly when they are discharged. They would be ideal storage systems.

▷ Green Power

Renewable energy sources are the subject of a great deal of research and commercial application, and we can expect to see all sorts of advances as we get farther into the transition. The cost of solar panels will drop as new materials are developed. Scientists are already talking about paint-on solar cells that would serve as the outer coating of houses or even as part of our clothing. Zoning battles will erupt over the placement of wind turbines—we have already seen resi-dents of Cape Cod objecting to the building of offshore wind towers. The shift to green energy, like all energy transitions, will not be smooth, but it will happen.

▷ Batteries

A significant fraction of American energy use is in the transportation sector, which is now dominated by the internal combustion engine (see page 216). Hybrid and all-electric cars represent the next step in ground transportation, but at the moment they are limited by what is called the range problem—the fact that the best batteries available often have to be recharged after less than 100 miles of driving. Using lithium-ion bat-teries, vehicles produced by Tesla Motors achieved ranges in excess of 200 miles. These vehicles are expensive, but they point the way to the future. Expect to see continuous improvement in battery technology as all-electric cars become more common. ■

A bank of capacitors like these might be used to store energy.

AGRICULTURE

▷ 10,000 B.C.

Nature Isn't Enough

The Invention of Agriculture

Around 12,000 years ago some people in the Middle East—probably women—realized that food could be grown, and that they didn't have to depend on hunting and gathering for nourishment. This was the beginning of agriculture. Anthropologists tell us that this technology developed independently in many parts of the world—perhaps as often as a dozen times. It wasn't a single "lightbulb" event, but the gradual accumulation of skills over time. People probably began by tending wild patches of grains, then moved on to planting and cultivation.

It's hard to overestimate the importance of the agricultural revolution. The increase in food supplies over what was available to hunter-gatherers made possible an increase in population, the founding of cities, and the division of labor—all of the hallmarks of modern society. Wheat, barley, and lentils were the first plants cultivated in the Middle East, with rice being cultivated in Asia. Although dogs became associated with humans during our hunter-gatherer days, cattle, goats, sheep, and pigs were quickly domesticated by farmers. In 4000 B.C. the horse was domesticated on the steppes of central Asia. A thousand years later pastoral societies appeared around the world, following herds of animals for their livelihood. Depending on the location, those animals might have been cattle or even yaks and reindeer. About the same time, one of the most important crops the world has even known—the potato—appeared in the Andes.

Below: A mural showing a grain harvest in ancient Egypt.

Opposite: Today's cow is the result of millennia of selective breeding.

Human beings invented agriculture 12,000 years ago and have been improving it ever since.

The movement of agriculture to Europe about 2,500 years after it appeared in the Middle East has been the subject of a long-standing scholarly debate. The two sides are those who think it came about because the ideas associated with agriculture spread (cultural diffusion) and those who think migrants brought the new skills with them (population diffusion). Modern DNA analysis seems to favor the latter view—that agriculture came to Europe because of the migration of farming peoples. □

🔍 The invention of **agriculture made it possible** for people to begin building cities and **developing specialized skills not related to producing food.**

We Can Do It Better

The Rise of Agricultural Technology

As soon as people developed agriculture, they began to find ways of improving it. The first farming implements were crude—a digging stick for planting seeds, a hoe for cultivating. Soon after the agricultural revolution we see farming techniques developed that persist to the present day. The earliest farmers, for example, probably stayed in one place until the soil was depleted, at which point they moved on. The use of crop rotation, irrigation, and fertilizers were all techniques aimed at maintaining the productivity of farmland. Perhaps the most important improvement in agricultural techniques was the development of the plow, a device that could turn over the soil and bring fresh nutrients to the surface. Primitive plows—basically an upright stick attached to a frame that could be dragged—appeared around 2000 B.C. The major advance, however, was the moldboard plow, a heavy, wheeled plow ideally suited to the soils of northern Europe. It may have appeared as early as A.D. 300 in Roman Britain, and it was in widespread use by A.D. 650. Agricultural technology improved slowly through the Middle Ages, but it wasn't until the 19th century that a fundamental change in farm technology occurred.

> 🔍 Today humans **make more fixed nitrogen** than is produced by nature.

The basic change was that people began inventing ways to have machines do the farm work that had been done by human beings from time immemorial. Nothing symbolizes this transition better than the McCormick reaper, a horse-drawn machine that harvested grains. Demonstrated in 1831 by the American inventor Cyrus McCormick (1809–1884), it cut the grain and threw it onto a platform. Later improvements led to the modern combine, which not only cuts the grain stalks, but threshes the grain kernels as well. In 1902 McCormick's son participated in founding International Harvester, a company that dominated the field of agricultural machinery for almost a century. The horse-drawn machines were replaced by machines with internal combustion engines, and in 1924

the Farmall—the first machine we would recognize as a modern tractor—was introduced.

While these changes were going on in farm machinery, other important changes were going on in the use of fertilizers. Plants need nitrogen to grow, and historically this had been supplied by adding manure, ash, and vegetable wastes (compost) to soils, as well as by growing legumes in crop rotation schemes. There is plenty of nitrogen in the air in the form of N2—two nitrogen molecules bound together. To be useful, however, the nitrogen atoms have to be separated, a process called fixing. (Legumes harbor bacteria that fix nitrogen, which is what makes them so valuable in crop rotation schemes.) Typically, fixed nitrogen is found in a chemical compound like ammonia (NH3). By the latter part of the 19th century the demand for fixed nitrogen fertilizer was recognized as a major problem worldwide.

In 1909 the German chemist Fritz Haber (1868–1934) demonstrated a process by which atmospheric nitrogen could be used to produce ammonia, and in 1910 the German chemist Carl Bosch (1874–1940) showed how Haber's process could be scaled up to industrial levels. Although the first use of this technology was to provide explosives for Germany in World War I, today it is used to produce hundreds of millions of tons of fertilizer annually. Without it, it has been estimated that we would need to have almost four times as much land under cultivation to feed the world population as we do now. □

Above: The dish shown contains a mixture of manufactured fertilizers and agricultural chemicals.

Left: A mass soybean harvest is a symbol of modern agriculture.

▷ 1492

It Went Both Ways

The Columbian Exchange

One of the most important events in the history of agriculture was what has come to be called the Columbian Exchange—the two-way flow of plants and animals that followed the entry of Europeans into the Americas. Before this time, agriculture had developed separately in the Old and New Worlds. A complete list of everything involved in the two-way flow would be much too long for this book, but we can look at a few important items.

> 🔍 In 1820 **a man ate a tomato outside a New Jersey courthouse— a ceremony still reenacted.**

West to East

The main crops that were introduced to Europe were corn (often called maize), potatoes, and tomatoes. The potato eventually replaced turnips as a staple for Europe's poor, to the point that, when a disease ("potato blight") attacked the Irish crop in 1845–1852, it caused a major famine, with a million people dying and another million emigrating.

The tomato has a very interesting history. When it first came to Europe it was thought to be poisonous, probably because it is related to nightshade, and was grown mainly as an ornamental plant. It wasn't until the 19th century that it was considered fit to eat.

East to West

The main crops that came the other way were oranges, bananas, and coffee. By far the most interesting import, however, was the horse. Horses had actually been present in North America at one time, but had gone extinct long before humans arrived. Once they were reintroduced by Europeans, however, they completely changed the social structure of Native Americans. The animals were used as beasts of burden and, more important, for transportation. The popular image of an Indian on horseback, then, a fairly recent historical development. ☐

Left: "The Potato Eaters," a painting by Vincent Van Gogh, illustrates the importance of the potato in the European diet. The potato came to Europe from South America as part of the great exchange that followed the voyages of European explorers.

▷ Late 1960s

Food for Everyone

The Green Revolution

During the late 1960s, people worried that the world's burgeoning population would soon outstrip the world's food supply. In his 1968 book *The Population Bomb*, for example, Stanford University scientist Paul Ehrlich stated that hundreds of millions of people would starve in the 1970s, despite any efforts that governments might make to avoid famine. That this predicted disaster, and other Doomsday scenarios put forward at the time, never happened was the result of decades of patient research leading to what has come to be called the Green Revolution.

American agricultural scientist Norman Borlaug (1914–2009) is the man generally associated with this revolution. Working in Mexico, he used traditional cross-breeding techniques to develop strains of wheat that were more productive than those in widespread use. For example, one problem with ordinary wheat is that

the plants tend to have tall stems. These plants not only shade their neighbors but are susceptible to falling over, thereby making it impossible to harvest the grain. Borlaug developed dwarf plants to overcome these difficulties, a development that, together with the introduction of modern fertilizers and pesticides, greatly increased grain production. A couple of statistics will make his point. When India introduced Borlaug's techniques, cereal production increased from 10 million tons in the 1960s to 73 million tons in 2000. By 1976, just six years after Ehrlich's prediction of massive famine, India became self-sufficient in cereal production. Green Revolution technology was applied to other crops, most notably rice. It has been estimated that Borlaug's techniques have saved a billion lives over the years. He was awarded the Nobel Prize in 1970.

There are, of course, downsides to the Green Revolution. It requires fertilizers and pesticides, and tends to produce what biologists call monocultures—large areas in which only one kind of crop is grown. This makes the system vulnerable to diseases like the potato blight that wiped out the potato crop in Ireland in the 19th century. It is expected that modern techniques in molecular biology will be able to deal with this threat. □

Above: Norman Borlaug, the father of the Green Revolution. The use of selective breeding led to vastly increased food production and the ability to feed the world's growing population.

Now What?

Are GMOs a New Green Revolution?

The crops that gave rise to the Green Revolution were produced by traditional cross-breeding techniques. This means that the DNA of two plants was scrambled, essentially at random, to produce offspring with a new genome. This technique has been used from time immemorial to improve agricultural crops and livestock.

Genetic engineering techniques (see page 117) offer a new way of improving crops. In essence, a single useful gene is inserted into the DNA of a plant, and that gene is transmitted, in the usual way, to future generations. In 1987 a gene from the bacterium *Bacillus thuringiensis* (Bt) was

> 🔍 The pattern of colors in kernels of corn helped scientists **unravel the behavior of genes** in the plant's DNA.

introduced into tobacco plants. This gene produces an insecticide that kills any insect that eats the plant (it does not affect humans). The idea is that plants with this gene do not require spraying with insecticides, and hence avoid the problem of insecticides entering the environment accidentally. The Bt gene has been added to the DNA of many food crops.

Another genetic engineering technique in agriculture is the production of plants that are resistant to specific herbicides. The idea is that fields can be sprayed with those herbicides to kill weeds without affecting the crops being grown. This means that the process of plowing fields to eliminate weeds—a process known as fallowing—can be avoided, thus reducing soil erosion.

In the United States today, over 60 kinds of genetically modified foods have been approved for consumption by the Food and Drug Administration. The majority

Above right: Different patterns in the coloring of corn kernels distinguish genetic differences in the plants. On the left is an ear of ordinary hybrid corn; on the right an ear of genetically modified corn. Genetic modification can, but does not have to, result in different coloration.

of plantings of many major crops—soy, corn, and cotton, for example—are genetically engineered. The use of genetically engineered crops has spread around the world, particularly in developing countries, where the increased production and lower cost of growing GMOs are extremely important.

One final point: in a technical sense, genetic modification has been going on since the beginning of agriculture 12,000 years ago. The difference is that with genetic engineering techniques we have a lot more control over the changes being made in crop DNA. □

On the Horizon

▷ The GMO Pipeline

Once the technique involved in genetic modification has been mastered, a wide variety of options become available. Some of the things that scientists are thinking of include producing bananas which carry genes that can counter the effects of cholera, producing pigs whose meat includes omega-3 fatty acids, and producing rice that contains vitamin A and other supplements. In addition, familiar crops will be modified so that they can grow in changed climate conditions. They will, for example, be able to handle higher temperatures and drought. As more and more of the function of various genomes becomes known, there will be more advances like these.

▷ GMO Regulation

As often happens with new technologies, the legal system is having difficulty keeping up with the introduction of GMOs. Furthermore, the kinds of legal and regulatory responses to GMOs vary from place to place. In most of the world, the use of genetically modified crops is unregulated. In the United States, for example, the main regulatory question at the moment is whether genetically modified foods should be labeled. In Europe, on the other hand, genetically modified foods, with few exceptions, are banned pending further research on health effects.

▷ CRISPR

A new tool has recently been added to the geneticist's repertoire. Called CRISPR (an acronym formed from its technical name Clustered Regularly Interspaced Short Palindromic Repeats), it allows scientists to edit genomes. They can, for example, remove genes that cause fruit to spoil quickly once it is picked. Because it does not involve transferring genes from one species to another, many of the objections that have been raised to GMO do not apply to the new technique. ■

Genetically modified plants are tested in a laboratory in Berlin.

COMMUNICATION

▷ 3200 B.C., A.D. 1439

In the Beginning Was the Word

Writing

In the beginning human communication had to be face to face, but with the invention of writing by the Sumerians in about 3200 B.C., that changed. Writing provided a way of communicating not only over distance but through time. Systems developed independently in Egypt, China, and Mesoamerica all fulfilled this purpose. For millennia, writings could be passed on only through the tedious process of copying texts by hand. The process of copying books by hand was used throughout the Middle Ages in Europe. It not only made books rare, but introduced errors as mistakes by one scribe were copied by his successors. In 1439, however, Johannes Gutenberg (ca 1390–1468) invented movable type printing and opened a new era of mass communication. □

Above: Cuneiform writing on a Sumerian wall—the oldest form of writing known.

To communicate is human; the urge to encode, transmit, and preserve those communications equally so.

▷ 1439 A.D.

Font of Knowledge

Movable Type Printing Press

For most of recorded history, people passed on their knowledge by writing on materials like clay tablets, papyrus, or parchment (treated sheep hide). The transition to the modern world depended on the invention of movable type. This kind of type is a block of material with a raised symbol on its surface. It works by spreading ink on the raised symbol and then pressing a piece of paper to it. The symbol then appears on the paper—a process we call printing.

The printing process was first developed in China, in 1040 A.D. and, a few hundred years later, in Korea. Neither of these countries uses an alphabet, however, so producing a book was a difficult and tedious process—there are over 1,000 characters in Chinese, for example, compared to 26 letters in English. Thus, it wasn't until German inventor Johannes Gutenberg developed his printing press that the full impact of the technology could be seen.

Gutenberg made his movable type by casting a mixture of lead, tin, and antimony—a formula that would endure for over 500 years. The point is that once a block of type has been assembled, it can be used to produce many copies of the original text. Books, for the first time, became common and accessible to the literate public. One of the most interesting results of the spread of printing was the need to produce new designs for letters in different languages—we call these fonts. Thus, Gutenberg is responsible for all those fonts on your computer. □

🔍 There are **over 600 fonts available** in Microsoft Word and thousands more can be installed.

Above: An old wooden printing press of the type developed by Gutenberg. It's hard to imagine, but the advent of movable type ushered in a communications revolution much bigger than computers.

Top: A young woman operates a telegraph during World War I.

Above: Samuel Morse invented the telegraph.

▷ 1837

Universal Code
Telegraph

In its most primitive form, telegraphy has been around for a long time in the form of signal fires, smoke signals, and large mirrors. The first system we would recognize as a telegraph, however, was the so-called optical telescope system built in France at the end of the 18th century. The system consisted of a series of towers about 20 miles apart, each with a large semaphore-type structure on its roof. An operator in one tower would use a telescope to determine the orientation of the arms on the upstream tower and duplicate them in his own system. This system was capable of sending about two words per minute and

many such systems were built in the early 19th century. The first system in the United States connected Boston and Martha's Vineyard, and Telegraph Hill in San Francisco got its name from the optical telegraph that was used to announce the arrival of ships.

In 1837 Samuel Morse (1791–1872) demonstrated the first electrical telegraph in Morristown, New Jersey. This was a system that sent electrical (rather than optical) signals between distant locations. Using a code, known as the Morse code, that converted different sequences of long and short electrical pulses into letters of the alphabet and numbers, messages could be sent quickly and cheaply. The original system translated the

Above: An old telegraph machine. The operator presses the lever on the left to send a signal.

incoming message to indentations on a paper tape, but later the signals were converted into the familiar audible dots and dashes.

The electric telegraph had obvious advantages over its optical predecessor—it didn't require intermediate stations, was faster, and, probably most important, it could operate at night and in bad weather. By 1861 a telegraph connection was established between the east and west coasts of the United States, eliminating the colorful Pony Express. In 1866 the first transatlantic cable was laid (after several failed attempts), and the world began to be connected for the first time.

But all technologies are replaced sooner or later. Driven by developments we'll discuss in a moment, in 2006 Western Union discontinued telegraph service, and the electrical telegraph joined its optical counterpart in the museum of vanished artifacts. ☐

🔍 The first message Samuel Morse sent was **"What hath God wrought?"**

Talking Wires

Telephone

The question of who invented the telephone is one of those issues that is clouded by a series of claims, counterclaims, and lawsuits. What we can say, however, is that the awarding of the telephone patent to Alexander Graham Bell (1847–1922) opened the way to our modern communication system. Bell first demonstrated a telephone in his Boston laboratory in 1876. The first words spoken were "Mr. Watson, come here. I want to see you." Since Thomas A. Watson (1854–1934), Bell's assistant, was in the next room, it was an easy request with which to comply.

There were two problems associated with the early telephones: finding an efficient way to convert the varying air pressure of sound waves to an electrical signal that could be sent out over wires, and finding an efficient way to connect large numbers of telephones to each other. In 1876 Thomas Edison solved the first of these with the invention of the carbon microphone. Basically, the device consisted of carbon granules packed behind a metal plate. As the plate moved in response to sound waves, the electrical resistance of the carbon changed, and this change was used to produce the electrical signal. Edison's microphone remained the industry standard until the 1980s.

The connection problem was solved by the invention of the telephone exchange. Basically, wires from all the telephones in a system are brought to a central location. Originally, an operator (usually a woman) would then manually plug a wire into two sockets, one from the caller, one from the destination, thereby establishing contact. The first such exchange was constructed in New Haven, Connecticut, in 1879. Today, of course, the connections are made electronically. In any case, the technology obviously worked since there were over three million telephone subscribers in the United States by 1904.

You wouldn't recognize one of the first mobile phone systems introduced in 1946—it weighed 80 pounds and had to be carried in a car. It wasn't until 1973 that the first modern mobile phones were introduced. They worked by sending microwave signals to towers located in hexagonal grids, with the towers sending the message on to the intended recipient. The grids were called cells, hence the term "cell phone." ☐

Left: As telephone systems developed, operators, usually women such as this worker in the late 1940s, had to manipulate wire to produce a connection. Today, this is all done electronically.

▷ 1899

The Wireless Arrives

Radio

The existence of radio waves was predicted by the men who developed the theories of electricity and magnetism. Unlike other kinds of electromagnetic radiation (such as x-rays) radio waves can travel long distances through the atmosphere, and hence are ideal tools for communication.

In 1888, the German scientist Heinrich Hertz (1857–1894) detected radio waves, and in 1899 the Italian scientist Guglielmo Marconi (1874–1937) was able to send and receive the first radio transmission—he called it wireless telegraphy. Both men received a Nobel Prize for their pioneering work.

Commercialization followed quickly. In 1920 a station in Detroit aired the first news broadcast, and the first sporting event—a football game between West Virginia and Pittsburgh—was broadcast the next year. Radios quickly became the focus of family living rooms across America, and President Franklin Roosevelt's (1882–1945) "Fireside Chats" marked the entry of radio into the political arena. In 1937 the scope of commercial radio was expanded by the introduction of frequency modulation (FM) broadcasts.

More changes followed. In 1954 the transistor radio was introduced, greatly expanding the radio listenership, and in 1963 the first Telstar satellite, the world's first communication satellite, was launched. In less than a century, then, radio went from being a theoretical possibility to an omnipresent backdrop to modern life, bringing us news, music, sports, and commentary. □

Above: The radio became a major mode of communication in the 1930s, as illustrated by this farm family in Michigan enjoying a broadcast.

▷ 1927

The Box That Roared
Television

As was the case with the telephone, there are many who can claim to have built the first television. The first to scan a picture electronically, convert the scan to radio waves, and reassemble a picture at a remote location was the largely self-taught American inventor Philo Farnsworth (1906–1971) in San Francisco in 1927.

If you imagine a TV screen broken up into a square grid, then each square is called a picture element, or pixel. This is the key concept of a TV display. In the original black and white TV sets, the back of the screen was coated with a material that would emit light if it was hit by an electron beam—the stronger the beam, the more light emitted. When the electron beam scanned across the screen it produced a series of dots that the eye integrated into a picture. Color TV works the same way, except that there are three primary colors in each pixel, and mixing them produces the colors we see. Modern flat screen TVs replace the electron beam with liquid crystals or light-emitting diodes to produce the same effect.

The beginning of commercial television was spearheaded by RCA, the nation's largest broadcaster. In 1939 the company broadcast the opening ceremonies for the World's Fair in New York. The first TV sets offered for sale after that had screens that measured 5 × 12 *inches*!

Improvements followed rapidly. In 1951 color TV sets went on sale, and in 1955 the first wireless remote control—the enabling technology for the couch potato—was sold. By the 1990s, fully 98 percent of American households had TV sets, and, for better or worse, the average American watched about 5 hours of television a day. ☐

Above: The progression of TV sets from black and white to color. The first commercially available color TV sets went on sale in 1954.

🔍 The first TV image **Philo Farnsworth** sent was a straight line, but he later changed it to a dollar sign ($) when his investors **asked when they would see some dollars.**

Never Getting Lost

GPS

The Global Positioning System (GPS) is not, strictly speaking, a means whereby people communicate with each other, but it is built into so many communication systems that it is worth mentioning here. Like many technological advances, the GPS started as a military venture. In 1959 the navy launched a fleet of six satellites (later expanded to ten) to help submarines find their location. This so-called NAV-STAR system measured the distance from several orbiting satellites to allow submariners to determine their position, but because of the small number of satellites, the boats often had to wait in vulnerable situations on the surface for hours to complete the measurement.

With the downing of an off-course Korean airplane that had wandered into Soviet air space in 1983, the need for accurate positioning information for civilian aircraft became important. President Ronald Reagan (1911–2004) ordered that the military satellite system be made generally available, and the modern GPS era was born.

> 🔍 The first car to have **a GPS system was the Toyota Soarer** in 1991.

Here's how the system works: The modern GPS is a network of 34 satellites, of which 24 are always operational, in orbits 20,000 km (12,000 miles) above Earth. On each of these satellites is an atomic clock. In order to find its position on Earth, a GPS receiver reads the time from several satellites (typically four) and combines this with knowledge of each satellite's position to determine the location of the receiver. Today even a cheap handheld receiver can locate its position to within 10 to 20 feet, and more sophisticated receivers can do even better. This level of accuracy requires that the time on the clocks in the satellites must be known to a level of accuracy of around 20 nanoseconds, which means that these systems also serve as test beds for the theory of relativity.

Starting in the late 1990s, the advance of miniaturization led to the availability of GPS receivers that could be installed in cell phones and cars, a trend that is expected to continue. ☐

Left: GPS pinpoints your location by measuring the distance from you to several satellites orbiting the Earth.

....

▷ 1965

Hitting Send

E-mail

Few technologies have been as widely adopted as e-mail, which we can define as the sending of messages in an electronic format. Modern e-mail systems started in 1965 at the Massachusetts Institute of Technology, where people using the same mainframe computer could leave each other messages—a process that one author compared to leaving a note on someone's desk. By 1972 systems began to appear that allowed individuals to communicate from one computer to another. From that point on, a rapid evolution took place so that now people routinely send and receive electronic messages on their cell phones as well as their computers. ☐

🔍 **The first e-mail message,** sent in 1971, was **QWERTYUIOP** (look at your computer keyboard).

Right: Artist's conception of the e-mail universe. In broad use by 1972, e-mail became the first of many electronic communication systems available to us today.

▷ 1977

Bundle of Power

Fiber Optics

The idea behind modern optical fiber communication systems was well known to scientists in the 19th century. The easiest way to understand the idea is to think of the last time you saw a friend standing in a swimming pool. It appeared to you that your friend's legs were shorter than you knew them to be. The reason is that light rays are bent when they pass from a dense medium (like water) to a less dense medium (like air)—a phenomenon known as refraction.

If you imagine a light ray in the water approaching the water–air interface at a smaller and smaller angle, you reach a point where the refracted ray in the air is moving parallel to the water. If the angle is smaller than that critical angle, the light beam won't enter the air at all, but will be reflected at the surface and go back into the water. This phenomenon, known as total internal reflection, is what makes fiber optics work.

Imagine a light entering one end of a thin glass fiber. In general, the beam will be tilted with respect to the axis of the fiber, so that eventually the beam will come to the

outer edge of the fiber. If its angle of approach is shallow enough, the beam will be reflected back into the glass. In fact, the beam will just bounce its way down the fiber until it emerges at the other end. This, in essence, is how all fiber optic systems work.

The first advance in fiber optics occurred in 1930, when a medical student in Munich used a bunch of optical fibers tied together to transmit an image (the filament of a lightbulb). But the most important application of fiber optics had to wait for the development of the laser and improved methods of producing pure glass fibers. With these developments, the major use of fiber optics—in communication systems—opened up.

The point is that, just as a telephone converts sound waves into electrical impulses that can be sent out over copper wires, a fiber optic system converts them into light waves that can be sent over a fiber. And because light has a very short wavelength, fiber optic systems can transmit information much more efficiently than copper wires.

The first fiber optic transmission of this type took place in Long Beach, California, in 1977, and in that same year fiber optic systems were installed to link major telephone exchanges in Chicago. Other advances followed quickly. In 1989 the first undersea fiber optic cable was laid to the Isle of Wight in England, and in 1990 the first transatlantic fiber optic system came into operation. Today, of course, the entire world is tied together by fiber optics. □

Above: Light can be trapped and transmitted in fiber optic threads like these.

A World of Friends

Social Media

There has seldom been a development so profound—and so completely unexpected—as the emergence of social media from the coming together of the Internet and the smart phone. The latter, of course, was made possible by the miniaturization implicit in Moore's law (see page 62), so that each of us can now carry a sophisticated computer around in our pocket or purse, and the existence of the Internet allows us to connect all those miniature computers together.

Like many technological advances, the concept of an integrated network of computers began as a military exercise—in essence, experiments in the 1960s with command and control systems. The first major move in the civilian sector occurred with the appearance of bulletin boards in the 1970s and 1980s. This was a time, remember, when computers were still relatively rare and difficult to operate.

The bulletin boards allowed people with similar interests to communicate with each other through text messages and primitive e-mail systems, using phone lines to transmit messages. A social networking system similar to today's was created in 1995, when Classmates.com was created so people could contact old schoolmates and have virtual class reunions.

The most important step toward our modern system occurred at Harvard University, and the system went public in 2006. Today Facebook has over a billion users worldwide and includes many platforms that are intricately interwoven with modern life; it includes everything from recipe exchanges to Islamic State recruiting. ☐

Below: A student interacting with friends on social media— a common sight. Accounts at the ten largest social networking sites tally to almost 4 billion—with Facebook as the largest single company at almost 1.4 billion.

⊕ Social scientists argue whether virtual **interactions through social media** are as valuable as **face-to-face** meetings.

On the Horizon

▷ Augmented Reality

Walk down a street and look at a restaurant. Immediately the restaurant's menu pops up on the glasses you are wearing. Ask to find the nearest gas station or pizza parlor and a map pops up on those same goggles. These are examples of "augmented reality," which is basically the next step in smart phone technology. The idea is that it makes information already available on the Internet accessible in an easily used format. It is also a step on the way to the development of virtual reality systems.

▷ Virtual Reality

We interact with the world through our senses, and what we normally mean by "reality" is the messages those senses bring to us. But do those messages have to correspond to what is actually out there? That is the deep question posed by the current push to provide communication systems that supply a "virtual" reality.

Take visual reality as an example. What you see when you open your eyes is a complex swirl of shapes and colors, but as we saw with TV, it can also be thought of as a collection of pixels. If you substitute a pair of goggles for your unaided eye, you can imagine a computer system that will produce images by manipulating pixels on those goggles. Prototype systems like this already exist and are being marketed to first users, but mass-market availability cannot be far away. In fact, high-quality virtual reality goggles are expected to cost $300 or less by 2020.

An idea to ponder: We already have systems capable of reproducing sounds that the human ear cannot differentiate from the original. We have virtual reality gloves that allow us to feel things that aren't really there, and high-definition TV comes close to blurring the distinction between the image and reality. How far away are we from systems that can produce sensations indistinguishable from reality? If we enter these virtual worlds, will we ever come out? ■

A graphic designer uses a virtual reality headset. With this sort of equipment, the designer can visualize what the object being designed will look like from different angles and, in some cases, what it would be like to be inside it.

ABOUT THE CONTRIBUTORS

James Trefil, Clarence J. Robinson Professor of Physics at George Mason University, is internationally recognized not only as a distinguished scientist but also as an expert in making complex scientific ideas understandable. In 2007 the American Institute of Physics honored him with its Science Writing Award. In addition to publishing more than 100 scholarly papers, he is the author of numerous popular magazine articles and more than 50 books on science for the general public, including National Geographic's *Space Atlas: Mapping the Universe and Beyond.* He lives in Fairfax, Virginia, with his wife.

Destin Sandlin is the host of the wildly popular YouTube channel Smarter Every Day, now with more than four million followers. A single episode, "The Backwards Brain Bicycle," garnered 14 million views in one year. A rocket flight-test engineer, Sandlin was one of three YouTube personalities invited to interview President Obama after his State of the Union address in January 2016. He lives in northern Alabama with his wife and four children.

ILLUSTRATIONS CREDITS

INDEX

Since 1888, the National Geographic Society has funded more than 12,000 research, exploration, and preservation projects around the world. National Geographic Partners distributes a portion of the funds it receives from your purchase to National Geographic Society to support programs including the conservation of animals and their habitats.

National Geographic Partners
1145 17th Street NW
Washington, DC 20036-4688 USA

Become a member of National Geographic and activate your benefits today at natgeo.com/jointoday.

For information about special discounts for bulk purchases, please contact National Geographic Books Special Sales: specialsales@natgeo.com

For rights or permissions inquiries, please contact National Geographic Books Subsidiary Rights: bookrights@natgeo.com

Library of Congress Cataloging-in-Publication Data

Names: Trefil, James, 1938-
Title: The story of innovation : how yesterday's discoveries lead to
    tomorrow's breakthroughs / James S. Trefil.
Description: Washington, D.C. : National Geographic, [2017] | Includes
    bibliographical references and index.
Identifiers: LCCN 2016053109 | ISBN 9781426217050 (hardcover : alk. paper)
Subjects: LCSH: Science--Popular works. | Life sciences--Popular works. |
    Medical care--Popular works. | Astronomy--Popular works. |
    Technology--Popular works.
Classification: LCC Q126 .T74 2017 | DDC 509--dc23
LC record available at: https://lccn.loc.gov/2016053109

ISBN: 978-1-4262-1705-0

Printed in Hong Kong
17/THK/1